CW01272151

Ferment
Pickle
Dry

Good luck with your fermenting adventures!

Simon Poffley
&
Gaba Smolinska-Poffley

Frances Lincoln Limited
A subsidiary of Quarto Publishing Group UK
74–77 White Lion Street
London N1 9PF

Ferment, Pickle, Dry
Copyright © Frances Lincoln Limited 2016
Text © Simon Poffley and
Gaba Smolinska-Poffley 2016
Photographs © Kim Lightbody
Food stylist: Marente van der Valk
Design: Glenn Howard
Commissioning editor: Zena Alkayat

First Frances Lincoln edition 2016

All rights reserved.
No part of this publication may be reproduced, stored in a retrieval system, or transmitted, in any form, or by any means, electronic, mechanical, photocopying, recording or otherwise without the prior written permission of the publisher or a licence permitting restricted copying. In the United Kingdom such licences are issued by the Copyright Licensing Agency, Barnard's Inn, 86 Fetter Lane, London, EC4A 1EN

A catalogue record for this book is available from the British Library.

978-0-7112-3778-0

Printed and bound in China

1 2 3 4 5 6 7 8 9

FRANCES LINCOLN

Quarto Knows

Quarto is the authority on a wide range of topics.
Quarto educates, entertains and enriches the lives of our readers – enthusiasts and lovers of hands-on living.
www.QuartoKnows.com

Ancient methods,
modern meals

Ferment
Pickle
Dry

Simon Poffley and
Gaba Smolinska-Poffley

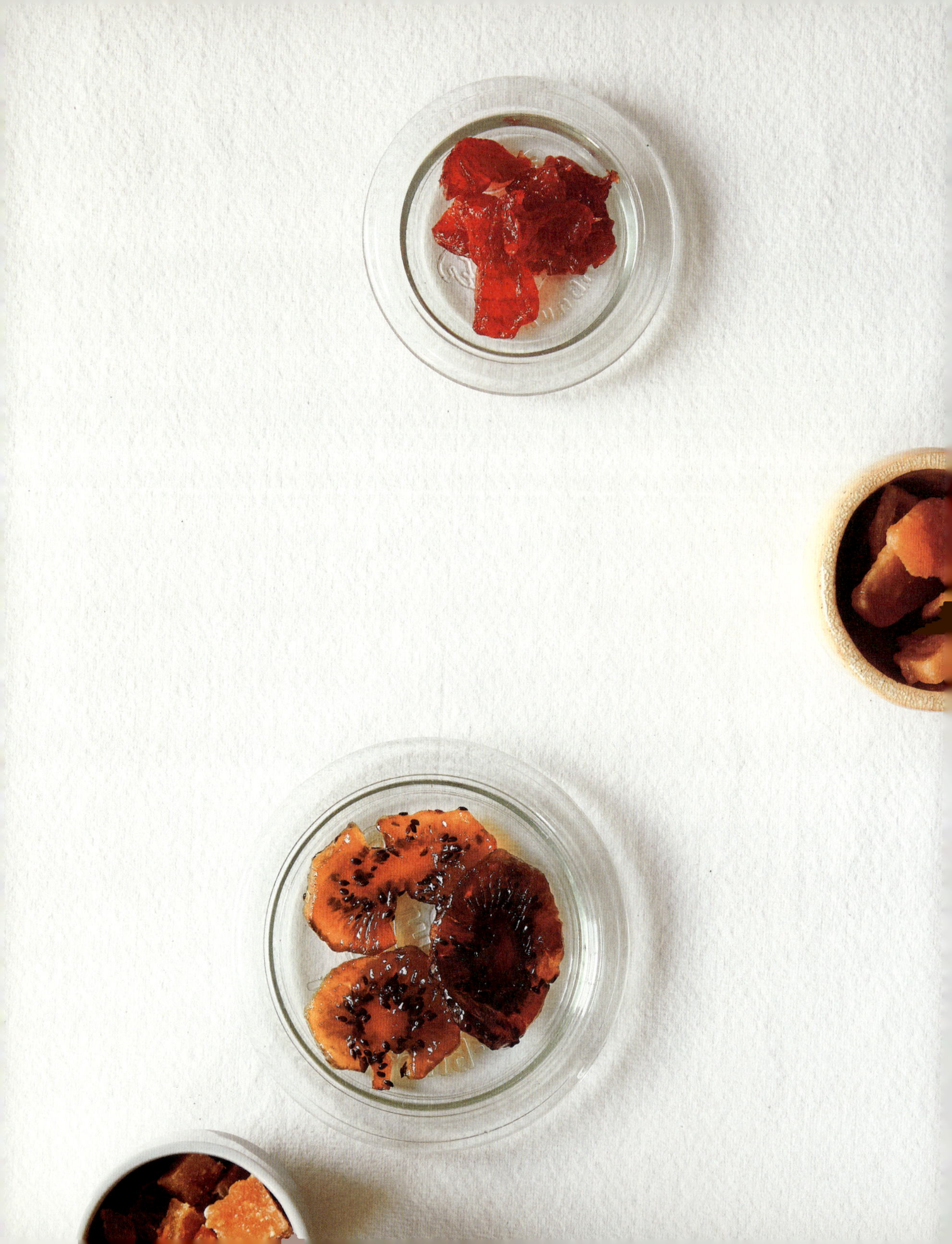

7
Ancient methods, modern meals
The centuries-old story of preserving continues to evolve as fermented, pickled and dried food is used to create exciting and flavourful dishes

8
Why ferment, pickle and dry?
Preserving is so much more than saving seasonal surplus and homemade gifts. These ancient methods leave you with jars of tasty, long-lasting, natural ingredients ready to use in cooking

11
How to use this book

12
Key techniques and ingredients

17
Ferment

103
Pickle

169
Dry

252
Index

256
Acknowledgements

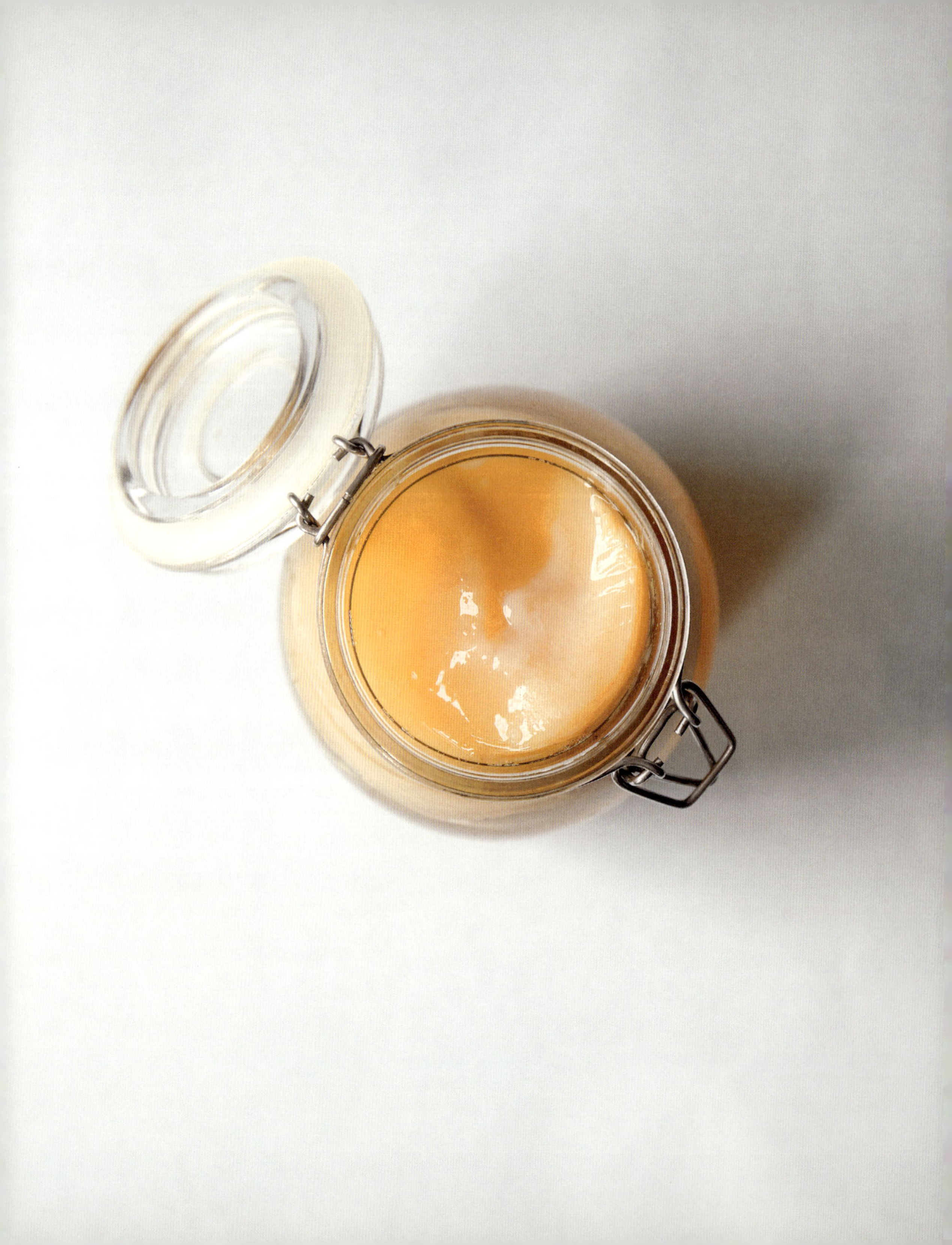

Ancient methods, modern meals

Ancient civilisations may be lost in the mists of time, but the methods our forebears developed to enrich and preserve food millennia ago are still with us today. Certainly the more recent industrial processes such as pasteurisation, homogenisation and the use of a multitude of chemical compounds would baffle a citizen of Mesopotamia or the prehistoric Indus Valley – but the processes we know as fermentation, pickling and drying would ring a familiar bell.

It wasn't that long ago that the space race promised to usher in a brave new world of synthetic food, in which a pill would be a whole meal. While that didn't quite happen, there has been a definite and determined move from small-scale to large-scale and industrial food production. This shift has helped create our fast-food, ready-meal culture, as well as today's additive-fuelled bread-making industry and the many companies churning out an array of sugar- and fat-stuffed packages that fill the supermarket shelves, contributing to an increase in obesity and poor health.

In parallel with the industrialisation of food production, our cities are getting bigger, and urban life is increasingly disconnected from agricultural and rural land. The thought of growing our own food or foraging can seem alien to city-dwellers with busy lives and long commutes. Equally the pressure on our time and energy has meant that preserving and cooking techniques have become neglected. This all makes it very hard to avoid bland, uninspiring and forgettable mass-produced food.

But it's worth remembering, wherever we are, whatever our budget and however busy we get, we have the power to reinvent our meals with new flavours, textures and colour by reclaiming simple ancient preserving methods.

This book brings together the techniques of fermenting, pickling and drying from across the world that have been passed down through the millennia. It is neither a comprehensive compendium or an in-depth investigation into a single technique. Instead, it is a set of doorways to new experiences.

It's intended to be a gentle guide and should help you overcome any obstacles, because while we have better equipped kitchens than at any time in history, we have become encumbered with the fear and anxiety that comes from not being connected with the production of our own food. There's a timidity about DIY preserving, and a prevalent fear of microbes. But we need bacteria; without them we would not be able to digest food. We hope this book will help you welcome good bacteria into your life, kitchen and diet.

Another aim of this book is to show you how fermenting, pickling and drying foods will create a fantastically varied range of ingredients that you can use to transform ordinary dishes and everyday snacks into modern, flavoursome meals. You won't end up with ten jars of kimchi or chutney you have to give to friends – instead you'll find yourself armed with new and exciting ingredients to use in your kitchen.

Why ferment, pickle and dry?

Preserving is more than just a solution to seasonal surplus going to waste. It actually positively transforms fruit and vegetables, bringing out new flavours and textures. This transformation is really the most exciting thing about taking up these techniques – it means you end up with an enormous variety of brand new ingredients to use in your cooking.

As well as that, making your own preserved foods ensures that no unnecessary or questionable additives sneak into your diet – something that can't be said of shop-bought foods. Fermenting, pickling and drying are also very cheap and do not require much space, equipment or technical ability. It means anyone can have a go – and we're certain most people will be hooked.

The three processes are very different from each other. Fermentation and pickling often get confused and have become entangled over time because some ferments and pickles fall between the two processes. The main difference is that fermentation is a live process which involves metabolic change, while pickling usually relies on an acid solution (vinegar) to prevent change in the ingredient that's being pickled. Meanwhile, drying or dehydrating preserves food by removing moisture, which creates an environment unfavourable to yeast and bacteria.

Fermenting, pickling and drying are all great in their own right but they don't form a natural triptych. Some people will love pickling but will not ferment, while there are some avid fermenters who wouldn't touch pickling. If we could only do one we would ferment, but luckily we enjoy all three. It is variety that engages us with food.

To ferment, pickle and dry, we often set off on a quest to find certain varieties of fruit and vegetables, or seek out quality herbs and spices. If we can't find something, we try our hand at growing it. We look for new recipes, join forums and swap methods. Ferments, pickles and dried foods make great gifts, but sharing preserving knowledge is infinitely more rewarding.

It's something we've noticed other people enjoying too, and there's been many signs of a mainstream revival of these ancient techniques. Since the 1970s, Camra (the Campaign for Real Ale) set out to fight for live, secondary-fermented beer in casks rather than the pasteurised and carbonated version so prevalent then and now. The Real Bread Campaign has sought to do the same for bread. And there has been a phenomenal growth in people's interest in the provenance of food, in shopping for organic and seasonal foods at farmers' markets, and in small-scale artisanal food producers. At the beginning of the twenty-first century Sandor Katz also did much to help reignite interest in fermentation in the US, UK and beyond. Indeed there are now so many different food movements and trends grounded in traditional values that it can be hard to keep up.

We're sure that this return to fermenting, pickling and drying is more than just a passing fad – and once you crack open your first jar, we're sure you'll agree.

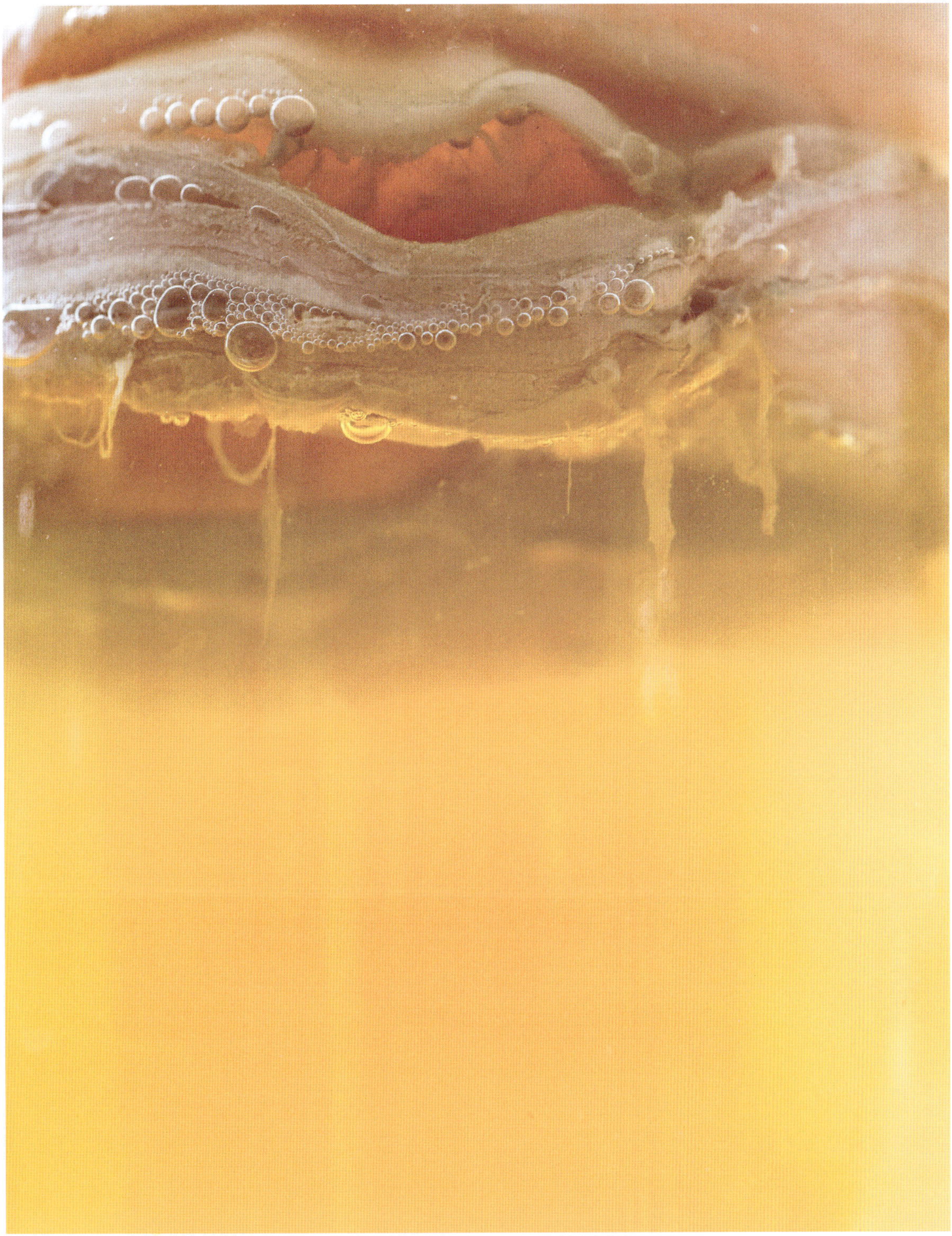

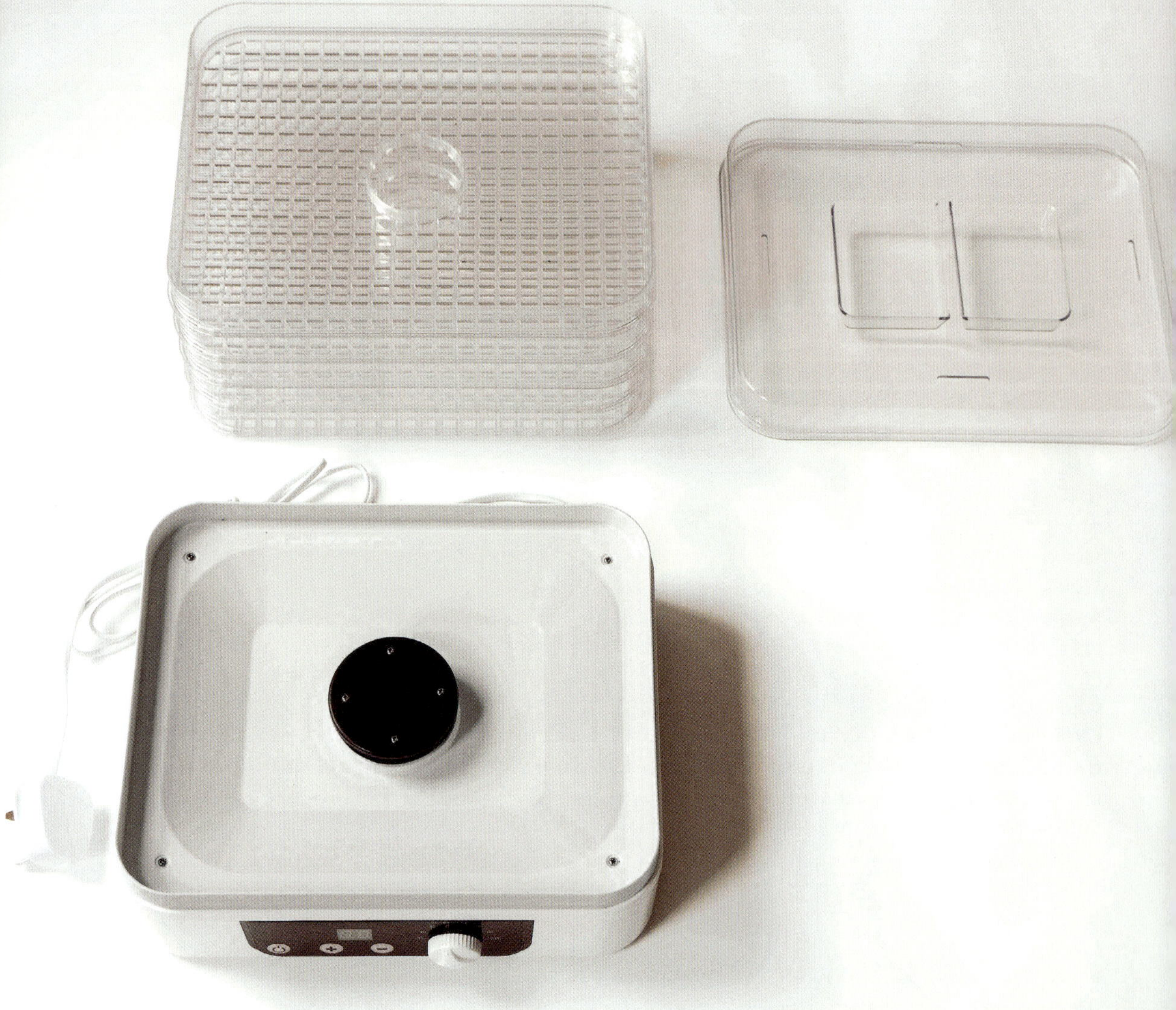

How to use this book
What you need

HOW TO USE THIS BOOK

This book is not meant to be comprehensive; it's a wide selection of simple (and some adventurous) preserving recipes for you to dip into. And for every fermented, pickled or dried recipe, you'll find various 'partner' recipes that show you how you can use these preserved foods in your cooking. So if you make the fermented gherkins on P38, you might want to try cooking with them and make the partner recipe of fermented gherkin caponata on P41, or dry the gherkins and turn them into a sour gherkin salt on P190. The partner recipes are identifiable by a knife and fork symbol beside the recipe names, and where possible we've tried to cross-reference the page numbers to help you find the partner recipes easily. The idea is that you don't end up with shelves packed with jars of preserves that never get eaten or have to be given away. We want you to learn to use them as everyday ingredients, and we hope these recipes will inspire you to do just that.

WHAT YOU NEED

Dehydrator

If you have one, great. But if not, it is possible to use a domestic oven instead. If you wish to invest in a dehydrator, it doesn't have to be expensive. All the recipes in this book were achieved using a very cheap and basic dehydrator.

Food thermometer

This is one piece of equipment that is worth investing in: it is inexpensive and essential for some of the recipes in this book.

Fermenting crock and/or fermenting jars

You can easily get away without using specialist equipment, but a fermenting crock with a drop weight will make things easier. Fermenting jars have an airlock, but you can also use ordinary jars or ceramic crocks (pictured on P14), just make sure your fermented vegetables are submerged in brine.

Jars

Twist-top jars (or any jar that creates an airtight seal) are necessary for some of the recipes. It's useful to have a few different sizes, including some very large ones. However we haven't been too specific about jar sizes as many people like to use the various empty jars they have to hand. We've tried to indicate roughly what volume you'll end up with, so you can use a series of smaller jars if that's what you've got. Whatever jar you use, just be careful to leave 1cm/½in space at the top of your jar (after adding the ingredient to be pickled and the pickling solution).

Mandolin slicer

A very useful tool for thinly slicing fruit and vegetables ready for drying.

Spice/coffee grinder

Perfect for grinding dried foods into salts or stock. Blenders and food processors aren't as efficient.

Other useful equipment
- Muslin or cheesecloth
- Sieve or jelly bag
- Handheld blender or food processor
- Jam funnel

Sterilising and sealing

For some of the recipes it will be necessary to sterilise equipment and pasteurise preserves. It's not hard and you don't need any specialist equipment.

STERILISING JARS AND UTENSILS
Different techniques can be used to sterilise jars and utensils. First prepare the equipment by washing it in hot, soapy water and rinse well. Then use one of the following techniques.

Oven
- Preheat oven to 120°C/250°F/gas mark ½.
- Place the jars on a baking tray. If using Kilner jars, remove the rubber seals and boil them in water. Any metal lids should be placed in boiling water for around 5 minutes.
- Place the baking tray with jars in the oven.
- Leave in the hot oven for 30 minutes.

Boiling in water
- Line the base of a big saucepan with a tea towel and stand the jars upright on it.
- Fill the saucepan with water so all the equipment is submerged completely.
- Cover with lid, bring the water to boil, then boil for at least 10 minutes.

Dishwasher
Place the clean jars, lids and utensils in a dishwasher and run on the hottest cycle. Dishwasher powder/tablets are not needed.

Microwave
- Remove and set aside any metal lids. Half fill clean jars with water and heat on full power until the water has boiled and bubbled for 1 minute.
- Carefully remove the jars from the microwave and swish the water around the jar before draining and allowing to dry.
- Metal lids should be placed in boiling water for around 5 minutes.

HOW TO SEAL JARS
To make sure your pickles are safely preserved, you need to carefully seal your jars closed to create an airtight vacuum.

- Preferably use twist-top jars.
- Always use a pickling solution that has just boiled. Do not let it cool down.
- Leave approximately 1cm/½in space at the top of your jar of pickles (after adding the pickle and the hot pickling solution).
- Close the jar with the lid immediately.
- Turn the jars upside down — this will help to create a vacuum. Leave the jars upside down for 24 hours.
- Most twist top-lids will seal with a 'pop' sound while they're cooling. This happens as the lid gets sucked down by the vacuum created by the contents cooling and contracting inside the jar.

TESTING FOR A SEAL
Important: don't test lids for seal until they are completely cooled and you've given them several hours to seal. If you test them before the jars are completely cool you might create a false seal and end up with unsafe food. Once completely cool, test jars for a seal using one of these methods:

Finger test method
Press and release the middle of the jar lid with a finger or thumb. If the lid 'pops' up and down with your finger when you press, it's not sealed.

Teaspoon test method
Tap the lid with the bottom of a teaspoon. If it makes a clear ringing sound it means there's a good seal. If it makes a dull sound, the lid is not sealed. However, if you did not leave the recommended 1cm/½in space at the top of the jar (and food is touching the lid) it will create a dull sound anyway.

Eye method
Hold the jar at eye level and look across the lid. The lid should be curved down slightly in the centre. If the centre of the lid is either flat or bulging, it probably isn't sealed.

WHAT TO DO IF JAR IS NOT SEALED
If a jar is not sealed, refrigerate it and use within 2 days. You might have longer to use the food, but it really depends on what you were preserving.

Or you can try to re-jar your pickle – for that you will need to start again with a sterilised jar and a hot pickling solution. But before re-jarring, remove the lid and check for tiny nicks or damage. If necessary, change the jar and/or lid for a new one. Another option is to pasteurise the food within 24 hours.

PASTEURISATION
Pasteurisation preserves food by heating it at a specific temperature for a certain length of time – this kills off bacteria and yeast. By pasteurising, you can extend the length of time that your pickled and fermented food will keep. Jars which are already properly sealed do not need to be pasteurised. However if you're planning to store pickles in a cupboard for a prolonged period of time, it's best to pasteurise them for saftey, even if they've already been sealed successfully.

- Place your filled jars (with the lid tightly closed) in a saucepan lined with a tea towel.
- Fill the saucepan with water – up to about ⅔ of the jar's height. Turn on the heat, bring to boil, and boil for 15 minutes.
- Turn off the heat and leave the jars to cool in the pan. Once cool, the jars are pasteurised.

Low-temperature pasteurisation treatment
This is another way to pasteurise fermented or pickled products. The jars must be held in a canner or saucepan completely covered with water that's heated between 82-85°C/185°F. Using a thermometer to ensure accuracy, you must maintain this steady temperature for 30 minutes to kill harmful bacteria. Low-temperature pasteurisation is often the preferred method for processing some pickled and fermented foods because it does not soften vegetables and helps them retain their crunch.

STORING PRESERVED FOOD
Store sealed or pasteurised jars in a dark, cool and dry cupboard. If any jar smells bad, or the contents are mouldy or look slimy or damaged, discard without tasting. Store dried food in airtight containers in a dark, cool and dry cupboard.

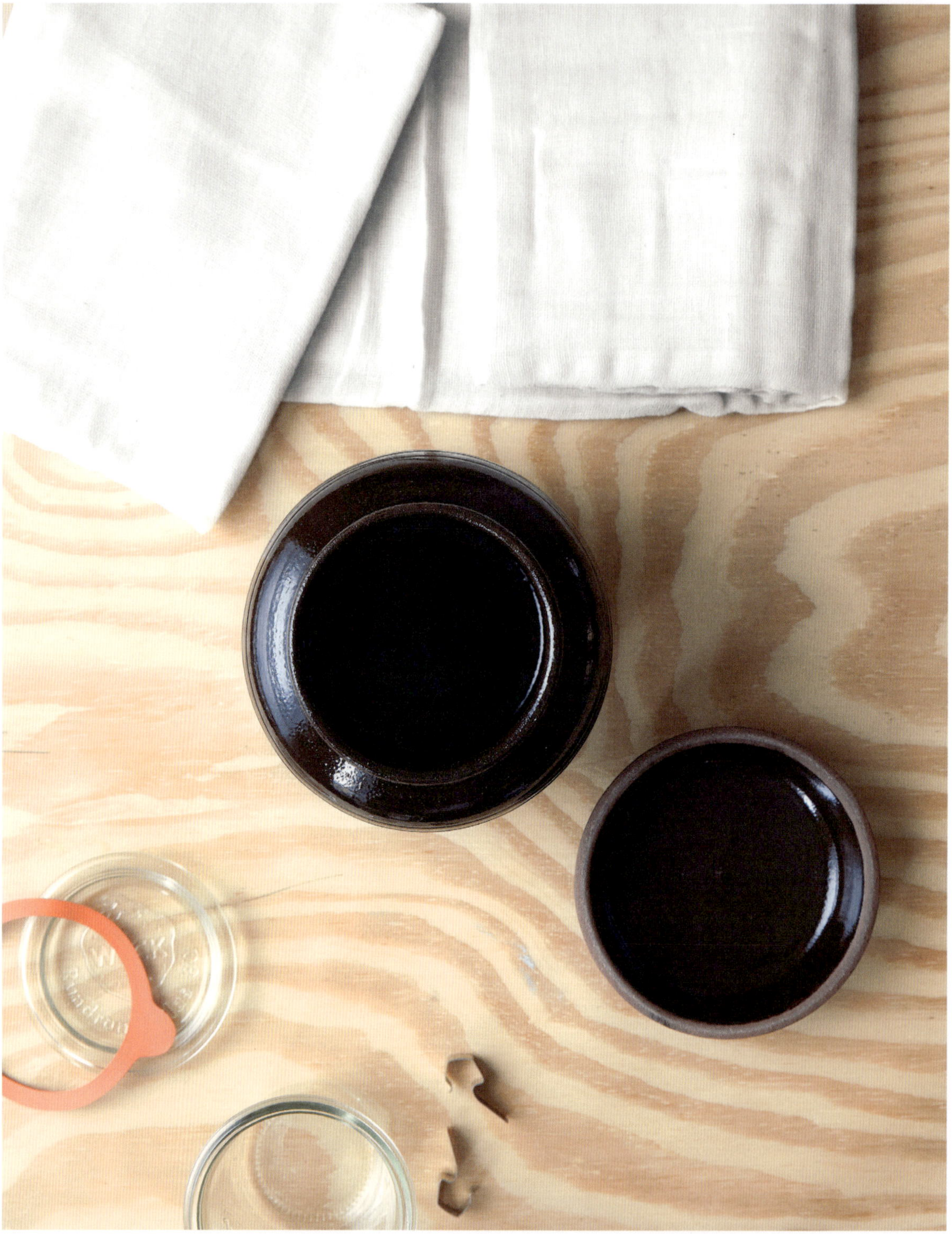

Key ingredients

Salt
It's best to use a pure salt such as rock or sea salt. Always check the ingredients and avoid iodised salt or salt containing anti-caking agents – they can cause spoilage, cloudy brine and a bitter flavour in some types of food.

When fermenting and pickling it's important to stick to the quantity of salt given in the recipes: salt is there to ensure food safety by preserving properly. Too little salt may cause the item you are fermenting or pickling to go soft and slimy.

Don't use salt substitutes as they will not behave in the same way as real salt, and your preserves might end up spoiled or unsafe for consumption.

Vinegar
Vinegar is the most important component in pickling. Unless you are planning to keep your pickles refrigerated and use them within a few days, use only store-bought vinegar which clearly states its acid content. It's best not to use homemade vinegar as it's hard to be certain of the acid content. To make a pickling solution that will ensure a safely preserved pickle, you need to use vinegar which has a minimum 5% acid content. A mixed pickling solution should end up with a minimum of 2.5% overall acid content.

Different types of vinegar such as apple cider, raw apple cider, wine, rice, malt and distilled spirit vinegars can be used, but always check the acidity level on the label. If you're not sure you've used a vinegar with a high enough acid content, be sure to refrigerate and consume your pickles within a few days as they may not be safely preserved.

Raw honey
Raw honey is a honey which has not been heated beyond 35°C/95°F, the temperature found in a beehive. As long as honey is not significantly heated above that temperature, the nutritional and beneficial qualities are preserved. Filtered, strained or pressed honey can be treated as raw as long as heating has been avoided. The label will usually indicate whether the honey is raw.

Pickling leaves
Blackcurrant leaves, grape vine leaves, sour cherry leaves and oak leaves are all used in fermenting fruit and vegetables such as gherkins, tomatoes and plums. The tannin present in these leaves prevents the fruit and vegetables from going too soft, and ensures fermented foods are still crisp and firm to the bite. You can usually find these leaves in a friend's garden, in parks and public spaces – trim off a few leaves and wash before use.

Pickling spices
Spices and herbs such as caraway (commonly used in sauerkraut), dried dill, dried horseradish root and leaves, garlic, tarragon, black pepper, bay leaves, mustard seeds and cloves can be used in fermenting and pickling to add flavour. In addition to flavour, some of the spices and herbs will also help create an environment hostile to harmful bacteria. The spices we've suggested are to our taste, so do experiment with flavours you like.

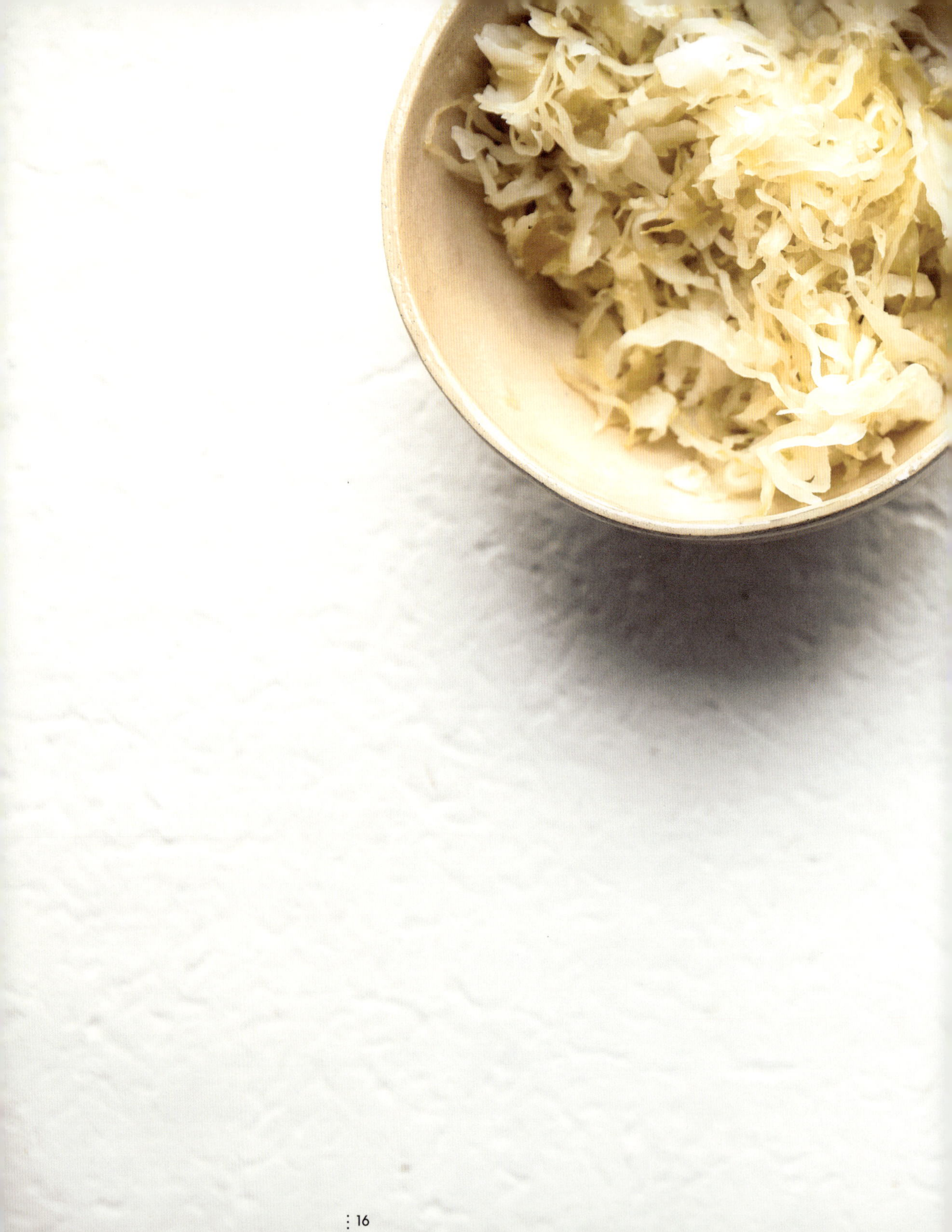

Ferment

Everyday life would not be the same without fermentation. Our cupboards and fridges would be bare if there was no bread, beer, cider, wine, coffee, tea, cheese, yoghurt, kefir, miso and soy sauce, among many other everyday favourites.

Fermentation is the result of micro-organisms converting carbohydrates or sugars into alcohol or acid. Yeast cells create alcohol, while bacteria creates lactic acid. For this to happen it is necessary to create the right moisture and temperature conditions.

Fermentation got its name from the Latin *fervere*, 'to boil', because vats of fermenting wine and beer appeared to boil as carbon dioxide bubbled to the surface. The word yeast comes from Old English meaning 'to foam', but an understanding of yeast's integral role was not fully understood until the nineteenth century when French microbiologist Louis Pasteur discovered yeast could be responsible for fermentation – he went on to invent pasteurisation.

This chapter covers 'wild' fermentation, which harnesses the power of naturally existing yeasts which are already present in the air (rather than adding commercially produced yeast). This ancient method is used to make sourdough P82 and is known for giving bread superior flavour and texture, and often more minerals. Sourdough starters P80 (which use this naturally occurring yeast) will end up containing different strains of yeast, but there will almost certainly be some Saccharomyces cerevisiae present. Most commercial beers, wines and breads are made using different strains of this yeast.

The chapter also looks at 'lactic' fermentation, which is the work of lactobacillus bacteria. The lactic bacteria convert sugar into lactic acid which acts as a natural preservative and improves the digestibility of food. This category covers sauerkraut P67, kimchi P42, nukadoko P62 and other sour vegetable and fruit ferments.

Ferment

Once you have had a go at fermenting with yeast and bacteria, why not have a go at fermenting with mould? Overcoming the initial trepidation is the hardest part – after that it is fairly easy and there are some very nice moulds to choose from. Perhaps the most prolific is Aspergillus oryzae, which is used to ferment rice and is used in the production of soy sauce, miso, sake and amazake P94. For truly full-on mouldiness though, there is Rhizopus oligosporus, which is used to make tempeh from soya beans P70.

Fermentation helps to create many drinks, but not all of them need to be alcoholic. There are several varieties of fermented soft drinks to try and they're all a welcome alternative to carbonated drinks. Each uses different types of fermentation: for example, kvass P75 and ginger beer P88 use lactic fermentation, while kombucha P90 uses a scoby (which stands for 'symbiotic culture of bacteria and yeast').

Many fermented foods are probiotic and contain 'good' live organisms, like in live yoghurt – they're healthy for the digestive tract and the immune system. Fermentation also breaks down phytic acid, which can be difficult to digest. By eating fermented foods, our bodies are more able to absorb the vitamins and minerals present in the food.

Fermented food will usually be sour, but it should have a clean flavour and aroma. If something smells or tastes unpleasant it is best discarded. See the information on sealing and pasteurisation P12 to be sure you are storing your food safely.

If you are planning to get stuck into this chapter and experiment with a few of the recipes at the same time, we have one last tip: keep them in separate rooms or on opposite sides of a room while fermenting to avoid cross contamination.

Plain live yoghurt

Yoghurt is so simple to make. Without the aid of a yoghurt-making machine (or even a thermometer) you can easily make it taste fantastic. And it's very satisfying to unwrap the pot from its cocoon of blankets and find your yoghurt has set perfectly. Use it to make ice cream P24.

Prep 15–25 minutes
Ready 20–24 hours
Makes approx 1.5 litres/50fl oz

1.5 litres/50fl oz/6¼ cups whole milk
6 tbsp plain live yoghurt, which acts as a starter culture (for your first batch use shop-bought yoghurt, but your next batch can be made using your homemade yoghurt)

— Fill a large pan with about 2.5cm/1in water and bring to the boil over a medium heat.
— Pour the milk into a heatproof bowl that will comfortably fit over the large pan and place on top making sure the bowl doesn't touch the water below. Heat the milk, stirring constantly, to 85°C/185°F, or until it is frothy, then remove the bowl from the heat.
— Leave the milk to cool until it reaches 43°C/110°F on a thermometer. Alternatively, cover with a tea towel and leave to cool for about 2 hours, or until it feels warm but is no longer hot.
— Pour the yoghurt (which acts as a starter culture) into the warm milk and stir well, then pour the mixture into a ceramic bowl with a lid or a lidded saucepan, wrap it tightly in 3 or more thick blankets and leave in a warm place for 12–20 hours until it is thick.
— Once the yoghurt has cooled completely, stir, cover and place in the fridge for a few hours until chilled. The yoghurt can be kept it in the fridge for about 7 days.

You can also use a large vacuum flask (like a Thermos) to make yoghurt. Once the heated milk is cool enough mix it with the yoghurt, then pour into a 1.8 litre/61fl oz (or larger) flask, close tightly and leave for 8–12 hours.

Make sure you sterilise your flask before use, and clean the flask thoroughly after use. A long-handled bottle brush works well.

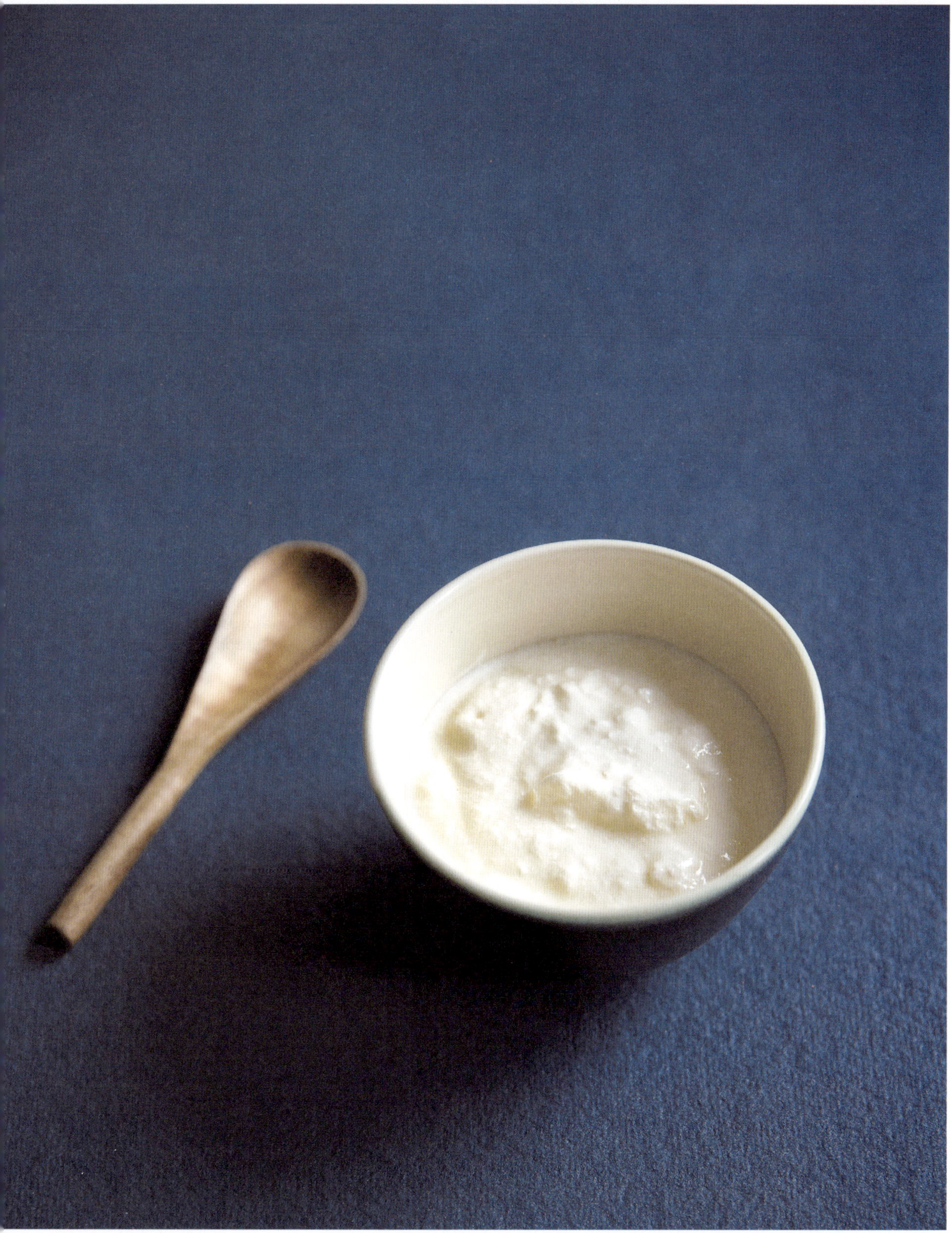

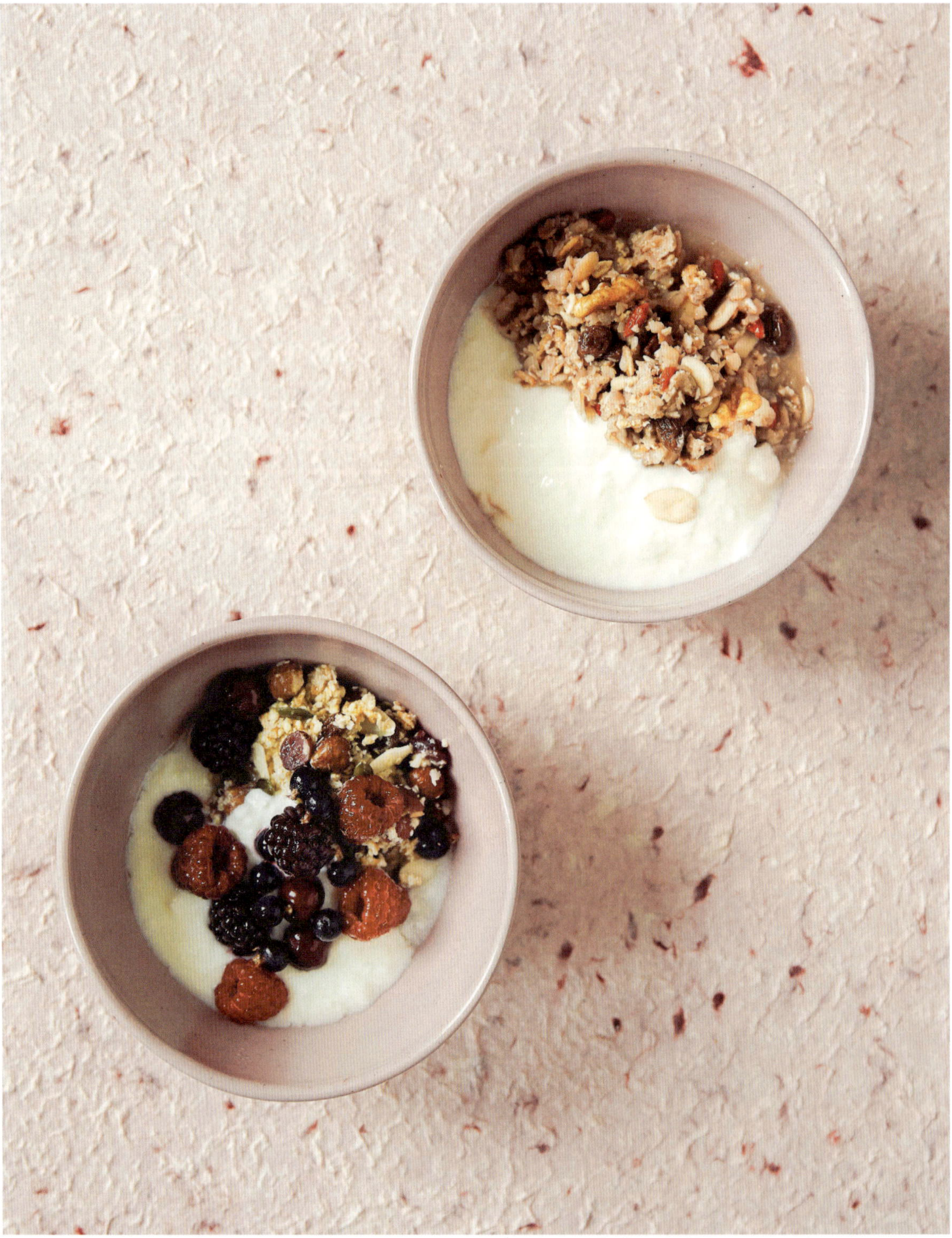

Whey-fermented muesli

Humans across the world have soaked grains since the days of early civilisation, although the practice has declined in the West since the industrial revolution. Soaking kickstarts the fermentation process and improves our ability to digest grains by reducing phytic acid, which prevents the absorption of vitamins and minerals. Whey P34 is very easy to make and adds richness to the muesli.

Prep 10 minutes
Ready 8–10 hours
Makes approx 300g/10½oz

3 tbsp oats (rolled or porridge)
3 tbsp millet flakes
3 tbsp spelt flakes (rolled)
3 tbsp quinoa flakes
2 tbsp hazelnuts (whole or chopped into large chunks)
1 tbsp pumpkin seeds
1 tbsp cranberries
1 tbsp sultanas (golden raisins)
1 tbsp flaked almonds
150ml/5fl oz/⅔ cup whey P34

— Mix all the dry ingredients together in a bowl or large 700ml/24fl oz jar.
— Add the whey, then cover the bowl or jar with kitchen paper, a lid or a plate.
— Leave to soak for 8–10 hours, or ideally overnight in the fridge. This muesli will keep for up to 24 hours.

Other ingredients can be added, including roasted buckwheat or rye flakes, walnuts, sunflower seeds and raisins.

Whey-fermented muesli with plain yoghurt and fruit

Serves 2–3

1 portion (300g/10½oz) whey-fermented muesli above
400ml/14fl oz/1¾ cups plain live yoghurt P20 or shop-bought)
200g/7oz/1⅓ cups fresh or frozen and defrosted raspberries, blackcurrants or blueberries (or any fresh fruit of your choice)

— Place the whey-fermented muesli into a bowl and top with the plain live yoghurt. Pop the fruit on top and serve.

Blackcurrant smoothie or yoghurt ice cream

This is a quick and simple recipe to liven up plain yoghurt P20 with the zing of fresh blackcurrants. Blackcurrants give a wonderfully deep purple colour, but this also works really well with raspberries or redcurrants.

Serves 4

For the smoothie
1 litre/34fl oz/4 cups plain live yoghurt, chilled P20
150g/5½oz/1⅓ cups blackcurrants
3 bananas, peeled and sliced
3–4 tbsp raw honey (optional)

For the ice cream
2 level tsp agar agar (a vegetarian gelling agent)
8 tbsp hot water

— Place all the ingredients for the smoothie in a large bowl or jug and blend with a handheld blender until smooth. Alternatively, use a blender.
— The smoothie is best served immediately, but it can be kept overnight in the fridge. If it begins to separate simply stir well to combine.
— To turn the yogurt smoothie into ice cream, put the agar agar, in a pan along with the hot water to dissolve it (it is insoluble in cold water). Bring it to the boil, then reduce the heat and simmer for about 5 minutes. Add to the smoothie and mix well.
— Pour the mixture into an ice-cream machine and churn.
— Alternatively, pour into a freezerproof container and freeze for 20 minutes, then remove and stir vigorously with a whisk or spoon, or use a food processor. Return to the freezer and repeat at 30-minute intervals until frozen.

You can use this smoothie to make ice lollies, rather than ice cream, by simply pouring the mixture into moulds and freezing for at least 5 hours, but preferably overnight.

Alternatively, pour the smoothie over a bowl of whey-fermented muesli P23.

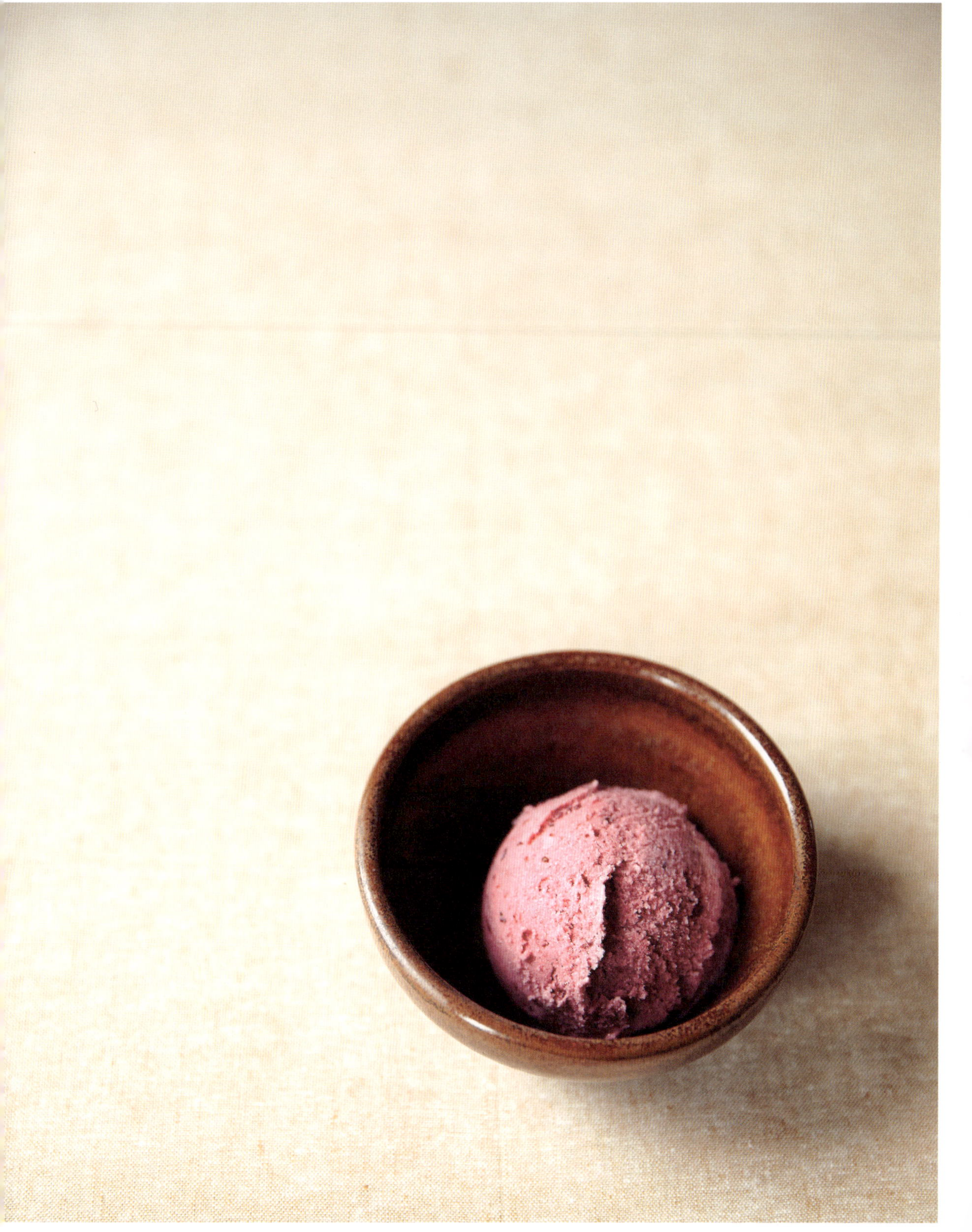

Tartar sauce
Viili cream
Sweet and spiced viili cream P28

Viili cream

Viili is a viscous fermented milk popular in Finland. It has a mild, delicious flavour, and can be quite stringy. It's easier to make than ordinary yoghurt P20 and you can use it in place of sour cream as well as in the sauce below.

To make viili yoghurt rather than cream, replace the single cream in this recipe with more milk.

Prep 10 minutes
Ready 18–48 hours
Makes approx 600ml/20fl oz

3–4 tbsp unpasteurised viili cream, which acts as a starter culture (you can buy some from a specialist supplier online, but your next batch can be made using your homemade viili cream)
300ml/10fl oz/1¼ cups pasteurised milk (non-homogenised)
300ml/10fl oz/1¼ cups single (light) cream (non-homogenised)

— Combine the viili starter, milk and cream in a bowl, then pour the mixture into a sterilised 1 litre/34fl oz jar P12. Cover with kitchen paper and secure with a rubber band.
— Keep the jar on the work surface or other warm place, ideally between 21–25°C/70–77°F, until the cream has set. This can take up to 48 hours.
— To check if it has set, take off the paper and gently tip the jar sideways as if to pour it out: if it looks like it will pour in a stream like milk, it isn't ready. If it looks like it will dollop off the side of the jar and seems thickened, then it is ready.
— Once set, stir, then seal the jar with a lid and refrigerate.
— Consume within 3–4 weeks. The flavour gets stronger the longer you keep it.

Tartar sauce

We had assumed this sharp, mayonnaise-based condiment originated in Russia, as it is ubiquitous there and it shares its name with a local ethnic group. As it turns out, it probably migrated there from France.

Serves 4

3 eggs, hard-boiled
1 tsp olive oil
3–4 tsp mustard
2 tsp mayonnaise
250ml/9fl oz/generous 1 cup viili cream above, or sour cream
75g/2½oz/⅓ cup whole pickled mushrooms, finely chopped P110
3–4 pickled cucumbers, finely chopped P124
1 tsp sugar
Salt and freshly ground black pepper

— Separate the cooked egg yolks from the cooked egg whites and put the yolks into a bowl. Set the whites aside.
— Add the olive oil to the egg yolks and, using a wooden spoon, pound until smooth.
— Add the mustard and mayonnaise and mix until smooth. If the mustard is fiery it is best to add it at the end by the teaspoonful, mixing and tasting as you go.
— Add the viili cream, chopped mushrooms and chopped cucumbers and mix well.
— Chop the egg whites finely, add to the sauce and mix well.
— Season the sauce with the sugar, salt and black pepper.
— Store the sauce in the fridge and use within 5 days. Try using with the mackerel dish on P110.

Fermented pumpkin syrup

This works well in recipes that ask for date or maple syrup, or you can combine with viili cream below. The key ingredient is ginger bug P88.

Prep 20 minutes + cooling
Ready 24 hours
Makes approx 500ml/18fl oz jar

250ml/9fl oz/generous 1 cup water
250g/9oz/1¼ cups brown sugar
300g/10½oz pumpkin (or butternut squash), peeled, deseeded and grated
2 tsp ground cinnamon
½ tsp ground allspice
1 tsp ground ginger
½ tsp ground nutmeg
½ tsp ground coriander
60ml/2¼fl oz/¼ cup ginger bug P88

— Mix all the ingredients, except the ginger bug, together in a medium saucepan. Bring to the boil, then reduce the heat and simmer for 15 minutes.
— Remove from the heat and leave to cool to room temperature, then strain the liquid into a medium sterilised jar P12.
— Add the ginger bug, cover loosely and leave to ferment for at least 24 hours before chilling in the fridge.
— Shake well before using and use within a month.

Sweet and spiced viili cream

This is a rich, sweet and slightly sour sauce with a viili cream P27 base.

Serves 3-4

100ml/3½fl oz/scant ½ cup freshly made viili cream P27
50ml/2 fl oz/scant ¼ cup fermented pumpkin syrup above
½ tsp ground cinnamon

— Combine all the ingredients together in a glass bowl and stir well.
— Store in the fridge and use within 2 weeks.

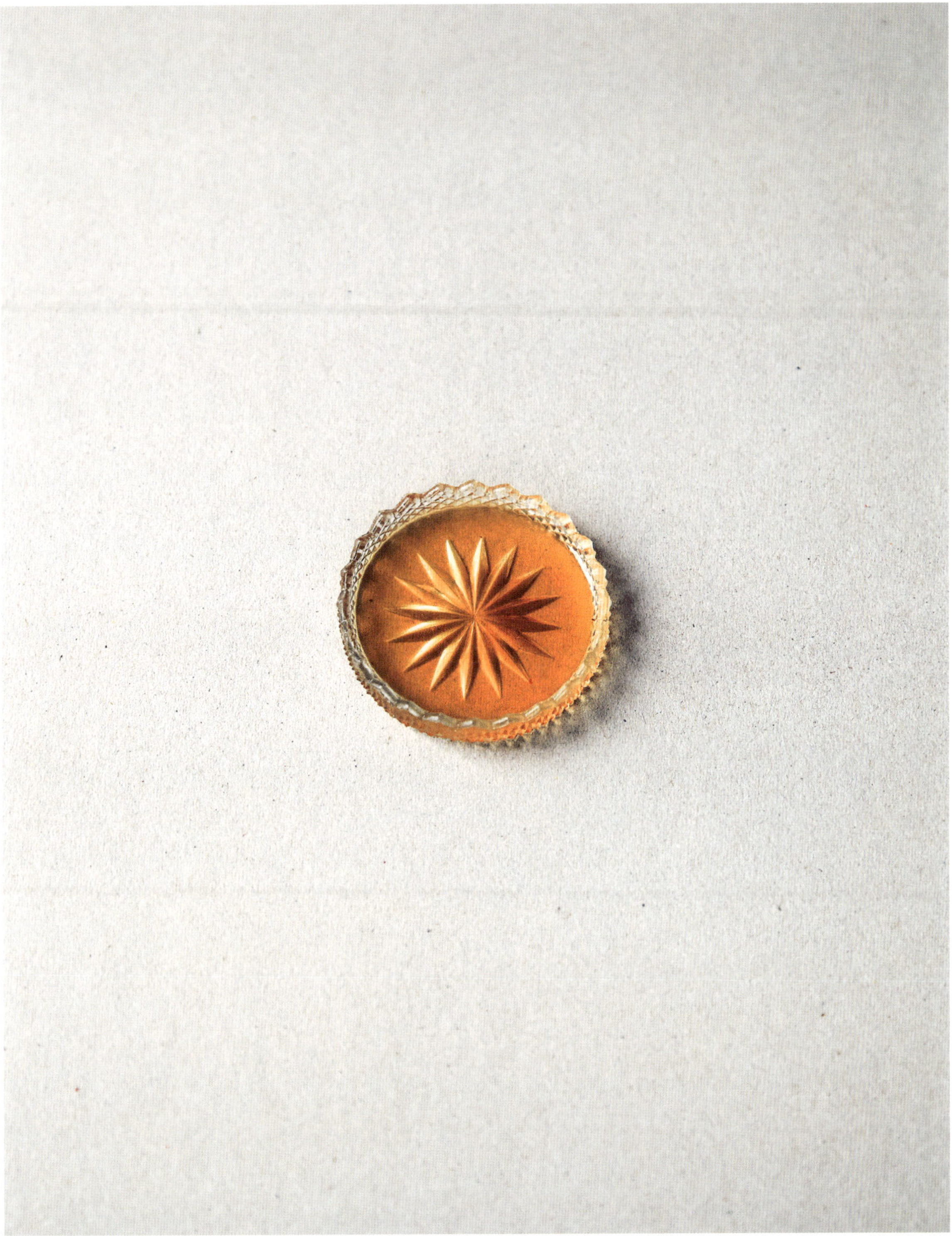

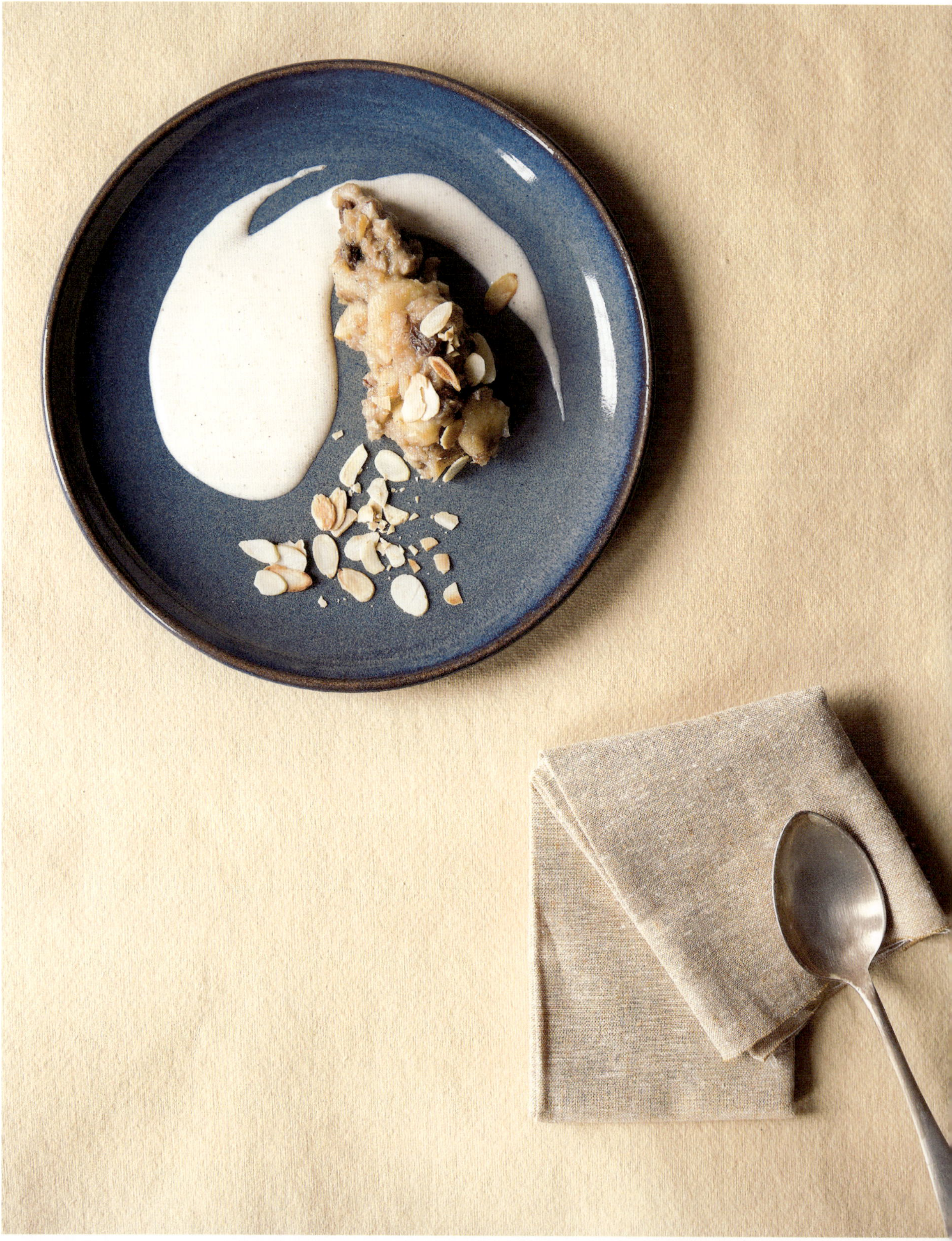

Baked apple with sweet and spiced viili cream

Baked apples go brilliantly with the mild, sour tang of spiced viili cream and fermented pumpkin syrup P28.

Serves 3–4

5 large cooking apples such as bramley (peeled, cored and cut into 2cm/¾in cubes)
30g/1oz/¼ cup walnuts, chopped
30g/1oz/¼ cup hazelnuts, chopped
30g/1oz/scant ¼ cup raisins
½ tsp ground cinnamon
2 tbsp fermented pumpkin syrup P28 (or honey)
30g/1oz/⅓ cup flaked (slivered) almonds
Sweet and spiced viili cream P28, to serve

— Preheat the oven to 250°C/480°F/gas mark 10.
— Mix all the ingredients, except the almonds, together in a large bowl.
— Place the apple and nut mixture in a medium baking dish and bake for about 25 minutes, or until the apples are very soft. Check the apples every 10 minutes and stir all the ingredients.
— Meanwhile, heat a small frying pan over a medium heat, add the flaked almonds and stir constantly until the almonds turn light brown in colour. Remove from the pan immediately and set aside.
— Once the apple pieces are baked mash them with a fork. Some larger pieces can be left, if you like.
— Serve the apples drizzled with the sweet and spiced viili cream and the toasted almonds.

Milk kefir

Milk kefir is tangy, thick and slightly effervescent. It is one of those fermented drinks that people rave about as being life-changing. If we had to choose between kefir and yoghurt, we would choose kefir: yoghurt is eaten or drunk, but kefir is sipped like a fine ale. Use in to make blinis P37.

Prep 10 minutes
Ready 24 hours
Makes approx 300ml/10fl oz

1 tbsp milk kefir grains (this is a yeast/bacteria starter you can buy from a specialist supplier online, but your next batch can be made using your homemade kefir grains)
300ml/10fl oz/1¼ cups whole milk, semi-skimmed milk or goat's milk

— Place the kefir grains in a 500ml/18fl oz jar and pour the milk over them, making sure there is a space of 1cm/½in at the top. Stir well and cover the jar with a lid.
— Leave to ferment at room temperature, between about 18–24°C/32–75°F, for 24 hours. Swirl, shake or stir the jar from time to time for a more even ferment.
— After this time taste the milk to see if it has become tangy and thick.
— Using a nylon sieve, strain the kefir into a sterilised container P12 and drink or use as it is. Chill and use within a week.

— The grains collected in the sieve can be reused to make more batches and should multiply in quantity. They don't need rinsing, just keep them covered in milk in the fridge for up to a week. When you want to reuse them, refresh with fresh milk. Semi-skimmed will work, but whole is preferable and goat's milk is also a good option. Alternatively, start a new batch.

In the warmth of summer the grains will go to work quicker than in winter.

Don't use metal containers or utensils when making kefir as it can react with it.

Kefir goes very well with new potatoes that have been covered in butter and sprinkled with chopped dill.

Water kefir

This lemonade-like drink is made using water kefir grains, which are crystal-like clumps of different yeast and bacteria strains. You can buy grains online, or use leftover grains from your first batch of kefir. Kefir grains prefer mineral-rich water, so hard water (from the tap) is fine as it contains minerals, but it can contain chlorine and fluoride so is best filtered. Lemon is usually added to water kefir to make the solution more acidic, which helps prevent it from spoiling. You can add dried fruit for flavour (steer clear of fruit that contains preservatives or added oil), and you can stir in white sugar for sweetness – darker sugars such as demerara, muscovado, jaggery and molasses are even better because they contain more nutrients like potassium, magnesium and zinc which are beneficial to the yeast. Use water kefir to make fermented hummus P66.

Prep 20 minutes
Ready 1-2 days
Makes approx 500ml/18fl oz

- 1 tbsp water kefir grains (this is a yeast/bacteria starter you can buy from a specialist supplier online, but your next batch can be made using your homemade kefir)
- 500ml/18fl oz/2 cups water (filtered, or tap water boiled for around 15 minutes to remove the chlorine)
- 40g/½oz/scant ¼ cup muscovado or brown sugar
- ⅓ lemon, sliced (or 1 tbsp of water kefir from a previous batch)
- 3 tbsp raisins (optional)

— Place the water kefir grains in a sterilised 1 litre/34fl oz jar P12 and add the water. Add the sugar and stir until it has dissolved, then add the lemon and raisins, if using.
— Cover the jar with a piece of muslin or cheesecloth and secure with a rubber band. Leave for 24 hours.
— Taste it, if it's as you like it, then go to the next step. Alternatively leave for another 12-24 hours first and taste again.
— Using a nylon sieve, strain the liquid into a clean container. The water kefir can either be drunk now or bottled in sterilised flip-top glass bottles to make it fizzier and kept in the fridge or at room temperature.
— The grains can be reused. Place them in a sterilised jar and repeat the process or put them in a mixture of water and sugar and chill (see notes).

The grains need to be fed every 48 hours. Strain and put in a fresh mix of water and sugar. You can take a break from this process by transferring them to the fridge and refreshing them weekly (rather than every 48 hours) with fresh water and sugar.

The grains multiply, especially in summer, so it is good to pass on extra to friends.

After 2 days, water kefir can contain a little alcohol, but it is usually below 0.5%. After 3-4 days it may increase to 2% or slightly more.

Although water kefir and milk kefir grains look similar they are not interchangeable.

Labneh and whey

Labneh originates from the Middle East and is thicker than Greek yoghurt – it's essentially yoghurt without the whey. Traditionally this quick-to-make curd cheese is eaten with bread, olive oil, spices and herbs. The extracted whey is rich in lactic bacteria and makes a powerful starter culture for use in other recipes such as fermented muesli P23.

Prep 10 minutes
Ready 2–3 hours
Makes approx 200g/7oz

500ml/18fl oz/2 cups plain live yoghurt P20

— Place a sieve over a bowl, making sure there is 10cm/4in space between the base of the sieve and the base of the bowl, then drape a piece of muslin or cheesecloth (folded once or twice) over the sieve, making sure it's hanging over the sides.
— Pour the yoghurt into the sieve and leave to drain for 2–3 hours to allow the whey to drip into the bowl.
— Gather up all the edges of the muslin and hold them together tightly with one hand. The yoghurt should be enclosed in the muslin.
— Still holding the edges of the muslin with one hand, twist the muslin-covered yoghurt a few times to squeeze out as much of the whey as you can.
— Pour the whey into a clean jar and chill. It will keep in the fridge for up to 4 weeks and the remaining curd cheese will keep chilled for 3 days.
— You can drink the whey straight from the fridge or you can use it in other dishes, such as fermented muesli P23, fermented ketchup P57 and fermented hummus P66.

Labneh cream cheese

Turn your labneh into a cream cheese spread. The herbs are optional, and more garlic can be added to make it into a garlic cream cheese. Add to blinis as a dip P37.

Serves 2–3

100g/3½oz fresh labneh
1 garlic clove, chopped
Salt and freshly ground black pepper
1–3 tbsp plain live yoghurt P20
  or viili cream P27 (to achieve the required consistency)
1 tsp chopped thyme (optional)
1 tsp chopped marjoram (optional)

— Place all the ingredients, except the fresh herbs, in a large bowl and mix well with a fork until combined. Alternatively, blend for 2 minutes in a food processor.
— Add the herbs and mix well.
— Transfer to a lidded plastic container and store in the fridge. Use within 3 days.

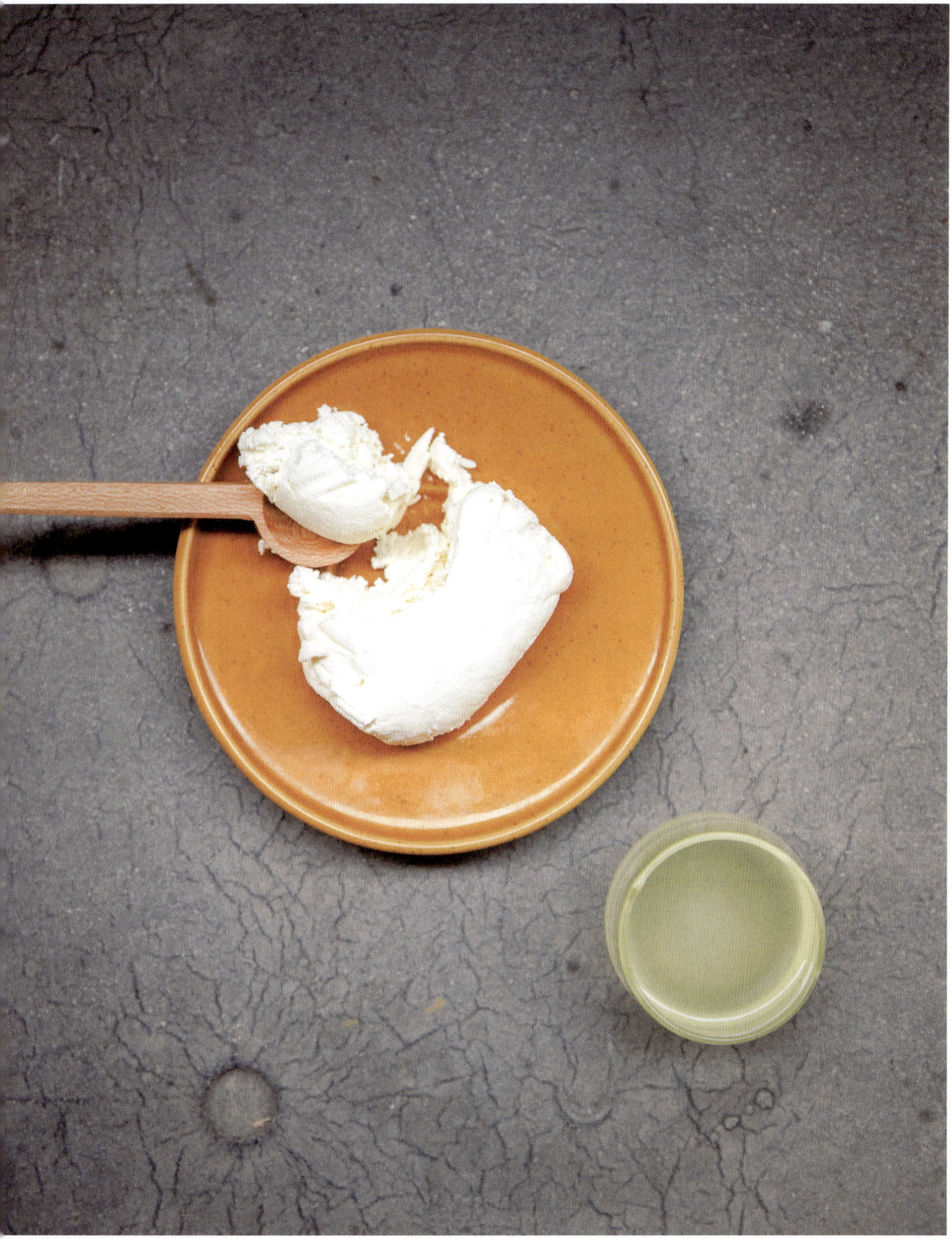

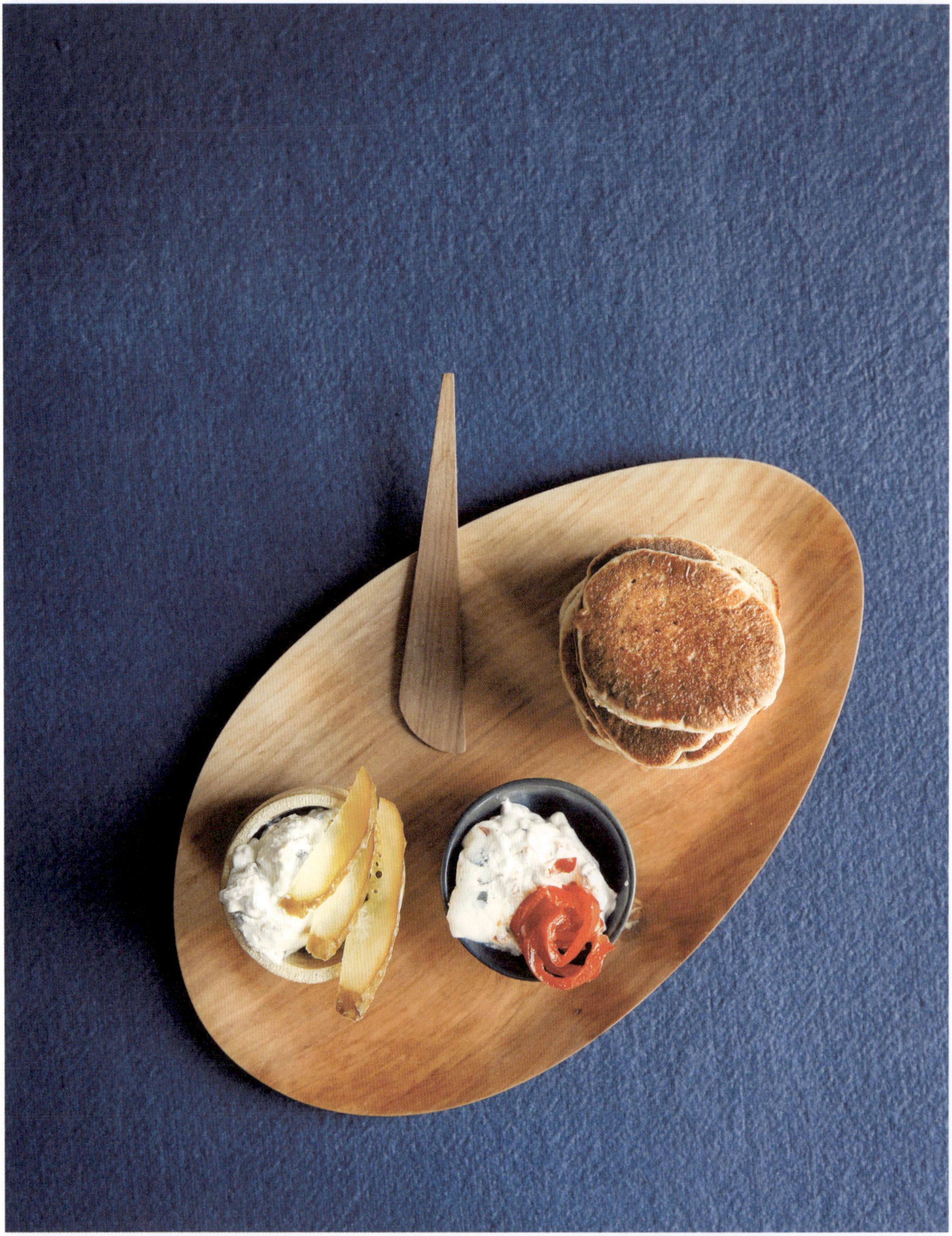

Blinis

Blinis are particularly popular in Russia, where they are often served with caviar, but they were first made in pagan times to celebrate the coming of spring, probably partly because the golden discs reminded people of the sun. In this recipe we use milk kefir P32 and a sourdough starter P80, but if you prefer you can use a teaspoon of fresh yeast. If you do this, replace the water with lukewarm milk and mix the milk with the flour that would have gone into the production leaven.

Prep 1 hour
Ready 10–11 hours
Makes about 40

30g/1oz wheat or spelt starter P80
100ml/3½fl oz/scant ½ cup water
100g/3½oz/¾ cup strong white flour
200ml/7fl oz/scant 1 cup milk kefir P32
150ml/5fl oz/⅔ cup milk
1 tsp salt
2 large eggs, separated
150g/5½oz/1¼ cups buckwheat flour
Vegetable oil, for frying

— First make a production leaven by mixing the starter and water together in a large bowl. Sift in the white flour and mix until smooth.
— Cover and leave in a warm place to ferment for 5–8 hours, or overnight, until bubbles appear.
— Add the kefir, milk, salt, egg yolks and buckwheat flour and mix well.
— In a separate bowl, beat the egg whites until stiff, then very gently stir into the flour mixture.
— Leave in a warm place for a further 1–2 hours.
— The blinis will need to be cooked in batches. Heat a little of the oil in a large frying pan. Using a tablespoon or small ladle, drop in spoonfuls of the batter and cook until small bubbles start to appear. Turn over and cook for 1 minute, or until starting to turn golden, then transfer to a plate and keep warm. Repeat until all the batter is used up.
— Serve immediately or keep in the fridge for up to 2 days. Blinis can be served warm or cold.

Blinis with labneh dips

Pickled pepper labneh dip, will top about 20 blinis

6 tbsp labneh curd or labneh cream cheese P34
4 pieces pickled pepper P106 (or more if you prefer a stronger pickled flavour), chopped

Gherkin and mushroom labneh dip, will top about 20 blinis

1 tbsp butter or oil
1 small (or ½ large) shallot, finely chopped
100g/3½oz chestnut (cremini) mushrooms, chopped
Salt and freshly ground black pepper
6 tbsp labneh curd or labneh cream cheese P34
1 fermented gherkin P38, finely chopped

— For the pickled pepper dip, combine the labneh with the peppers and mix well. Chill in the fridge for at least 1 hour before serving.
— For the gherkin dip, melt the butter in a small frying pan over a low heat. Add the shallot and fry for about 5 minutes until soft and golden. Add the mushrooms and fry for a further 5 minutes. Season and allow to cool.
— Place the labneh, fermented gherkins, shallot and mushrooms in a bowl and mix well. Chill for at least 1 hour before serving.

Fermented gherkins & grapes

After cabbage, the most popular fermented vegetable across Poland, Ukraine and Russia is the gherkin. This is a twist on the usual recipes with the addition of grapes.

Prep 25 minutes
Ready 5–7 days
Makes approx 2 litre/67fl oz jar

600ml/20fl oz/2½ cups water
3 tbsp Himalayan pink salt
2 vine leaves (optional)
2 blackcurrant leaves (optional; the tannin in grape, blackcurrant, horseradish and oak leaves helps keep the gherkins crunchy)
2 tbsp dill seeds
800–900g/1¾–2lb small tender gherkins
5 garlic cloves
1 tbsp white mustard seeds (optional)
5–6 black peppercorns (optional)
1 tsp dried chilli flakes (optional)
1 tbsp dried horseradish root P177 (optional)
200g/7oz black grapes

— To make the brine, pour the water into a large bowl, add the salt and stir until it has dissolved.
— Place 1 vine leaf, 1 blackcurrant leaf and 1 tablespoon dill seeds in the base of a sterilised jar P12. Pack the gherkins upright, tightly, into the jar.
— Add the garlic, the remaining dill seeds, the mustard seeds, black peppercorns, chilli flakes and horseradish root (if using), then place the grapes on top.
— Cover the grapes with the remaining vine and blackcurrant leaves, then pour over the brine.
— Cover the jar with the lid and leave in a warm place for 5–7 days.
— Once ready, chill in the fridge and use within 2 weeks or pasteurise P13 to keep for several months.

You can omit the grapes if you prefer, just add a couple more gherkins.

You can use 2 or more smaller jars instead of a large one. This is useful if you plan to pasteurise them.

Use the gherkins in a fermented gherkin caponata P41, dry it and turn it into a salt P190, or add to a labneh dip P37. Use the grapes in a dirty martini below.

Sour grape pickle-tini

The brine from sauerkraut and fermented gherkins above makes a lovely, sometimes full-on, tonic drink by itself. It can also be used as part of cocktails to great effect. Here is a take on a 'dirty martini'.

Serves 1

75ml/2½fl oz/5 tbsp gin
1 tbsp dry vermouth
2 tbsp fermented gherkin brine above
Ice cubes
1 fermented grape above

— Pour the gin, dry vermouth and gherkin brine into a cocktail shaker, fill with ice and shake well.
— Strain the contents of the cocktail shaker into a glass and add a fermented grape. Serve.

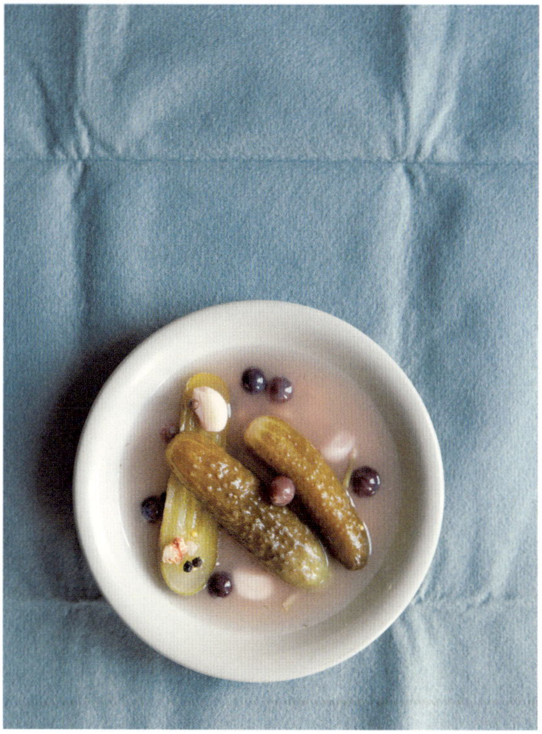

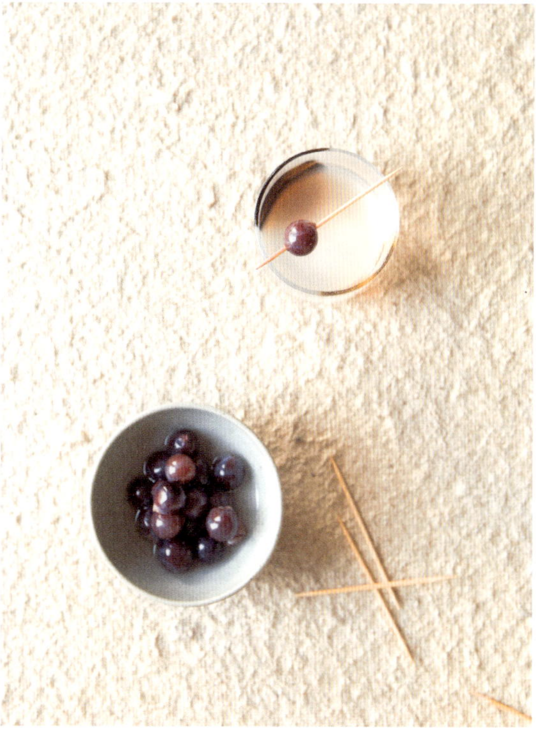

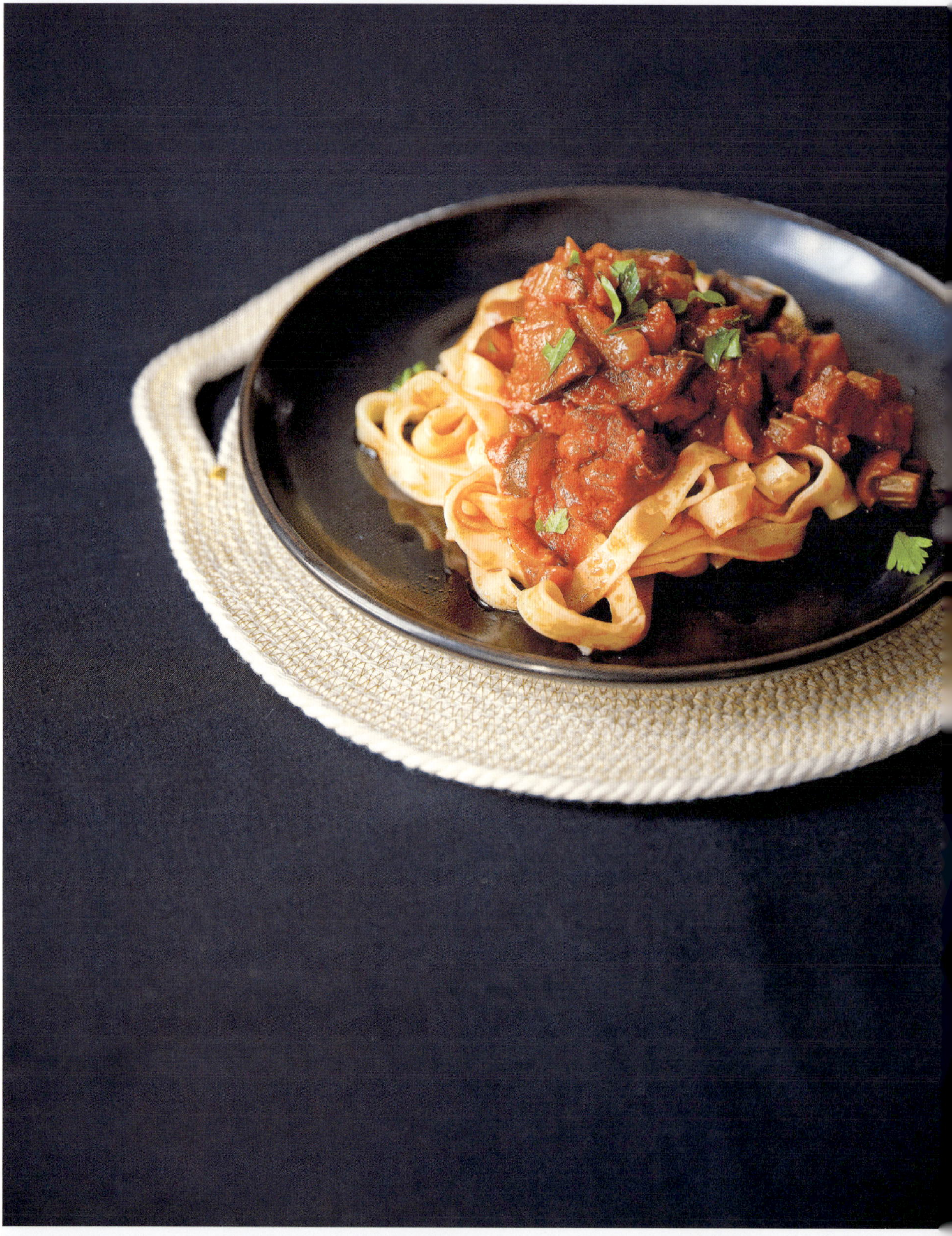

Fermented gherkin and nasturtium caponata

This Sicilian sweet-sour aubergine dish is great both as a main meal with bread or pasta, or served cold as a side dish. The gherkins P38 add a wonderful tang.

Serves 3

- 50ml/2fl oz/scant ¼ cup sunflower or rapeseed (canola) oil
- 1 medium onion, chopped
- 700ml/24fl oz tomato passata
- 2 tbsp honey
- 2 tbsp apple cider vinegar
- ½-1 tsp salt
- ½-1 tsp ground black pepper
- 500g/1lb 2oz aubergine (eggplant), cut into about 2- 2.5cm/¾-2.5cm chunks
- 4 celery sticks, washed and sliced into 1cm/½in wide pieces
- 50ml/2fl oz/scant ¼ cup olive oil
- 3 fermented gherkins, chopped P38
- 1 tbsp nasturtium capers P109
- Handful of green olives, pitted and halved
- 2 tbsp pine nuts or sunflower seeds, toasted
- Handful (about 10g/¼oz/6 tbsp) fresh flat leaf parsley or coriander (cilantro), chopped

— Heat 2 tablespoons of the sunflower oil in a large heavy-based saucepan or casserole dish over a low heat, add the onion and fry, stirring frequently, for 10-15 minutes, or until soft and golden brown.

— Add the passata, stir well and cook for a further 10 minutes.

— Add the honey, vinegar, salt and black pepper, stir well and simmer for a further 10 minutes.

— Meanwhile, heat the remaining sunflower oil in a large frying pan over a low heat. Add the aubergine and celery, in batches if necessary, and fry for 5-10 minutes, stirring frequently until the aubergine is golden brown and tender.

— Stir the aubergine and celery into the tomato and onion sauce, add the olive oil and simmer for 10 minutes.

— Add the gherkins, capers, olives and pine nuts or sunflower seeds and simmer for a further 15 minutes.

— Add the parsley or coriander and continue to simmer for 2-3 minutes.

— Serve with sourdough bread P82 or pasta. You can freeze the sauce for up to a month.

Classic napa cabbage kimchi

This is the most well-known type of Korean kimchi. In Korea this type of kimchi would contain fish paste, but we omit it to cater for vegetarians. If you like, you can add a tablespoon of fish sauce or a tablespoon of miso paste. For lovers of hot food, this kimchi works surprisingly well in stews, on burgers or in soups. You can also replace the cabbage with mooli (also known as daikon or white or oriental radish) to create a mooli kimchi. Simply use two medium-sized mooli in place of the cabbage, and omit the mooli from the paste. Kimchi can be added to a hearty solyanka P48.

Prep 20 minutes + 6-13 hours soaking
Ready 3-4 days
Makes approx 500ml/18fl oz jar

1 small head of napa cabbage (often called Chinese cabbage)

Brine
1 litre/34fl oz/4 cups water
8 tbsp (80g/3oz) coarse sea salt (pure, without iodine or anti-caking agent)

Paste
1 medium leek or bunch of spring onions (scallions), finely chopped
2 large garlic cloves, very finely chopped
1.5 cm/⅝in piece of ginger, skin scraped off and grated (1-2 tsp)
12 tbsp (50g/1¾oz) gochugaru (Korean hot chilli flakes)
80g/3oz (⅓ of medium) mooli (daikon)
2 tsp sea salt
2 tsp sugar

— To make the brine, pour the water into a large bowl, add the salt and stir to dissolve.
— Separate the cabbage leaves and place them into the brine, then weigh them down in a bowl with a heavy weight. Leave the cabbage to soak for at least 6 hours, or overnight (but not more than 24 hours).
— Drain and rinse the cabbage and squeeze out the excess water. The cabbage should now be soft and salty.
— Cut the cabbage into 4cm/1½in pieces.
— For the paste, blend all the ingredients together until smooth.
— Mix the cabbage and paste together, making sure that the cabbage is well coated all over.
— Pack the cabbage into a large sterilised jar P12 and knock down to remove any air pockets.
— Cover the jar and leave to ferment at room temperature for 2 days, then transfer to the fridge.
— The kimchi should be ready after 4-5 days.
— It can be kept in the fridge for about 6 weeks, but the flavour will develop and become more sour.

As there is a lot of chilli in the paste, it is best to wear plastic gloves when mixing the cabbage and paste together. If you do not have any gloves a couple of small plastic bags would suffice.

An alternative brining method is to cut the cabbage in half and rub each leaf with the salt, then submerge under water. The cabbage is then rinsed thoroughly after 6 hours and the paste rubbed over each leaf in turn. The cabbage halves are then packed into a jar cut side up. This method is popular in restaurants so people can be served a whole piece of kimchi rather than what looks like chopped-up leftovers.

Any brine left over can be used to kickstart a new batch of kimchi.

Baby courgette kimchi

Courgettes like you've never tasted before! One of these on the plate will change a meal. They are sure to please (or shock). Try adding turning into savoury biscuits P53.

Prep 20 min
Ready 3-4 days
Makes approx 500ml/18fl oz jar

8-9 baby courgettes (zucchini)
60g/2¼oz/¼ cup coarse sea salt (pure, without iodine or anti-caking agent)

Paste
1½ bunches spring onions (scallions) or 1 leek, finely chopped
1 garlic clove, very finely chopped
1cm/½in piece of ginger, skin scraped off and grated (1 tsp)
7 tbsp gochugaru (Korean chilli flakes) or dried chilli flakes
1-2 tbsp sea salt
1 tsp sugar

— Cut the courgettes lengthways 3-4 times, but don't cut them all the way through. Rub the salt into the cuts.
— Place the courgettes in a bowl and pour in enough water to cover.
— Leave to soak for about 1 hour, then rinse them well.
— Place all the ingredients for the paste in a bowl and mix with a fork.
— Work the paste into the cuts in the courgettes, then pack the courgettes upright into a large sterilised jar P12 and seal with the lid.
— Leave to stand at room temperature overnight, then transfer to the fridge and leave to chill for 2-3 days before eating.
— This can be stored in the fridge for up to 3 weeks.

Pumpkin kimchi

Prep 15 minutes + 3-day process
Ready 10-14 days
Makes approx 500ml/18fl oz jar

400g/14oz pumpkin
10 tbsp (100g/3½oz) coarse sea salt

Paste
1 tbsp gochugaru (Korean hot chilli flakes)
2 large leaves napa (Chinese) cabbage, chopped
50g/1¾oz (10cm/4in long piece) large leek or ½ bunch of spring onions (scallions), finely chopped
10 large garlic cloves, grated
2.5 cm/1in piece (25g) piece of ginger, skin scraped and grated
1 tbsp salt
1 tsp sugar
1 tsp white miso paste (optional)

Day 1
— Peel, deseed and cut the pumpkin into rough squares and rectangles of no more than 1cm/½in thick and place in a large bowl.
— Add the salt and mix together until the pumpkin is coated. Cover and leave to stand at room temperature overnight.

Day 2
— Rinse the pumpkin well, washing off all the salt.
— Place all the ingredients for the paste in a blender and blitz until smooth. Add the paste to the pumpkin and mix until it is coated.
— Place the pumpkin in a large sterilised jar P12, seal with the lid and leave to stand at room temperature overnight.

Day 3
— Place the jar in the fridge and leave to chill for 10 days, then taste to check if it has fermented enough for your liking.
— It can be stored in the fridge for 3-5 weeks. The flavour will become stronger over time.

Classic napa cabbage kimchi P42
Pumpkin kimchi curry P46

Baby courgette kimchi P43
Carrot kimchi P47
Pumpkin kimchi P43

Pumpkin kimchi curry

The addition of kimchi P43 to this almost tagine-style recipe creates a rich, spicy and unusual curry.

Serves 3-4

700g/1½lb pumpkin, peeled, deseeded and cut into large chunks
300g/10½oz (2 small) sweet potatoes, peeled and thickly sliced
250g/9oz (2 large) carrots, thickly sliced
2 tbsp coarse sea salt
1 tsp pink Himalayan salt (optional)
2 tsp ground cumin
2 tsp ground cinnamon
2 tsp ground coriander
2 tsp ground paprika
2 large red (bell) peppers, cut into large chunks
2 tbsp butter
3 large shallots, cut into 12 pieces
6 garlic cloves, sliced or crushed
40g/1½oz piece of ginger, skin scraped off and grated
2 bay leaves
6 green cardamom pods, split open and seeds lightly crushed
400g/14oz can chopped tomatoes
800ml/27fl oz/3½ cups water
50g/1¾oz/5 tbsp raisins
25g/1oz/2-3 tbsp dried cranberries P230, or shop bought
240g/8oz/1⅓ cups canned or freshly boiled dried chickpeas
150g/5½oz pumpkin kimchi P43
4 tbsp coriander (cilantro) or flat leaf parsley, chopped

— Preheat the oven to 220°C/425°F/gas mark 7. Put a roasting tin in the oven to heat up.
— Place the pumpkin, sweet potatoes, carrots, salt and half of each of the spices (cumin, cinnamon, coriander and paprika) in a large bowl and mix together. Add the vegetables to the hot roasting tin and roast for 25 minutes.
— Add the peppers to the tin and roast for a further 15 minutes.
— Meanwhile, heat the butter in a very large pan over a low heat, add the shallots and fry, stirring frequently, until beginning to soften and colour.
— Toss in the garlic and ginger and cook for a few more seconds.
— Tip in the other half of the spices (cumin, cinnamon, coriander and paprika) and fry for about 1 minute, adding a splash of water. The spices should start to turn into a paste.
— Add the bay leaves, cardamom, tomatoes, roasted vegetables and the measured water, stir well and bring to the boil.
— Stir in the raisins, cranberries and chickpeas, then reduce the heat and simmer for 20 minutes.
— Add the pumpkin kimchi and 2 tablespoons chopped coriander leaves and simmer for a further 20 minutes.
— Top with the remaining coriander leaves and serve with rice or preserved lemon couscous P79.

If using dried chickpeas soak them in plenty of cold water overnight. The next day, drain, put into a saucepan, pour in enough water to cover and bring to the boil. Reduce the heat and simmer for 1 hour. If you have too many chickpeas for this dish, the extra can be frozen for up to a month or could be used to make fermented hummus P66.

Carrot kimchi

This kimchi uses substantially less chilli than napa kimchi P42 and is therefore easier to use in salads and stews. Or try drying it and turning it into salt P188.

Prep 20 minutes
Ready 8 days
Makes approx 500ml/18fl oz jar

500g/1lb 2oz carrots, grated or finely chopped into thin matchsticks

Brine
1 litre/34fl oz/4 cups water
25g/1oz/5 tbsp coarse sea salt

Paste
½ bunch of spring onions (scallions) or 50g/1¾oz (10cm/4in piece of large leek), finely chopped
1 medium garlic clove, grated
1cm/½in piece of ginger, skin scraped off and grated (1 tsp)
½ tbsp gochugaru (Korean chilli flakes), or dried chilli flakes
½ tbsp sea salt

— To make the brine, pour the water into a large bowl, add the salt and stir until it has dissolved.
— Place the carrots in the brine and weigh down so that they are submerged. Leave for at least 6 hours but no longer than 12 hours.
— Drain the carrots, rinse well and squeeze out excess liquid.
— Place all the ingredients for the paste in a blender and blitz until smooth.
— Add the paste to the carrots and mix together making sure that the carrots are well coated.
— Pack the kimchi into a large sterilised jar P12 and knock down to remove any air pockets. Cover the jar with the lid and leave to ferment at room temperature for 2 days, then transfer to the fridge.
— The kimchi should be ready for eating after 4–5 days.
— Can be stored in the fridge for up to a month.

Carrot kimchi, beetroot and coriander salad

Serves 3–4

4 medium carrots, peeled and grated
1 small beetroot, peeled and grated
125–225g/4–8oz carrot kimchi above
35g/1¼oz/¼ cup sunflower seeds, soaked in water for 30 minutes (optional)
35g/1¼oz/¼ cup pumpkin seeds, soaked in water for 30 minutes (optional)
1 garlic clove, finely chopped
Juice of ½–1 lemon
2 tbsp light soy sauce
1 tbsp honey
3 tbsp sunflower oil
1 tbsp olive oil
Sea salt and freshly ground black pepper
½ bunch of fresh coriander (cilantro), chopped

— Mix the grated carrots, beetroot and carrot kimchi in a large bowl.
— Drain the sunflower and pumpkin seeds, then add to the vegetable mix.
— Add the garlic, lemon juice, soy sauce, honey and oils and mix well, then season with salt and pepper.
— Add the chopped coriander and mix well.
— Serve immediately or chill in the fridge for up to 24 hours.
— The quantity of carrot kimchi can be increased or decreased depending on personal preference. Kimchi will make this salad spicy – the more you add the hotter it will become.

Napa kimchi solyanka

This thick, hearty soup is both sour and spicy, and is very popular in Russia. Solyanka means 'salty', but the classic combination of pickled gherkins with fermented sauerkraut (in this recipe we've used napa kimchi P42) and lots of vegetables means the dish has a complex flavour. This recipe is based on one from our friend Heike, who learned it from her mum in the former East Germany.

Serves 3–4

2 tbsp olive oil
1 large onion, chopped
1 garlic clove, finely chopped
1 small carrot, chopped
1 large red (bell) pepper, chopped
100g/3½oz French (green) beans, chopped
100g/3½oz mushrooms, chopped
500–700ml/18–24fl oz/2–3 cups vegetable stock
400g/14oz can plum or chopped tomatoes
2–3 tbsp tomato purée
1 tsp black pepper
1 tsp salt
1 tbsp sweet paprika
3–5 allspice berries
1–2 bay leaves
1 tsp ground cumin
3 fermented gherkins, chopped P38 or 3 pickled gherkins
2 tbsp capers or nasturtium capers
100–200g/3½–7oz napa kimchi P42
Juice of 1 lemon or lime
35g/1¼oz/2¼ tbsp butter

To serve
2 tbsp flat leaf parsley, chopped
3–4 tbsp sour cream
Sourdough bread, sliced P82

— Heat the olive oil in a large saucepan over a low heat, add the onion and garlic and fry, stirring frequently, until the onion is soft and translucent.
— Add the chopped carrot, pepper and French beans and fry for a further 5 minutes.
— Add the mushrooms and fry gently for 5 minutes or so until the carrots, peppers and French beans have started to soften.
— Add the vegetable stock, canned tomatoes and tomato purée and stir well. Add all the spices and bay leaves, stir well, then simmer for 20 minutes stirring occasionally.
— Add the gherkins, capers and napa kimchi. Stir well, then simmer for a further 20 minutes, stirring occasionally.
— Add lemon or lime juice and the butter. Simmer for a further 10 minutes, stirring occasionally.
— Divide among serving plates and garnish with parsley. Add 2 teaspoons sour cream on to each, then serve with sliced sourdough bread.

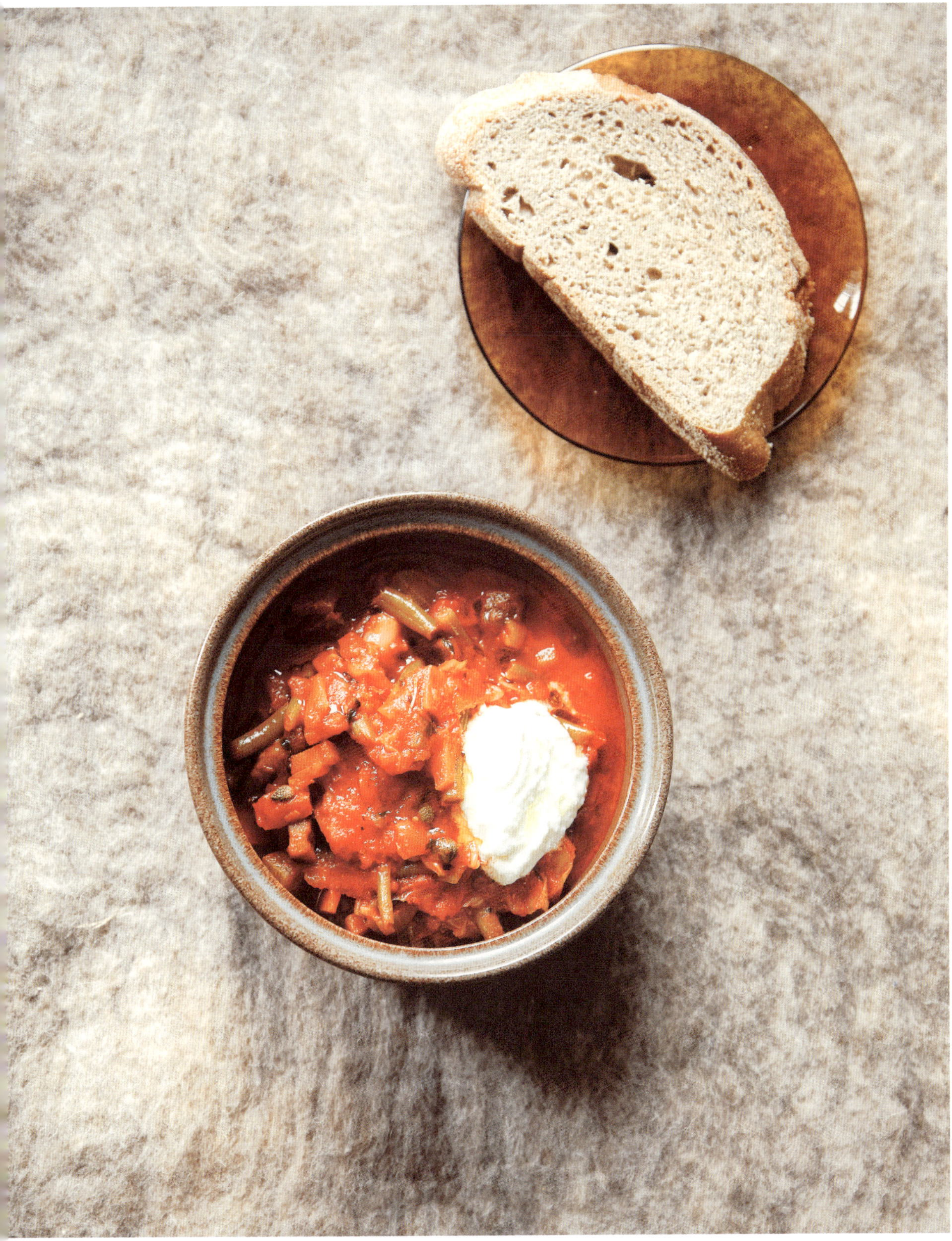

Fermented pink turnips

Turnip is pickled and fermented in many countries, but this recipe is a Slovenian-style one. You don't have to have pink turnips – it's the beetroot that produces the pink colour. Use to make savoury biscuits P53.

Prep 15 minutes
Ready 5–8 days
Makes approx 500ml/18fl oz jar

550g/1lb 4oz turnips (5 medium), peeled and grated using the large holes of a box grater
50g/1¾oz beetroot (beet), peeled and grated on the large holes of a box grater
15g/½oz/1 tbsp sea salt (pure, without iodine or anti-caking agent)

— Mix the turnips, beetroot and salt together in a large bowl. Leave for 1–2 hours, or until the excess water is drained out of the vegetables.
— Don't drain. Pack the mixture tightly into a sterilised jar P12, spooning it into the jar in batches and pressing each layer down hard to release as much liquid as possible. Make sure the salty liquid covers the vegetables.
— Leave to ferment in a warm place (about 21°C/70°F) for 5–8 days.
— Once fermented store in the fridge or keep in a cool place for up to a month.

If you're using fresh organic turnips, there's no need to peel them before grating.

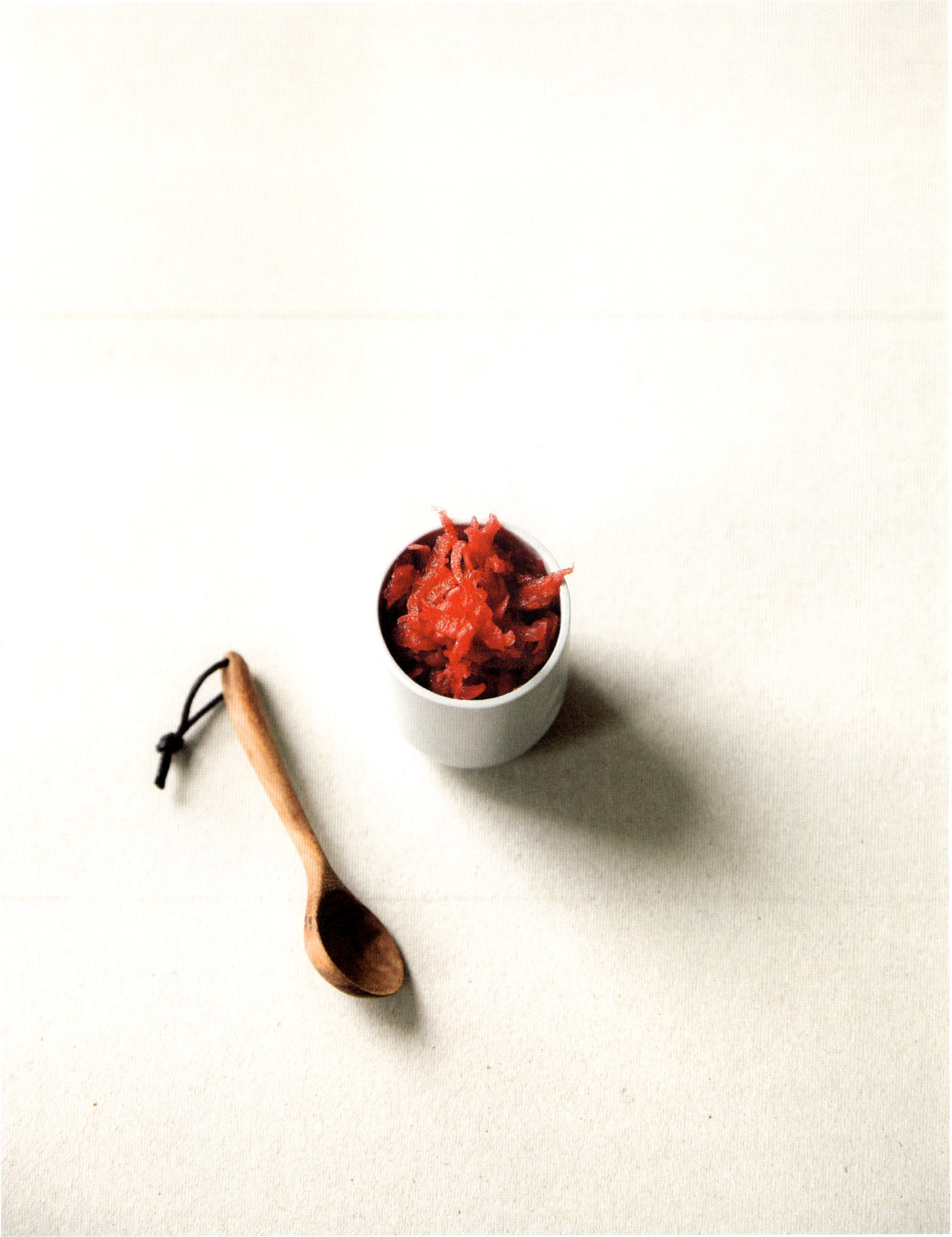

Carrot kimchi biscuits
Napa kimchi biscuits
Courgette kimchi biscuits

Kimchi or pink turnip biscuits

These moist, almost cake-like savoury biscuits are a brilliantly healthy and filling snack. They have the same satisfying bite of a falafel, but with a spicy kick. The recipe here uses napa kimchi P42 and fermented pink turnip P50. But you can also make these biscuits with carrot kimchi P47 or courgette kimchi P43 for variety in colour and flavour.

Makes 10-12 of each biscuit

100g/3½oz/¾ cup wholewheat flour, plus extra for dusting
50g/1¾oz/½ cup quinoa flour
50g/1¾oz/½ cup buckwheat flour
150g/5½oz/⅔ cup butter, softened
1 tsp pink Himalayan salt
100g/3½oz fermented pink turnip cut into small pieces P50
100g/3½oz napa kimchi P42 cut into small pieces

Replace the napa kimchi and pink turnip with the same quantities of carrot kimchi P47 and courgette kimchi P43 for biscuits with different flavour and hue.

If you make the courgette kimchi biscuits, try adding 2 tablespoons spirulina powder for a vivid green colour and health boost.

— Preheat the oven to 230°C/425°F/gas mark 7. Line 2 baking trays with baking parchment.
— Process the flours, butter and salt in a food processor until the mixture starts to turn into a dough, then remove half of the mixture and set aside.
— Add the pink turnip to the remaining mixture in the food processor and process until all the ingredients are well combined, about 2 minutes. Remove the turnip dough from the food processor and set aside on a floured work surface.
— Return the remaining half of the flour and butter mixture to the food processor, add the napa kimchi and process until all the ingredients are well combined, about 2 minutes. Remove the kimchi dough from the food processor and set aside on a floured work surface.
— Roll out the turnip dough on the floured surface into a 15cm/6in long, thick sausage, then cut into 2cm/¾in-long pieces.
— Roll each of these pieces into balls and place on the prepared baking tray. Use the bottom of a glass to gently press the balls into discs about 5mm/¼in thick.
— Repeat this process with the other kimchi dough.
— Place both baking trays in the oven and bake for 12–15 minutes. The biscuits won't go hard, but will crisp up slightly on the top.

Fermented mustard seeds

Prep 10 minutes
Ready 7 days
Makes approx 150ml/5fl oz jar

50g/1¾oz/5 tbsp white mustard seeds
Pinch of salt
100ml/3½fl oz/scant ½ cup green tea kombucha P90

— Put the mustard seeds into a sterilised jar P12 and add the salt.
— Cover with green tea kombucha, stir well, cover loosely and leave in warm place for a week to ferment.
— It will keep in the fridge for at least a month.

Fermented honey mustard

When we started to make fermented mustard we were amazed at how easy and tasty it is. The flavour is more intense than most commercial varieties. Different flavours such as chilli and horseradish can also be used.

Makes approx 150ml/5fl oz jar

1 batch fermented mustard seeds above
1 garlic clove, very finely chopped
½ tsp salt
3 tsp honey
1 tsp olive oil

— Blend the fermented mustard seeds in a food processor or blender, add the garlic, salt and honey and blend until smooth.
— Add the olive oil, mix well and transfer to a sterilised jar P12. Seal with a lid and chill in the fridge.
— Fermented mustard will keep in the fridge for at least a month.

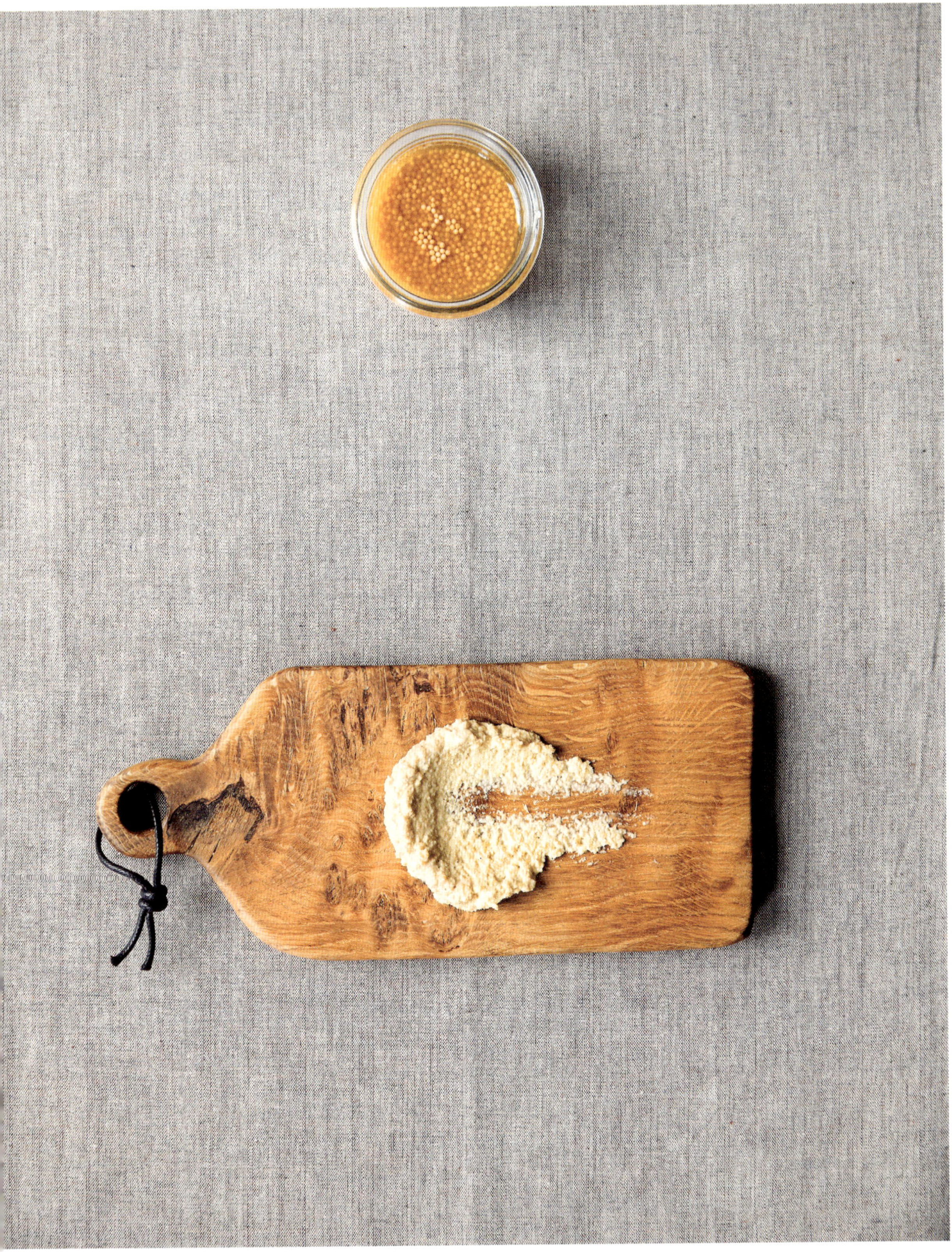

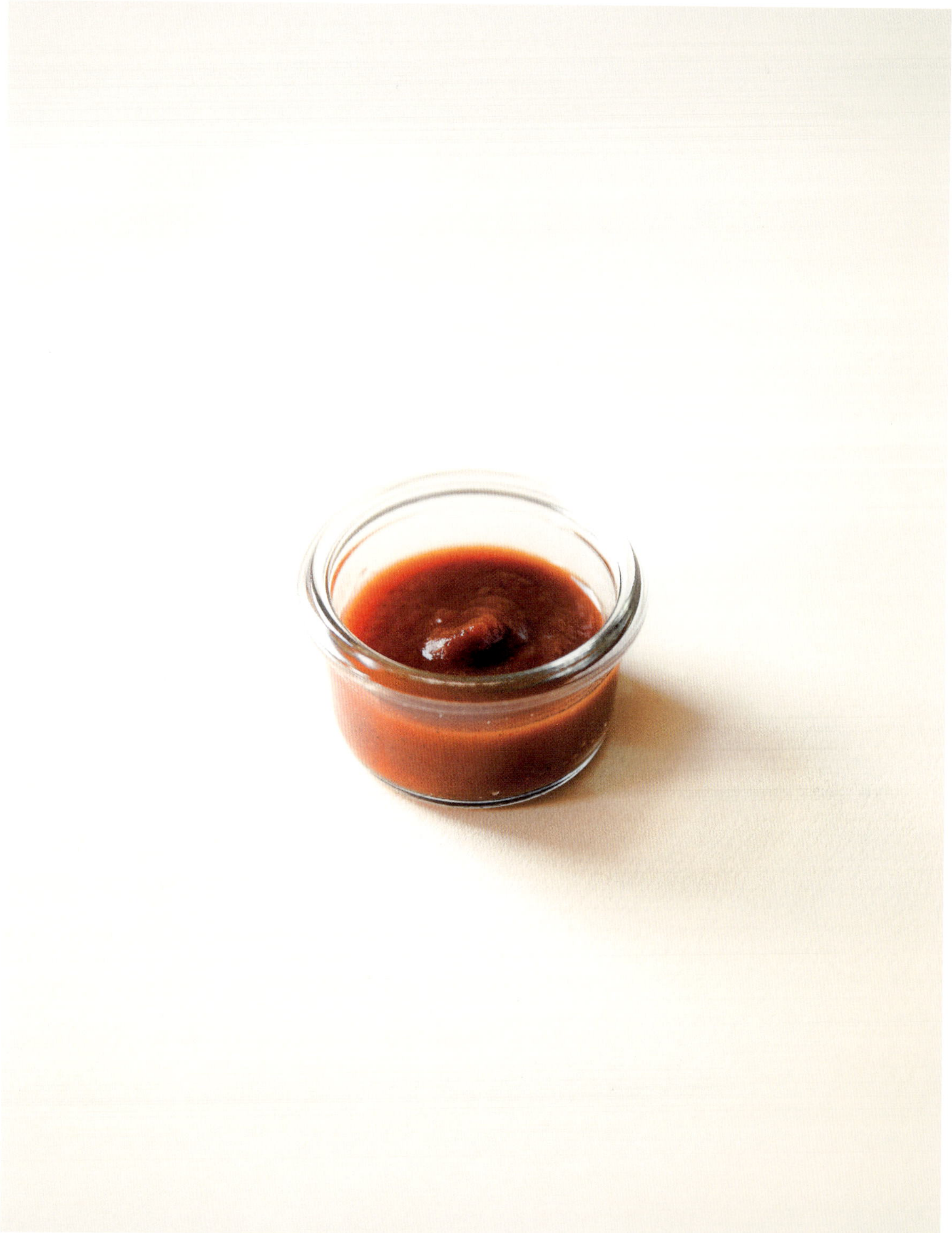

Fermented ketchup

The irresistible rise of chilli sauce is probably in part due to the blandness of ketchup, but this ketchup is something very special indeed.

Prep 1 hour
Ready 4 days
Makes approx 600ml/20fl oz

700ml/24fl oz/3 cups tomato passata
1 tsp ground cinnamon
1 tsp ground allspice
1 tsp ground paprika
2 cloves
4 black peppercorns
¼ tsp ground chilli (optional)
1 star anise (optional)
2 tsp sea salt
2 garlic cloves, very finely chopped
60ml/2¼fl oz/¼ cup raw cider vinegar
4 heaped tsp raw honey
½ tsp ground black pepper
120ml/4fl oz/½ cup whey P34, or water kefir P33

— Put the passata with all the spices in a saucepan and mix to combine, then simmer over a low heat for about 45 minutes. Remove from the heat and leave to cool.
— Once cold, add the salt, garlic, vinegar, honey, black pepper and whey or kefir and stir well.
— Transfer to a sterilised jar P12, cover loosely with a lid (or plate) and leave at room temperature for 4 days.
— After this time, seal the lid tightly and chill in the fridge and keep for up to a month.

Coriander and yoghurt dip

This is great served with spiced crackers P199 and as part of a thali P201. It's a good way to use leftover yoghurt P20.

Serves 2-3

40g/1½oz/1 cup chopped mixed coriander (cilantro) and mint
1 green chilli, sliced
1 cm/½in piece of ginger, skin scraped off and chopped
1 small garlic clove, very finely chopped
1 tsp honey
½ tsp ground cumin
½ tsp ground coriander
2 tbsp freshly squeezed lime juice
6 tbsp plain live yoghurt P20
Salt and freshly ground black pepper

— Place all the ingredients, except the yoghurt, salt and pepper, in a food processor and blend until smooth. Add the yoghurt and blend well, then season.
— Transfer the dip to a sterilised jar P12 and chill in the fridge.
— Use within 3-4 days.

Sourdough toasties with fermented toppings

Toast can fall short of its full potential – even Welsh rarebit can be too cheese-orientated – but the addition of tomato (or in this case a kimchi paste P42) and pickled vegetables P106 creates a treat every bit as satisfying as a mini-pizza.

Serves 1

2 slices of sourdough bread P82
2 heaped tsp leftover kimchi paste taken from the jar without the cabbage P42
6 slices of pickled pepper, cut into smaller pieces P106
8 slices of chorizo (optional)
6–8 slices of mature cheddar
Fermented ketchup, to serve P57

— Preheat the grill.
— Lightly toast the bread.
— On each slice, place 1 teaspoon leftover kimchi paste and spread evenly over the toast. Add a few pieces of pickled pepper, 4 slices of chorizo (if using) and a few slices of cheddar.
— Place under the hot grill for 3–4 minutes, or until the cheese has melted and is bubbling hot.
— Serve with fermented ketchup.

This recipe is also superb with ham and gherkin. Simply replace the pickled pepper with sliced fermented gherkins P38 and add 4 slices of ham, then top with cheddar and grill.

Fermented pizza sauce

Extra sauce can be frozen for up to a month. Freeze the sauce without the addition of the olive oil and garlic, then add the finely chopped garlic and olive oil after defrosting.

Makes about 700ml/24fl oz

1 tbsp sunflower or rapeseed (canola) oil
1 small onion, chopped
2–3 celery sticks, sliced
1 small carrot, cubed
2 garlic cloves, very finely chopped, plus 1 garlic clove, very finely chopped separately
½ tsp black pepper
¼ tsp hot paprika
½ tsp sea salt
100g/3½oz tomato purée (paste)
350–400ml/12–14fl oz/1½–1¾ cups water
2 rosemary sprigs
4 thyme sprigs
6–10 basil leaves
20ml/¾fl oz/4 tsp olive oil
100g/3½oz fermented ketchup P57

— Heat the sunflower oil gently in a heavy-based saucepan, add the onion and sauté for 5 minutes. Add the celery and sauté for 5 minutes, then add the carrot and sauté for 5 minutes. Add the 2 garlic cloves and spices and sauté for 1–2 minutes. Add the tomato purée and water and stir.
— Tie together the rosemary and thyme sprigs and add to the sauce along with the basil leaves. Bring to the boil, then reduce the heat and simmer for 15 minutes. Leave to cool.
— Remove the rosemary and thyme and use a handheld blender or food processor to blend until smooth.
— Add the remaining finely chopped garlic and the olive oil. Stir and leave to stand for 20–30 minutes. Add the ketchup and stir well. Use straight away or leave for 24 hours for the flavours to develop.

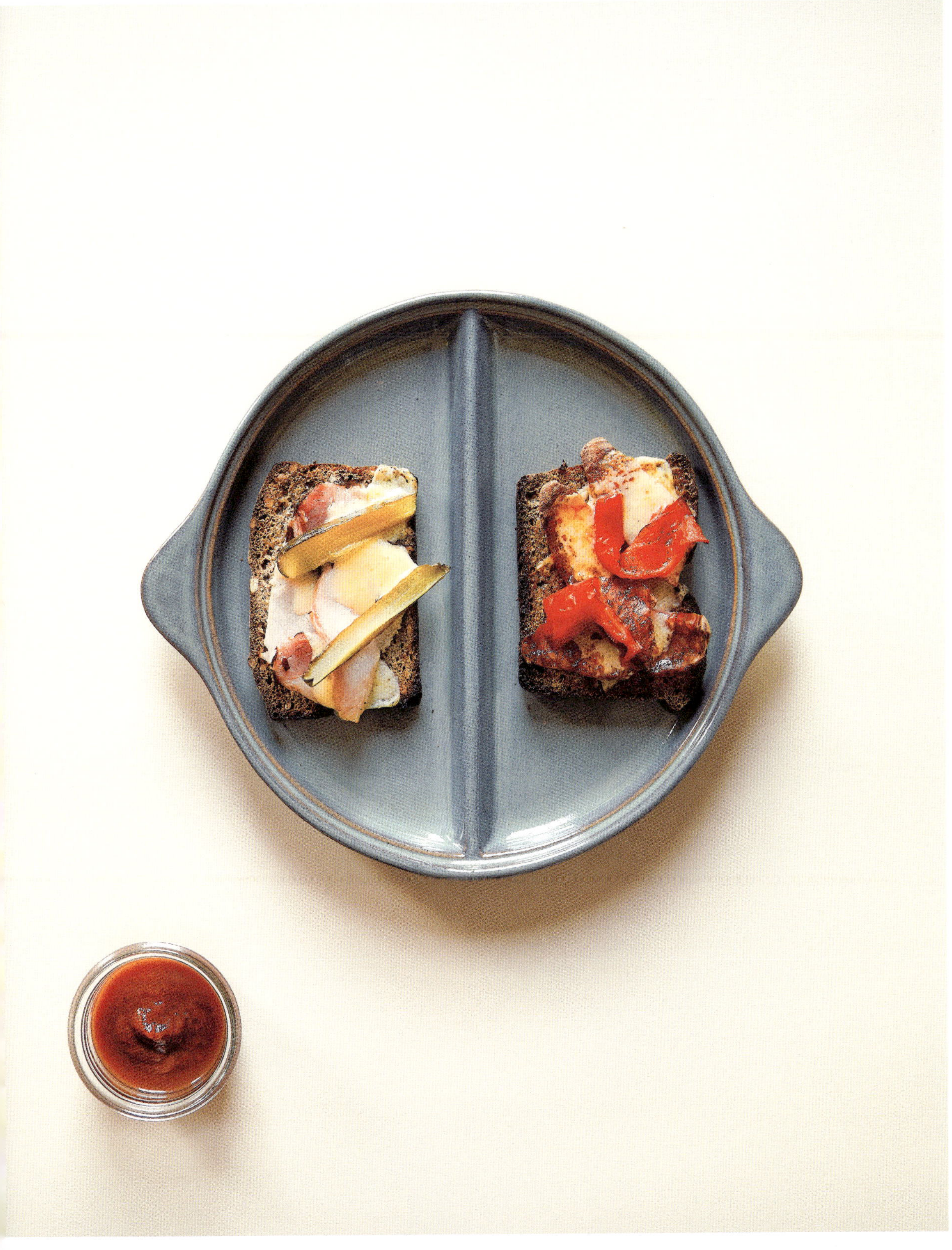

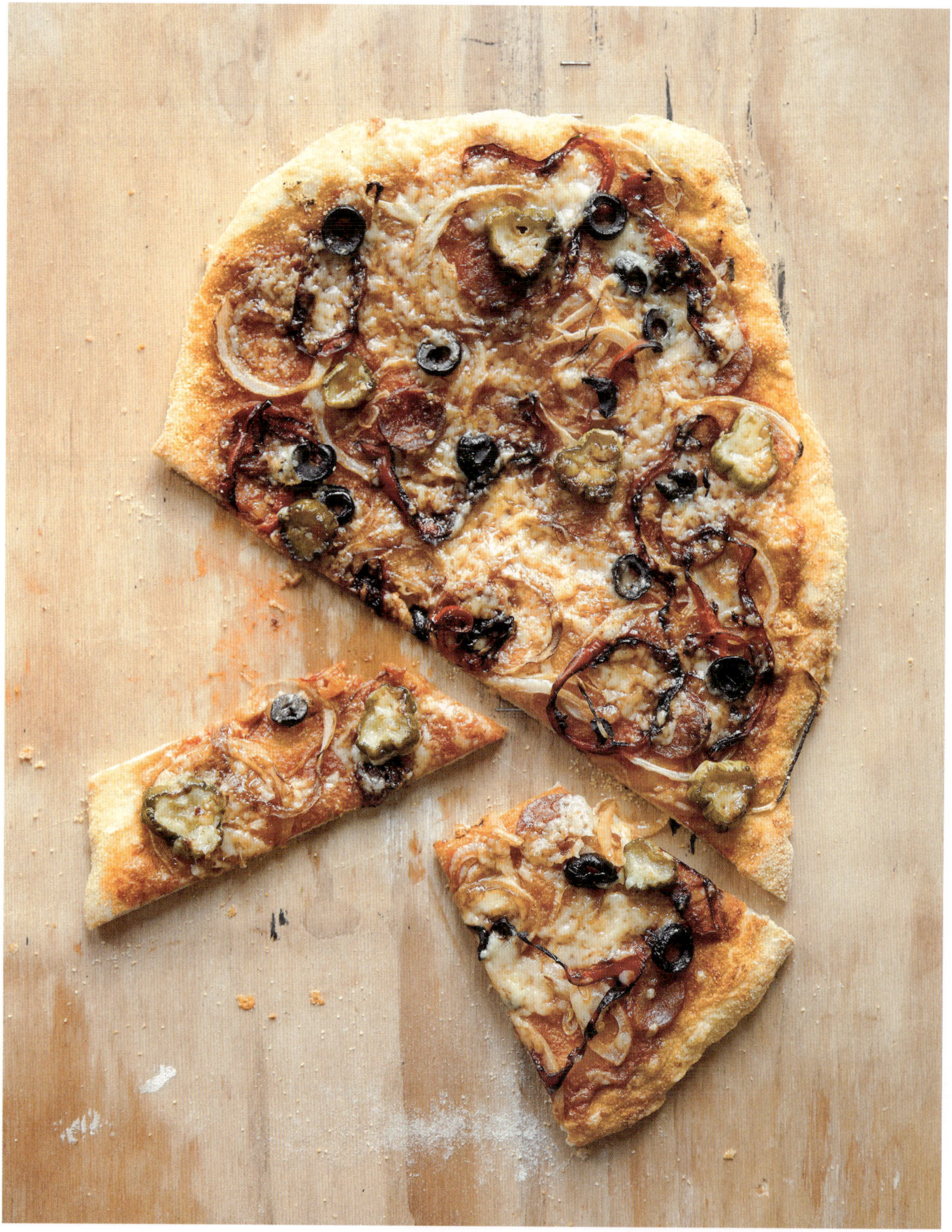

Long-fermented pizza dough

This dough uses a long-fermentation method with yeast. The longer fermentation gives time for the naturally occurring lactic bacteria to work on developing the flavour and texture.

Prep 20 minutes
Ready 1 day
Makes approx 800g/1¾lb (4 pizzas)

600g/1lb 5oz/4¼ cups strong white flour
3–4g/¾ tsp fresh yeast
2 tsp (10g/¼oz) sea salt
185ml/6½fl oz/¾ cup water
4 tbsp olive oil

— Place the flour in a large bowl, add the fresh yeast and rub it into the flour, then add the salt.
— Add the water and olive oil and mix until a dough has formed and there are no dry patches. Leave the dough to rest for 20 minutes.
— Knead the dough for 5–10 minutes, then cover and place in the fridge for 12 hours, or overnight.

This dough also makes a good white bread after the overnight rise. Shape the dough and place in an oiled 900g/2lb tin, leave to rise, then bake at 230°C/450°F/gas mark 8 for 15 minutes. Reduce the oven temperature to 200°C/400°F/gas mark 6 and bake for a further 20 minutes.

Peppe rosso 10-inch pizza

Makes 4, dinner plate size

175g/6oz/1 cup coarse semolina
800g/1¾lb long-fermented pizza dough, divided into 4 equal parts and formed into round balls above
About 12 tbsp pizza sauce P58
1 red (bell) pepper, thinly sliced
Handful of black olives, pitted and sliced
40 slices of chorizo (optional)
40 slices of sweet and spicy gherkins P116
120g/4oz/1 cup mature (sharp) cheddar, grated

— Preheat the oven to 230°C/450°F/gas mark 8.
— Prepare 4 flat baking trays and 4 sheets of baking parchment large enough to accommodate a 25cm/10in pizza.
— Place a sheet of baking parchment on the work surface and cover generously with semolina.
— Take 1 ball of pizza dough and place it in the middle of a sheet of baking parchment, then sprinkle generously with semolina.
— Flatten the dough, then using your hands, spread it out so you have roundish shape, about 25cm/10in (dinner plate size) in diameter. You can lift your dough and add semolina if it starts to stick. Avoid using a rolling pin if you can as it will change the dough structure and influence the texture and flavour of your pizza.

— Once the dough is ready carefully slide it from the baking parchment on to a baking tray.
— Spread 3 tablespoons of the pizza sauce over the pizza dough base, then add one-quarter of the sliced pepper, one-quarter of olives, one-quarter of chorizo slices (if using), one-quarter of the gherkins, and one-quarter of the grated cheddar.
— Bake for 15–25 minutes, checking after 15 minutes to make sure it's not burning. The crust should be crispy and golden brown.
— Repeat to make 3 more pizzas.

Nukadoko

Nukadoko is a Japanese rice-bran fermenting bed. Once made, it's used to ferment vegetables. It's fairly easy to make, but it does require maintenance, which makes it one of the more labour-intensive procedures. It also requires a leap of faith for those who have been waging war on bacteria, because this is basically a bowl of lactobacillus and wild yeasts. The resulting nukazuke are certainly worthwhile – vegetables that have been in a rice-bran bed remain crisp but become wonderfully tangy. This recipe shows you how to get the bed ready.

Prep 30 minutes
Ready 7 days
Makes 1 small fermenting bed (size of a large bowl)

375g/13oz/3¼ cups rice bran
50g/1¾oz/5 tbsp sea salt (pure, without iodine or anti-caking agent)
350ml/12fl oz/1½ cups cooled boiled water
40g/1½oz bread
3cm/1¼in piece of ginger, shredded
2 garlic cloves, crushed
10cm/4in square of kombu seaweed, soaked until soft
2 dried red chillies P193, or shop-bought
2 carrots, washed and quartered
4–5 cabbage pieces (about 4 cm/1½in square), washed

The bran should smell earthy and should not become mouldy, but if it does then discard it.

Once ready, the fermenting bed can be used indefinitely, but will need occasional top ups of bran and salt as it gets depleted.

— Heat a dry heavy-based frying pan over a medium-low heat. Add the rice bran and toast, stirring constantly, until it starts to dry and give off a nutty aroma. Be careful not to let It burn. Leave to cool.
— Dissolve the salt in the water. If it does not dissolve completely heat it gently and stir until it does.
— In a blender, blend the bread with the water and salt mixture. Allow to cool.
— Mix the rice bran with the cooled bread and water mixture in a large bowl. Add the shredded ginger, crushed garlic, kombu and chillies. The mixture should feel like wet sand but should not be waterlogged.
— Bury the carrots and cabbage pieces into the mix and press the surface of the bran down until smooth.
— Place a clean cloth over the top and tie a piece of string around it to secure it. Or use a lid to hold the cloth in place, but allow air to get in. Leave to stand at room temperature away from a heat source, such as a radiator, the oven or direct sunlight.
— The fermenting bed now needs to be turned over each day. Use clean hands to mix the bran well and turn it over to aerate it.
— After 2 days the carrots and cabbage can be removed and discarded and some fresh vegetables added. (This process continues to prepare the fermenting bed for the vegetables you will ferment later on.) It might take 2 weeks for the bed to get up to speed.
— As you continue to replenish these vegetables, they will become more salty and sour. After a few rounds, you will be able to eat the fermented vegetables you've used to get the fermenting bed ready.
— In summer the fermenting bed will work quicker. Smaller vegetables should ferment in hours while whole carrots and other large vegetables should ferment overnight.
— Once the fermenting bed is up to speed, it can be used to ferment many types of vegetables including carrot, cabbage, radish, cucumber and cauliflower.

Nukazuke with udon noodles

The delicate flavour of nukazuke made in a fermenting bed P62 is a perfect partner to udon noodles and miso.

Serves 3

4 tbsp white miso paste
1 tsp sugar
3 tbsp mirin
2 tbsp light soy sauce
125ml/4fl oz/½ cup boiled water
Juice of ½ lemon or lime
250g/9oz udon noodles
2 tbsp vegetable oil, for frying
1 onion, chopped
3 garlic cloves, finely chopped
2 nukazuke carrots, washed and sliced left
10cm/4in long piece of nukazuke mooli (daikon), washed and sliced left
9 nukazuke cauliflower florets, washed and cut into smaller pieces left
10cm/4in long piece of nukazuke cabbage, washed and sliced left
6 tbsp pine nuts, toasted

— Put the white miso paste, sugar and mirin in a large heatproof bowl set over a pan of simmering water and heat, stirring constantly until the sugar has dissolved.
— Add the soy sauce and boiled water, stir well and remove from the heat.
— Add the lemon juice, stir well and keep warm.
— Boil the udon noodles according to the packet instructions.
— Meanwhile, heat the oil in a wok over a medium heat. Add the onion and stir-fry for 5 minutes. Add the garlic and fry for another minute.
— Add the nukazuke vegetables and stir-fry for a further 2–3 minutes, then add the miso sauce and udon noodles and mix well.
— Serve immediately sprinkled with toasted pine nuts.

Fermented veggie sticks

This is a good way to try out a variety of fermented vegetables to see which you prefer.

Prep 30 minutes
Ready 7 days
Makes approx 2.5 litre/85fl oz jar

200g/7oz French (green) beans
200g/7oz carrots, washed, peeled and cut into 10cm/4in long, 1cm/½in wide sticks
200g/7oz celery, washed and cut into 10cm/4in long sticks
200g/7oz white cabbage, cut into thin wedges
200g/7oz cauliflower, divided into florets
1 red chilli, stalk cut off
3 garlic cloves, peeled
1 tbsp dried dill seeds
1 dried dill stalk with head
5-6 slices of dried horseradish root P177 (optional)

Brine
1 litre/34fl oz/4 cups water
50g/1¾oz/5 tbsp Himalayan pink rock salt or sea salt (pure, without iodine or anti-caking agent)

— To prepare the brine, bring the water to the boil in a medium saucepan, then add the salt and stir well until it has dissolved. Remove from the heat and leave to cool.
— Prepare the vegetables and place them in a large, sterilised jar P12. Add the garlic, dill and horseradish, then cover with the cooled brine.
— Cover the jar loosely with the lid and place in a warm place. Leave the vegetables to ferment for about 7 days before using.
— They can be kept in a cool place for up to a month.

Fermented veggie sticks
Fermented hummus P66

Fermented hummus

Tinned chickpeas will do, but for a very smooth hummus use freshly cooked dried chickpeas (they will need to be soaked overnight before cooking). It's the whey P34 or water kefir P33 that's responsible for the fermenting.

Prep 15 minutes
Ready 10 hours
Makes approx 250ml/9fl oz jar

250g/9oz/1½ cups chickpeas, cooked
1 small garlic clove, sliced
½ tsp fine sea salt
Freshly ground black pepper
Juice of 2 lemons
60ml/2¼fl oz/¼ cup olive oil
1 tbsp tahini
150ml/5fl oz/⅔ cup whey or water kefir P33

— Blend all the ingredients, except the whey or kefir, in a food processor or blender until smooth.
— Add the whey or kefir and mix well.
— Cover and leave at room temperature for about 10 hours, then transfer to an airtight container and chill in the fridge.
— Use within 3 days.

Alternatively, the hummus can be spiced up with pickled pepper P106. Simply follow the method, but at the blending stage add 60g/2oz/¼ cup chopped pickled pepper.

Aubergine hummus

This is great with sourdough pitta bread P87, pickled bean falafel P155 and Balkan pickles P153.

Serves 4

1 aubergine (eggplant), thickly sliced
½ tsp sea salt
Rapeseed (canola) oil
1 batch of fermented hummus above

— Sprinkle the aubergine slices with salt and coat in the oil.
— Preheat the oven to 230°C/450°F/gas mark 8 and put a baking tray in to heat up.
— Place the aubergine slices on the preheated baking tray and roast for about 15–20 minutes, or until golden and soft.
— Blend with the fermented hummus in a blender until smooth.
— Use within 3 days.

Cabbage and apple sauerkraut

Sauerkraut is a very easy example of lactic fermentation and is the ideal place to start if you are new to this. It's worth remembering that it's not *us* that makes delicious sauerkraut, it's lactic bacteria. We simply have to create the wet, salty environment that the lactic bacteria thrive in. Transform into sauerkraut bubble and squeak P69.

Prep 20 minutes
Ready 4–5 days
Makes approx 1.5 litres/50fl oz jar

1kg/2¼lb cabbage, finely chopped
200g/7oz apples, peeled, cored and grated
18g/¾oz/scant 2 tsp sea salt
½ tsp dried chilli flakes (optional)
½ tsp caraway seeds (optional)

— Put the cabbage and apple in a large bowl, add the salt and mix until the cabbage is coated. This will help release the liquid which will make up the brine. Sprinkle over the chilli flakes and caraway seeds (if using) then squeeze and turn the cabbage over.

— Pack the cabbage mixture into a large sterilised jar P12, knocking it down with a broad-based wooden spoon or a pestle as you go, so that the cabbage is submerged in the brine. Put a sterilised glass or stone weight on the cabbage, if available.

— Leave the sauerkraut to ferment at room temperature for 3 days. Check each day and push the cabbage down so it remains under the brine.

— From day 3 start tasting the cabbage to see how it is progressing. There is not an 'optimal' level of fermentation, as some people prefer a mild flavour while others like the more intense flavours that develop over time. Once you reach your ideal flavour, refrigerate and consume within 5 months.

You can use a fermenting lid with an an airlock on your jar, which will allow the escape of carbon dioxide (a by-product of fermentation) and restrict oxygen.

It's important that the sauerkraut remains under the surface of the brine. Released carbon dioxide will push up the vegetables. Check each day and push the vegetables back down under the brine.

If there is not enough brine to cover the vegetables, additional brine can be made by dissolving 1 teaspoon of salt per 200ml/7fl oz/ scant 1 cup water.

Experiment with other vegetables such as carrots, radishes, greens and onions. Other spices such as juniper and herbs are a good addition. Use these sparingly at first, as these flavours can be strong.

Sauerkraut bubble and squeak
Cabbage and apple sauerkraut P67

Sauerkraut bubble and squeak

Make good use of your sauerkraut P67 and dried mushrooms P172 in this satisfying small plate.

Serves 4

200g/7oz sauerkraut P67
1 bay leaf
5 allspice berries
225ml/8fl oz/1 cup water
8 medium potatoes, peeled and cut into pieces
Vegetable oil, for frying
1 medium onion, chopped
Dried mushroom sauce, to serve P175

— Place the sauerkraut, bay leaf and allspice in a small saucepan. Pour in the water to cover and bring to the boil.
— Reduce the heat and simmer for 30 minutes, then drain and remove the bay leaf and allspice. Chop the sauerkraut roughly.
— Boil the potatoes in another pan until tender, then drain and mash.
— Heat a little oil in a frying pan over a medium heat, add the onion and sauté until golden.
— Mix all the ingredients well in a large bowl.
— Heat 1–2 tablespoons of oil in a medium frying pan. Using a tablespoons scoop up some of the mix and with a second tablespoon form into an oval or rounded shape. Gently push each one on to the frying pan and fry until they are golden on both sides.
— Serve with dried mushroom sauce.

Tempeh

Tempeh is a protein-rich block of fermented soya beans. Although it isn't hard to make, it is on the more esoteric end of the fermenting spectrum because it's fermented by mould (created by the fungus Rhizopus oligosporus) rather than yeast or bacteria. The white mould encases the soya beans forming a block of nutty goodness which can then be used in to make spiced tempeh wraps P74.

Prep 1 hour 20 minutes
Ready 2 days
Makes 3-4 small blocks

500g/1lb 2oz soya beans
2 tbsp vinegar
2 tsp tempeh starter culture (you can buy this online)

— Soak the soya beans in a large bowl of water overnight.
— Next day, drain and put the beans through a rough grinder or crush them under a rolling pin to dislodge the hulls, then put them in a pan. Fill the pan with water and stir until the hulls from the beans float to the surface. Try to drain off as many of the hulls as possible, but don't worry if some remain.
— Bring the beans to the boil, then reduce the heat and simmer for about 30 minutes, or until the beans are nearly done, but still al dente.
— Drain the beans and spread them out on a tray. Dry them with a clean tea towel, kitchen paper or even a hairdryer, stirring them at the same time.
— When the beans have cooled to body temperature transfer them to a bowl and stir in the vinegar, then the tempeh starter culture.
— Using a thick, sharp needle, make holes about 1cm/½in apart all over 3-4 plastic ziplock bags and pack the beans into them. The beans should be lightly compacted to a thickness of between 2-3cm/¾-1¼in.
— Put the bags into a place where the temperature can be maintained at 30-32°C/86-90°F.
— Creating the right heat for the fermentation process is usually the hardest part. We have managed by putting the bean bags on a plate on the top of a dehydrator. Other methods include using an insulated picnic basket and adding a hot water bottle occasionally, or adding a microwaveable bean bag.
— Check the bags occasionally to ensure that the correct temperature is being maintained. After about 12 hours the incubating beans will start to create their own heat and might not require any additional heat source.
— After about 30 hours the beans should have developed a white coating. When the beans have become firm blocks or when grey/black marks appear by the holes then the process is complete.
— The tempeh blocks can now be stored in the fridge or removed from the bags and heated in an oven preheated to 170°C/325°F/gas mark 3 for 20 minutes to stop the fermentation process. They should be used within 4 days. Alternatively, the blocks can also be dipped in boiling water for a minute, then frozen and used within several months.

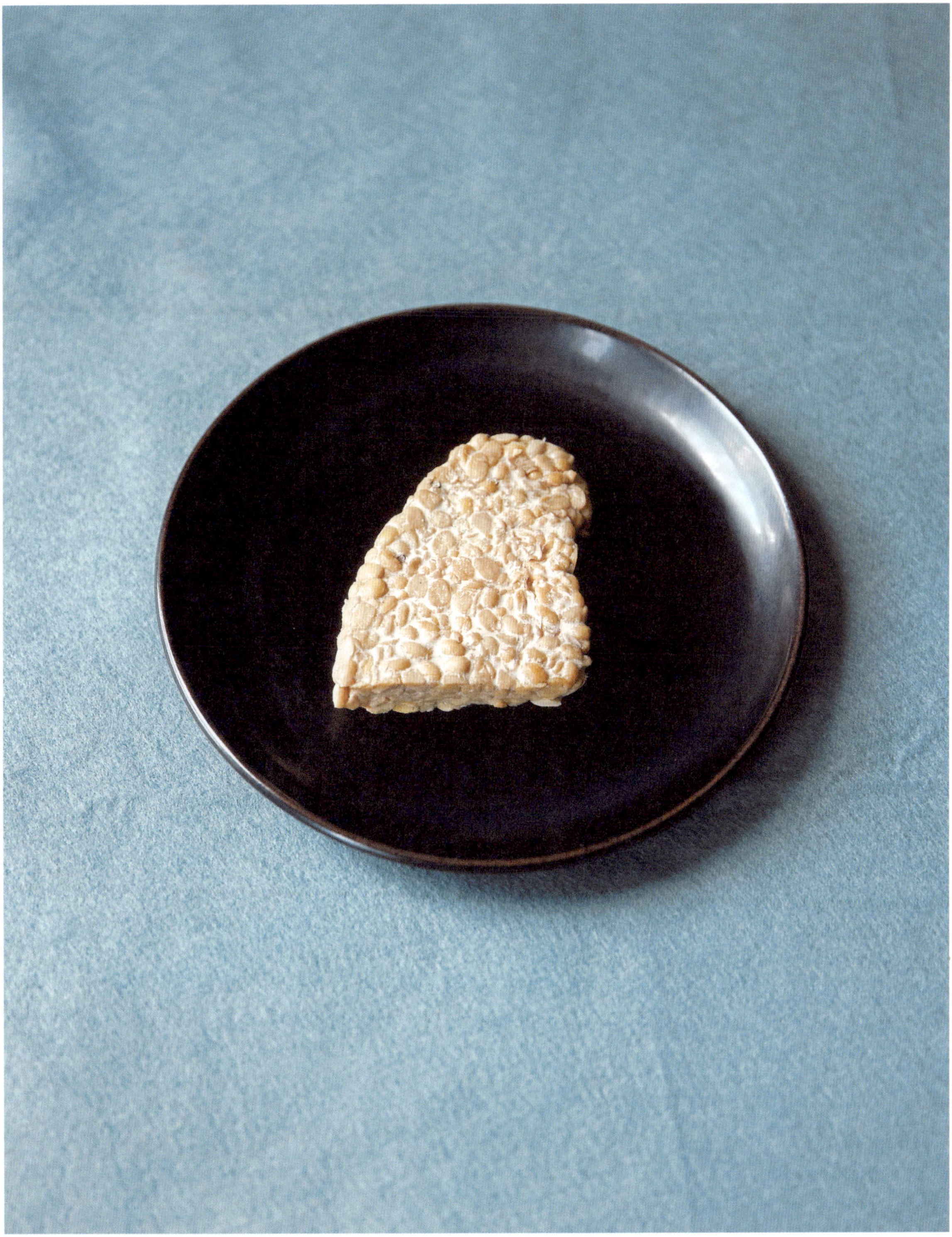

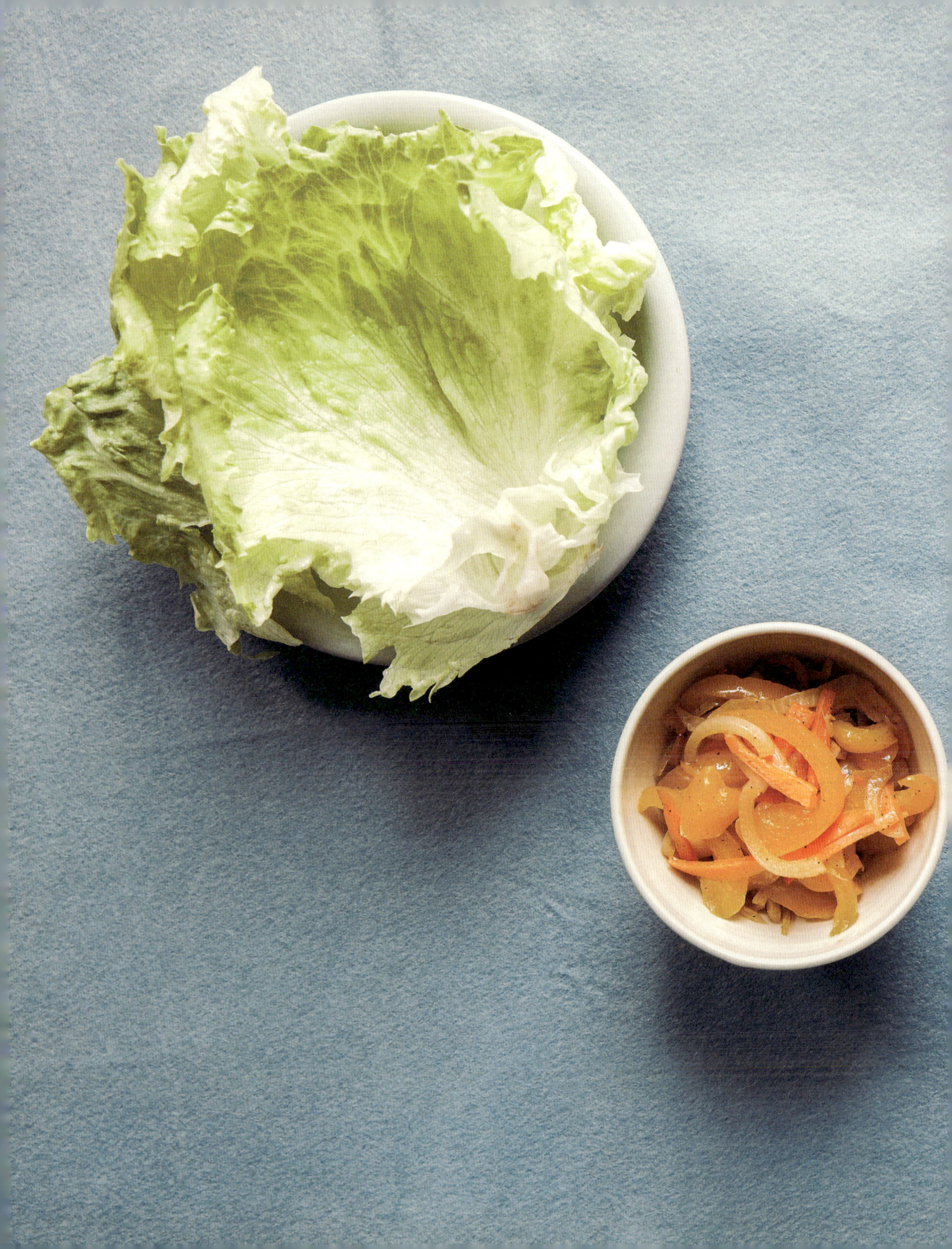

Spicy tempeh in Vietnamese wraps P74

Spicy tempeh in Vietnamese wraps

This is perhaps the most complicated dish, preparation-wise, but it is well worth it. Our friend Nel was taught this recipe by her Vietnamese friend Lotus.

Serves 4

230g/8½oz soya tempeh, sliced (1cm/½in thick) P70
Rapeseed (canola) oil, for frying
1 large onion, cut in half and sliced
2 red (bell) peppers, cut in half, deseeded and sliced
1 carrot, cut into matchsticks
1 garlic clove, chopped
2cm/¾in piece of ginger, skin scraped off, cut into matchsticks
1 red chilli, chopped
3 tbsp light soy sauce
1 tbsp freshly squeezed lime or lemon juice
½ bunch of mint leaves
½ bunch coriander (cilantro) leaves
½ bunch parsley leaves
8–9 large iceberg lettuce leaves

Tempeh marinade
2 tbsp light soy sauce
Juice of 1 lime
1 red chilli, chopped
5cm/2in piece of garlic, skin scraped off and very finely chopped

Pancake wraps (makes 8–9)
100g/3½oz/¾ cup plain (all-purpose) flour
100g/3½oz/scant 1 cup rice flour
50g/1¾oz/scant ½ cup potato flour
400ml/14fl oz/1¾ cups water
Pinch of salt

Dipping sauce
½ small red chilli, finely chopped, deseeded if preferred
2 garlic cloves, finely chopped
Juice of 1 lime or lemon
60ml/2¼fl oz/¼ cup water
2–3 tbsp honey

— Combine all the marinade ingredients together and mix well.
— Slice the tempeh and place in single layer in a flat-bottomed dish. Pour over the marinade to cover and leave for 2 hours.
— Blitz all the ingredients for the pancake wraps in a blender until smooth. Transfer to a bowl, cover and leave to stand for 10 minutes.
— Heat a little oil in a medium frying pan over a medium heat. Pour a small ladleful of the pancake wrap mixture into the pan and quickly tip the pan to spread the batter over the base. Cook until it is set and lightly coloured on the bottom side, then turn the wrap over and cook the other side.
— When the second side is done place on a warmed plate, cover with an upturned plate and place in a warm oven. Repeat until all the wrap mixture is used up.
— To make the dipping sauce, mix all the ingredients together in a bowl until combined, then set aside.
— For the tempeh, heat 1 tablespoon oil in a large frying pan over a medium heat, add the tempeh slices and fry until golden on both sides. Towards the end add the remaining marinade, then remove from the heat, transfer to an ovenproof dish, cover and place in a warm oven.
— Heat 1 tablespoon of oil in a wok over a medium heat, add the onion, peppers and carrot and stir-fry for 2 minutes. Add the garlic, ginger and chilli and stir-fry for a further minute. Add the soy sauce and lime/lemon juice and stir-fry for a further 1–2 minutes, then remove from the heat.
— To assemble, divide the stir-fried vegetables, tempeh and fresh herbs equally between the wraps, then roll up and enclose them in a lettuce leaf. Serve with the dipping sauce.

Beetroot kvass

This fermented beetroot juice can be drunk as it is or used to make borscht P76. 'Kvass' is an old word of Slavonic origin meaning a fermented drink. The most common kvass is a low-alcoholic version made with old rye bread.

Prep 15 minutes
Ready 6–7 days
Makes approx 3 litre/5¼ pints

2kg/4½lb beetroot (beets), peeled and thinly sliced
3 garlic cloves, peeled
3 litres/5¼ pints/3 quarts spring water, or boiled and cooled tap water
3 tsp rock or sea salt (pure, without iodine or anti-caking agent)

— Place the beetroot and garlic in a sterilised 4 litre/7 pint/3.5 quart jar P12 or fermenting vessel.
— Dissolve the salt in the water, then pour over the beetroot. Cover loosely with the lid and place in a warm place to ferment for 6–7 days.
— Strain the liquid into sterilised bottles or jars and store in a cool place or in the fridge.
— Use within 2–3 weeks.

Zur kvass

This is another form of kvass, but this one is made with rye flour and water. It's used to make a soup called zurek P77. It is possible to replace the rye flour with wholemeal wheat flour, but made with wheat, kvass is called *bialy barszcz* and has a slightly different flavour.

Prep 15 minutes
Ready 5 days
Makes 500ml/18fl oz

8 heaped tbsp/¾ cup wholemeal rye flour
1–3 garlic cloves, chopped
Slice of rye sourdough bread P82
500ml/18fl oz/2 cups boiled water
1 tsp dried marjoram (optional)
½ tsp black pepper (optional)
Pinch of salt (optional)

— Mix all the ingredients together in a sterilised 1 litre/34fl oz jar P12 and cover with a kitchen towel secured with a rubber band.
— Leave in a warm place for about 4–5 days, or until it is sour in flavour. Stir once or twice a day until ready.
— Keep in the fridge for up to 2 weeks.

Borscht

This beetroot dish can be found across Russia, Ukraine and Poland, and there are many regional variations. Many versions simply use raw beetroot with lemon juice, but this one uses beetroot kvass P75 which gives a richer and more intense flavour. For a milder version serve with one or two tablespoons of sour cream or crème fraiche per bowl.

The mushrooms from the stock can be used to make the filling for ravioli or dumplings you might want to make to go in the borscht.

This can be served with hard-boiled eggs cut in half, chunks of boiled potato or butter beans.

The mushroom stock can be replaced with fish stock.

Serves 4

8g/¼oz/⅓ cup dried mushrooms P172
700ml/24fl oz/3 cups water
4 medium beetroot (beets), thickly sliced
1 carrot, thickly sliced
¼ medium celeriac, peeled and thickly sliced
1 garlic clove, sliced
500ml/18fl oz/2 cups beetroot kvass P75
Pinch of salt
Freshly ground black pepper

— To make the stock, put the dried mushrooms in a medium saucepan, pour in the cold water to cover and leave to soak for 30 minutes.
— Add the beetroot, carrot and celeriac slices, bring to the boil, then reduce the heat and simmer for 1 hour.
— Add the garlic and simmer for a further 10 minutes.
— Strain the stock into a clean pan. Add the fermented beetroot juice and stir to mix, then reheat gently. Be careful not to let it boil as this would spoil the colour. Season to taste with the salt and pepper.

Zurek

For this recipe either rye or wheat flour zur P75 can be used. In this recipe we're using Polish streaky bacon which is sold in one piece rather than sliced. If it's not available, use ordinary sliced smoked bacon but omit the frying step. Instead of smoked sausage, any uncooked sausage can be used. Cook them whole rather than sliced. The vegetarian version of this soup is also very tasty. To make it, simply do not add any meat and increase the amount of dried mushrooms to 1½ cups and soak in two cups of water. Once cooked blend in a food processor or blender. Follow all the other steps.

Serves 4

16g/½oz/½ cup dried mushrooms, soaked in 225ml/8fl oz/1 cup water for at least 2 hours P172, or use fresh mushrooms
200g/7oz smoked bacon, cut into 1cm/½in cubes
200g/7oz smoked sausage, sliced
4 large or 8 small potatoes, cut into small chunks
700ml/24fl oz/3 cups water
1 bay leaf
4-5 allspice berries
1 tbsp vegetable oil, for frying
1 large onion, finely chopped
500ml/18fl oz/2 cups rye or wheat zur kvass P75
2 garlic cloves, chopped
1 tbsp dried marjoram
1 tsp salt
Freshly ground black pepper
4-5 tbsp sour cream
4 hard-boiled eggs, quartered (optional)
Juice of 1 lemon (optional)

— Place the soaked mushrooms together with their soaking water in a small saucepan. Bring to the boil, then reduce the heat and simmer for 20-30 minutes until cooked.
— Remove the mushrooms from the stock and finely chop.
— Meanwhile, fry the bacon cubes in a frying pan for 3-4 minutes, then place in a medium saucepan. Add the smoked sausage, potatoes, water, bay leaf and allspice berries. Bring to the boil, then add the mushrooms and mushroom stock and simmer.

— Heat the oil in a medium frying pan over a medium heat, add the onion and fry until soft and golden. Add to the soup.
— Once the potatoes are soft add the rye or wheat kvass, garlic and marjoram. Bring to the boil, then reduce the heat and simmer for 3 minutes. Season with salt and pepper.
— Add the sour cream, stir well and serve with quartered hard-boiled eggs. If the zurek is not very sour you can add the lemon juice.

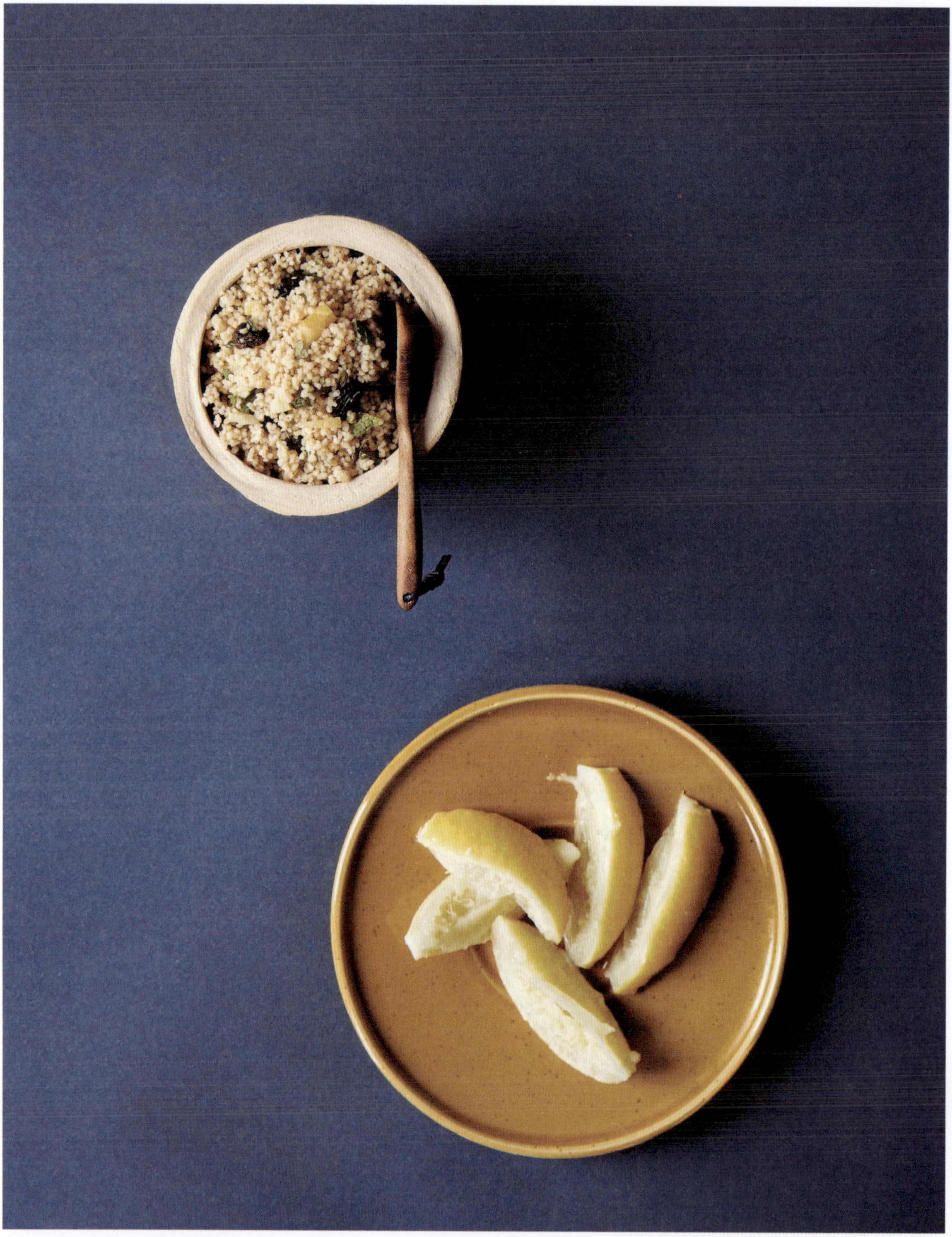

Preserved lemons

Lemon trees are said to have originated in India, and it's thought they were introduced to Europe by the Romans, before the Arabs helped lemons find their way to the Mediterranean and on to China. Wherever lemons went, new methods of preserving them for use out of season were invented, but this Moroccan style of fermenting is best known. It's simple and yields a vibrant result.

Prep 15 minutes
Ready 3-4 weeks
Makes approx 1 litre/34fl oz jar

600g/1¼lb (4-5) unwaxed lemons
40g/1½oz/¼ scant cup sea or rock salt (pure, without iodine or anti-caking agent)

— Wash and cut each lemon into at least 6 slices lengthways, then pack into a sterilised jar P12 in layers. Sprinkle each layer with salt before adding the next. Mash each layer with a fork to release the juice. As the juice is released, this forms the 'brine' in which the lemons will be preserved.
— When all the lemon slices are packed in, they should sit just below the surface of the brine. If there is not enough brine, make more by combining 250ml/9fl oz boiling water with ½ teaspoon of salt. Once the brine is cool pour over the lemons.
— Leave to ferment in a warm place (a cupboard is fine) for at least 3-4 weeks. The flavour improves over time.
— Once fermented, keep in the fridge for up to 3 months.

Preserved lemon couscous

North African-style couscous (made from semolina) tastes even better with preserved lemons above. This recipe is simple, but you can pack it with any flavours you love – think about adding pine nuts and pistachios, or replace the raisins with olives, which stand up equally well to the lemons.

Serves 2-3

180g/6½oz/1 cup couscous
6-8 slices of preserved lemon, finely chopped above
2 tbsp raisins
1 tsp ground cumin
1 tsp paprika
225ml/8fl oz/1 cup boiling water
4 tsp finely chopped mint
Sea salt and freshly ground black pepper
Olive oil, to serve (optional)

— Mix the couscous, preserved lemon, raisins, cumin and paprika together in a medium bowl, then pour in the boiling water.
— Cover the bowl with a lid or plate and leave to stand for 15 minutes.
— Mix well with a fork to separate the grains. Add the mint, season to taste and mix well (add a glug of olive oil if you wish) before serving.

Sourdough bread starters

Sourdough bread uses a starter instead of commercial yeast. In essence, a starter is a colony of naturally present wild yeast and bacteria. If you do not have one and are not able to get one locally, then you can make your own. To do this you simply need to create the right environment in which the wild yeast and bacteria can grow and multiply. It is a very easy process and although it will take about 5 days you will only need to do it once as it can then be kept in the fridge for future use. The rye starter is wetter and more active than the wheat and spelt starters so different proportions are used.

Prep 30 minutes + 5-day process
Ready 5–7 days

Rye sourdough starter
50ml/1¾fl oz/scant ¼ cup filtered water
25g/1oz/2 tbsp rye flour

Spelt/wheat sourdough starter
30ml/1fl oz/2 tbsp filtered water
30g/1oz/2 tbsp spelt flour

— Pour the water into a sterilised jar P12, add the flour and stir until there are no dry lumps. Cover loosely with a lid, then cover with a clean cloth to let it breathe. Place in a dry spot in the kitchen away from the oven, radiators or direct sunlight.

— Make the same additions of water and flour each day for 4 days. Don't worry if you do the refreshment at a different time or even miss a day.

— By day 5 the surface of the starter should be rippled showing that fermentation has begun. If not, then repeat the additions for another 2 days. It nearly always works but if it does not after a week, then it might be better to start again.

Production leaven

A production leaven is a necessary stage to create a larger body of active yeast and bacteria cells, which should be done before bread is made. It's simply taking some of the starter P80, which will have become dormant from sitting in the fridge, and refreshing it with new flour and water. This will bring the wild yeasts and bacteria into activity and help to ferment the dough and make it rise.

Prep 15 minutes
Ready 6–12 hours

Rye, makes 1kg/2¼lb – recipe can be divided to make different quantity
100g/3½oz rye starter left
600ml/20fl oz/2½ cups filtered water
300g/10½oz/2½ cups rye flour

Spelt/wheat, make just less than 1kg/2¼lb – recipe can be divided to make different quantity
320g/11½oz spelt starter left
240ml/8fl oz/1 cup filtered water
400g/14oz/3 cups spelt flour

— Weigh out the starter into a large bowl. Add the water and mix to form a thin soup or paste.
— Add the flour and mix well until there are no dry lumps. Cover the bowl and leave for between 6–12 hours.
— If you do not have a water filter then you can remove the chlorine from the tap water by boiling it for around 15 minutes.
— Sourdough starter is fairly hardy and will survive periods of inactivity. It is not necessary to feed it every day and it can survive for weeks in a fridge, but if you aren't baking and refreshing the starter it would be good to feed it by stirring in 1 tablespoon water and flour once a week.

— It is not necessary to have different starters on the go if you are not worried about making a 100% spelt or rye bread. You can have one starter and use it to make different production leavens, eg a wheat production leaven can be made from a rye starter or a rye production leaven from a spelt starter.
— It is necessary to work out how much production leaven is needed for a recipe. All the starters can be used to make the production leaven, but make sure there is enough production leaven left over to use as a new starter otherwise a new starter will need to be made.

Spelt sourdough

Spelt is a member of the wheat family and was a popular grain nearly two millennia ago when it sustained the Roman army in the British Isles. It fell out of favour partly due to its lower yield per acre compared to more hybridised wheat varieties, but has become more popular over the last decade as people find they can eat spelt without experiencing the intolerances they might have with wheat. It still contains gluten, so is not suitable for people who suffer from coeliac disease.

Makes 2 x 900g/2lb loaves

1 tsp sunflower or vegetable oil, for oiling
700g/1½lb/scant 5¼ cups wholewheat spelt flour
560ml/19fl oz/2½ cups water
14g/½oz/1 tbsp salt
540g/1lb 3oz spelt production leaven P81

— Oil two 900g/2lb loaf tins.
— Place the flour into a large bowl, add the water and stir until there are no dry lumps and a dough has formed. Leave the dough to rest for 30 minutes. This allows the starch in the flour to absorb the water and the gluten to begin to stretch.
— Add the salt, then turn out the dough on to the work surface and knead until it becomes smooth and stretchy, about 10 minutes.
— Add the production leaven and knead until the dough is well combined. Return to a clean bowl, cover and leave in a warm place for at least 1-4 hours.
— Knock the dough down again to deflate the air from it, stretch the dough into a rectangle, then roll it up like a Swiss roll and place it seam-side down in the prepared tins. Cover and leave to rise for at least 2 hours. This depends on the temperature of the dough, the room and the liveliness of the production leaven.
— Preheat the oven at 230°C/450°F/gas mark 8.
— Bake for 15 minutes, then for turn the oven down to 200°C/400°F/gas mark 6 and bake for a further 20-30 minutes.
— Using oven gloves, turn the loaf out of the tin and tap it on the bottom. If it is sounding hollow then it is ready. If not bake a little longer. It is good to bake the loaf for the last 5 minutes out of the tin as it firms up the sides of the loaf. Remove from the oven and leave on a wire rack to cool.

This recipe uses only flour, water and salt but there is an important fourth ingredient - time. Sourdough bread is improved by long fermentation times. The dough can be left in a fridge overnight before shaping or can be shaped in the tins and allowed to rise a bit before being stored in the fridge and then baked the next day.

The bread becomes sourer depending on the length of fermentation, so it is worth experimenting to find what tastes best for you.

Sourdough bread which has had a long fermentation process will keep very well. Even when it naturally stales (about a week after baking), it will make good toast. It will also freeze well either as a whole loaf, halved or sliced.

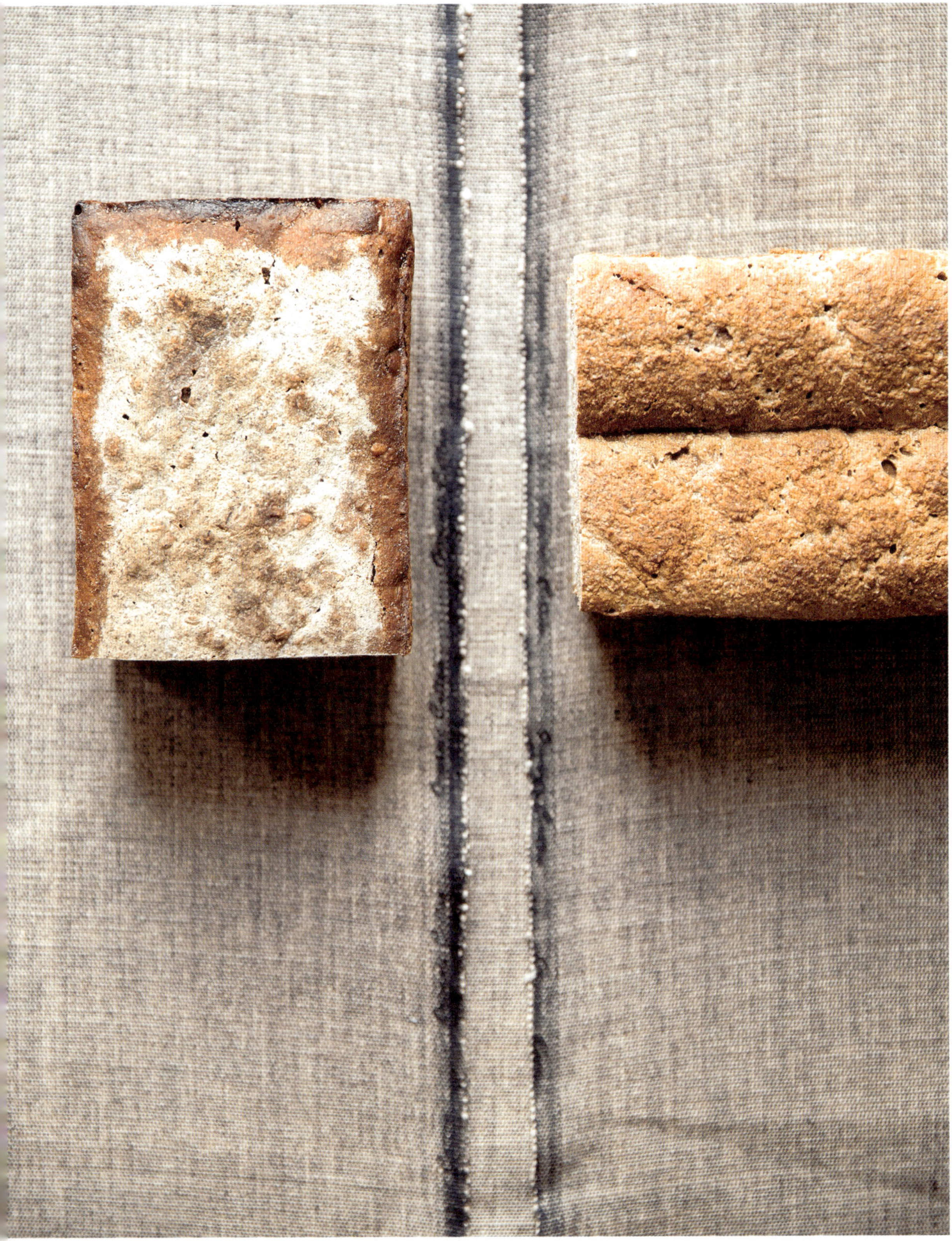

Sunflower rye sourdough

Rye bread has been a staple across much of Northern and Eastern Europe for centuries as rye can grow in conditions that are unfavourable to wheat. There are many so-called rye breads on the market which can contain as little as 15% rye, but this is the real deal: a 100% rye loaf. People who have been brought up on spongy supermarket bread can find rye sourdough challenging at first, but the wonderful flavour, texture and satiating qualities can convert the most sceptical. Rye bread is also very easy to make as it has a low gluten content, which means it does not require any kneading.

Makes 2 x 900g/2lb loaves

485g/17oz rye production leaven P81
425ml/15fl oz/scant 2 cups water
150g/5½oz/1 cup sunflower seeds
725g/1lb 9oz/6 cups rye flour (either dark or light rye or a combination)
15g/½oz/1 tbsp sea salt
1 tsp sunflower or vegetable oil for baking tin

— Pour the production leaven into a large bowl, add the water and mix well. Add the sunflower seeds, then the flour and salt and, using your hands, mix together making sure there are no dry lumps.
— Cover the bowl and leave for a minimum of 1–4 hours.
— Oil two 900g/2lb tins. This dough will be wet and resemble clay. Dampen your hands to shape it into a rough brick and put into the prepared tins. Dampen a couple of fingers and gently push the dough into the tins, then smooth the top so it is shiny and flat. Leave until it rises at least one-third of the way up the tins. The top of the loaves do not need to be cut.
— Preheat the oven to 230°C/450°F/gas mark 8.
— Bake the loaves for 15 minutes, then turn the oven down to 200°C/400°F/gas mark 6 and bake for a further 20–30 minutes.
— Using oven gloves, turn the loaves out of the tins and tap them on the bottom. If they are sounding hollow then they are ready. If not bake a little longer. It is good to bake the loaf for the last 5 minutes out of the tin as it firms up the sides of the loaf.
— Remove from the oven and leave on a wire rack to cool.

It is not necessary to do the whole process in one go. After the dough is ready in the bowl, the process can be slowed down by putting it in the fridge for the day or night.

Then the dough can be taken out and put in the tin and allowed to rise. This will take longer as the dough will need to return to room temperature, but the long fermentation time will improve the flavour and texture.

This bread is best left for a day before eating as the crumb can be sticky. The flavour also improves after a day or two.

Sourdough tortilla

As far back as the ancient Mayan civilisation, people were eating round maize flatbreads. Later the word 'tortilla' came from Spanish settlers and maize was replaced with wheat. If your sourdough starter has been recently refreshed and is active, it can be used to replace the production leaven stage.

Makes 4

100g/3½oz wheat or spelt production leaven, see method and P81
70ml/2½fl oz/5 tbsp filtered water
35g/1¼oz/2½ tbsp butter
½ tsp honey
170g/6oz/scant 1¼ cups strong white flour, plus extra for dusting

— Make up the production leaven by adding 35g/1¾oz starter, 25ml/1fl oz/2 tbsp water and 40g/1½oz/⅓ cup white or wholewheat flour P81. Leave to stand for 6–8 hours.
— When ready to make the tortillas, mix the production leaven and water together in a large bowl. Add the butter, honey and flour and mix together until there are no dry lumps.
— Leave to rest for 20 minutes.
— Knead the dough for 5–10 minutes, then cover the bowl with a lid and leave to ferment for 6–8 hours, or overnight.
— Dust a work surface with flour and divide the dough into 4 balls. Roll each ball out into a circle about 2–3 mm/⅛in thick, then dust with flour and stack on a plate.
— Heat a cast-iron frying pan or other heavy-based frying pan. When hot, add the first tortilla and cook for about 30 seconds until bubbles appear and the edges begin to dry. Flip the tortilla over and cook for about 30 seconds on the other side. The tortillas can be kept on a plate with another plate on top in the oven on a low heat.
— Repeat with the remaining tortillas.

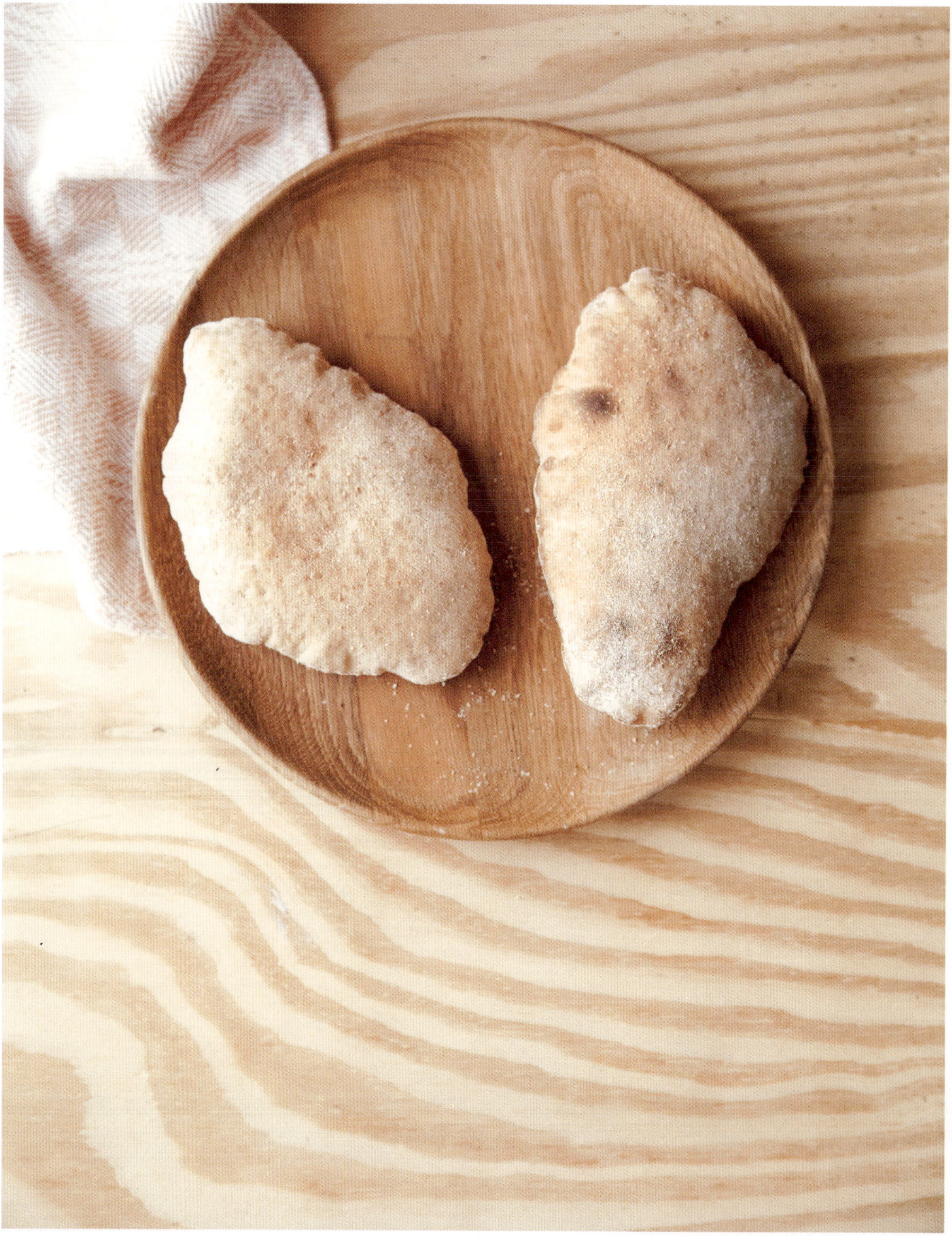

Sourdough pitta bread

When in a hurry it's probably best not to ask what the Mesopotamians did for us, as the answer would go on for some considerable time and include agriculture, irrigation, the wheel, beer, wine, sailboats and even the city. Helping to keep them going through this growth of civilisation was the humble pitta bread. It's certainly a contender for the oldest style of bread, having survived nearly five millennia. If your sourdough starter is fairly active the production leaven stage can be skipped.

Makes 4-5 pitta breads

80g/3oz wheat production leaven, see method and P81
75ml/2½fl oz/5 tbsp milk (or water)
1 tsp honey
1 tbsp melted butter
170g/6oz/scant 1¼ cups strong white flour (or a mix of white and wholewheat), plus extra for dusting
1 tsp salt

— Make the production leaven by mixing 25g/1oz starter, 20ml/¾ fl oz/4 tsp water and 35g/1¼oz/¼ cup white or wholewheat flour in a bowl P81. Leave for 6-12 hours, or overnight.

— When ready to make the pitta breads, mix the production leaven, milk, honey and melted butter together in a large bowl until they are well combined. Add the flour and mix until they are no dry lumps.

— Leave the dough to rest for 20 minutes.

— Add the salt and knead for about 10 minutes, then cover the bowl and leave to ferment for 6-12 hours, or overnight.

— Divide the dough into 4-5 pieces and roll up into balls.

— Lightly flour a work surface and roll out one ball at a time into an oval shape about 5mm/¼in thick. Dust with flour and stack on a plate. Cover the stack with a tea towel and leave to rise for about 2 hours.

— Preheat the oven to 230°C/450°F/gas mark 8. If you have a baking stone use that, if not heat a baking tray in the oven for 20 minutes.

— Place one of the dough circles on to a floured baking tray, open the oven door and slide the dough onto the baking stone/tray. Bake for 6-7 minutes until the dough puffs up and turns golden brown.

— Put the baked pitta on a plate and cover with a cloth and continue until all the pittas are baked.

— Pitta breads are best eaten fresh as they tend to dry out, but they can be sprinkled with water and reheated in the oven, if necessary.

Ginger bug

There are a number of different methods for making ginger beer, including buying a ginger beer plant (not actually a plant, but a mix of yeast and bacteria similar to kefir grains P32-3). Alternatively this method for making a wild fermentation at home can be used to produce ginger beer P89 and other sparkling drinks.

Prep 20 minutes + 5-day process
Ready 5 days
Makes approx 400ml / 14fl oz

1 tbsp grated ginger (not peeled)
1 tbsp sugar
4 tbsp water

— Put the grated ginger and sugar in a sterilised 500ml/18fl oz jar P12.
— Add the water and stir well, then cover the jar with a clean cloth or kitchen paper and secure it with a rubber band. Alternatively, cover loosely with a lid. The jar should not be airtight.
— Add the same quantities for each to the mix repeating every day for 4 days – this is feeding the ginger bug. Give the jar a swirl from time to time.
— By day 5 the ginger bug should show signs of fermentation. The grated ginger will be pushed to the top of the liquid and there should be bubbles on the surface. If this has not happened continue the process for a few more days.

Ginger bugs seem to fluctuate quite a bit: they can become dormant and then pick up again. If yours seems to have stopped bubbling, give it another feed and see if it recovers.

When not in use the ginger bug can be stored in the fridge, but it should be fed with 1 tablespoon grated ginger, 1 tablespoon sugar and 4 tablespoons water once a week.

Ginger beer

The use of ginger as a flavour goes back to ancient India, but ginger beer became popular as a drink during the Victorian era. It has been growing in popularity lately but many of the commercial versions are more like ginger ale, which is an unfermented carbonated drink flavoured with ginger. This recipe may look like it contains a lot of sugar, but much of this gets eaten by the yeast and bacteria so it will not be sweet. This has more ginger than usual for a spicy finish, but adjust this to your taste.

Prep 25 minutes
Ready 7 days
Makes approx 2.5 litre/85fl oz

2 litres/67fl oz/8 cups water
150g/5½oz/¾ cup brown sugar or jaggery
180g/6½oz piece of ginger, skin scraped off and grated
Juice of ½ lemon
75ml/2½fl oz/5 tbsp strained ginger bug P88

— Bring the water to the boil in a large saucepan, then stir in the sugar until it has dissolved. Add the grated ginger and boil for 15 minutes. Leave to cool.
— Strain out the ginger root, add the lemon juice and the ginger bug and swish round to mix. Pour into a sterilised demijohn or any sufficiently large glass or ceramic container P12. If using a demijohn an airlock can be fitted, otherwise cover the opening with a fine-mesh cloth and secure with a rubber band.
— Leave to ferment for about 4–5 days. The ginger beer should still be a little sweeter than intended as some of the sugar will be needed to ferment and create the carbonation in the bottle.

— Strain the ginger beer through a muslin or cheesecloth or a sieve and decant into sterilised flip-top glass bottles and seal. Leave at room temperature for 2–7 days to become carbonated, then chill in the fridge.
— Stories abound of exploding ginger beer bottles so caution is advisable. This should not be bottled too early as there is still a lot of fermentable sugar to create CO_2.
— Leave 4–5 cm/1½–2in space at the top of each bottle and open them carefully over a sink. Plastic fizzy drink bottles can be used, but if they swell, release the pressure over a sink.
— The bottles can be kept in the fridge after 2 days to slow the fermentation down if you do not wish the ginger beer to become drier.

Kombucha

Kombucha is a fermented drink made from tea and is widespread across Japan, China, Russia and now the United States. It is fermented by a jelly-like disc called a scoby, which stands for 'symbiotic culture of bacteria and yeast'. Some of the bacteria create the jelly-like mass, while Saccharomyces cerevisiae (beer yeast) turn the sugars of the sweetened tea into alcohol, which is in turn gobbled up by bacteria and converted into acetic acid.

Prep 20 minutes
Ready about 7 days
Makes approx 2.5 litre/85fl oz jar

2 litres/67fl oz/8 cups tap water
15g/½oz (about 6 tea bags) black or green tea or combination
170g/6oz/¾ cup white sugar
1 medium kombucha scoby (you can buy this from a specialist supplier online, but your next batch can be made reusing the scoby created in your kombucha, see notes below)
300ml/10fl oz/1¼ cups kombucha from the previous batch (or the liquid the scoby came in)

— Bring the water to the boil in a large saucepan and boil well (about 15 minutes) to remove the chlorine.
— Add the tea and sugar, stir quickly to dissolve the sugar and leave to stand for 10 minutes.
— Remove the tea bags, then leave to cool to room temperature.
— Pour the solution into a large sterilised 3 litre/5¼ pint/3 quart jar P12 or other glass container.
— Add the scoby and the kombucha or liquid that the scoby has been sitting in. Cover the jar with a cloth and secure with a rubber band.
— Leave to ferment for 5 days at room temperature away from radiators, the oven or direct sunlight.
— On day 5 taste the kombucha to see how it is doing. At this stage you can do a 'secondary ferment' by pouring off the kombucha and adding a fruit syrup to it and sealing it in pressurised jars for 2 days. It will then be fairly fizzy and can be stored in the fridge for drinking.
— If you wish to drink the kombucha in its plain form then keep trying each day until it reaches your favoured point between sweetness and acidity. The speed of the fermentation process depends on the temperature as well as the health of the scoby.

The scoby 'mother' will produce a new scoby each time you make a batch of kombucha. The new one can be separated with a clean plastic utensil. It is recommended not to use metal.

Extra scoby can be given away to friends or used for experiments with different flavours or teas.

See P6 and P9 for pictures of kombucha and a scoby mother.

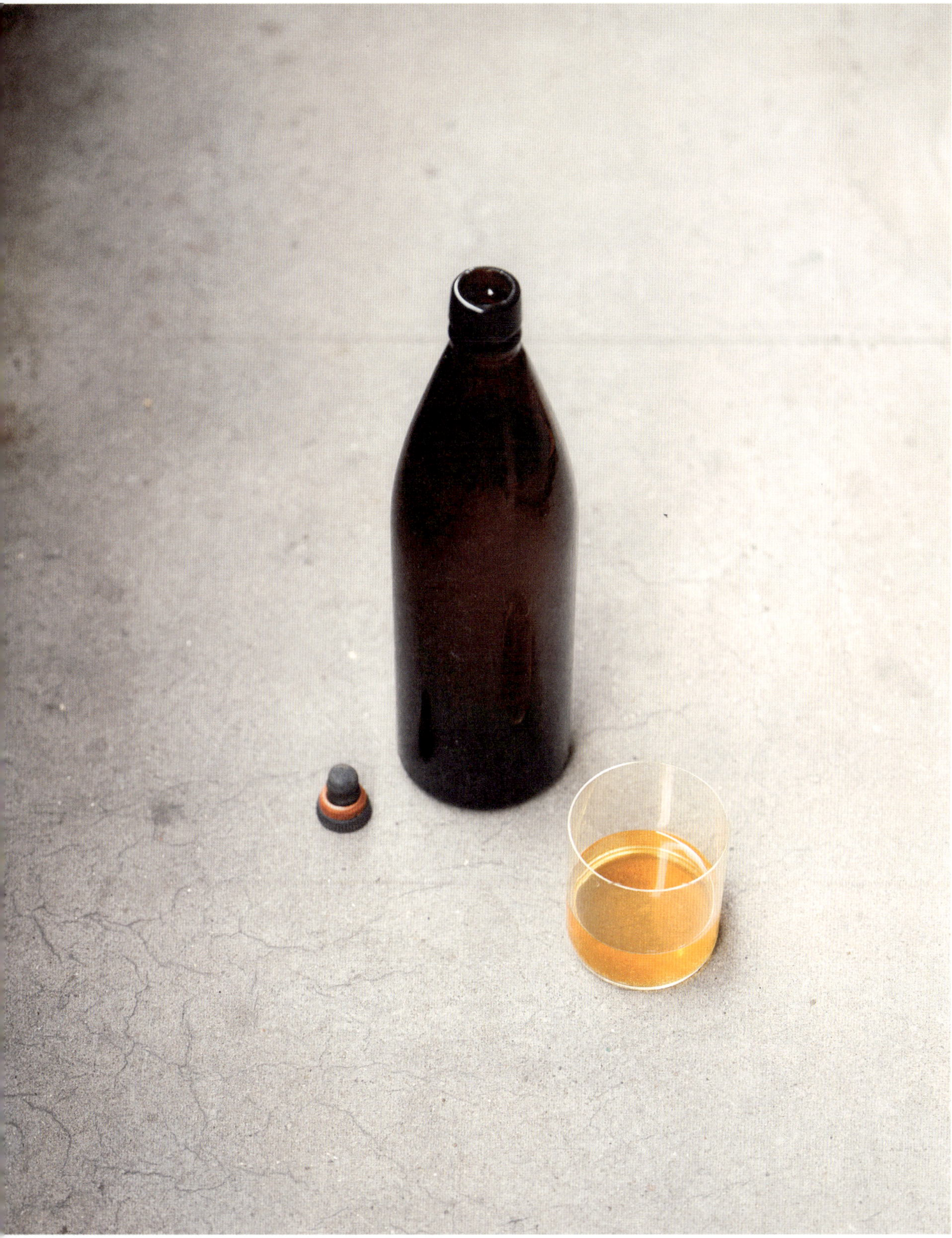

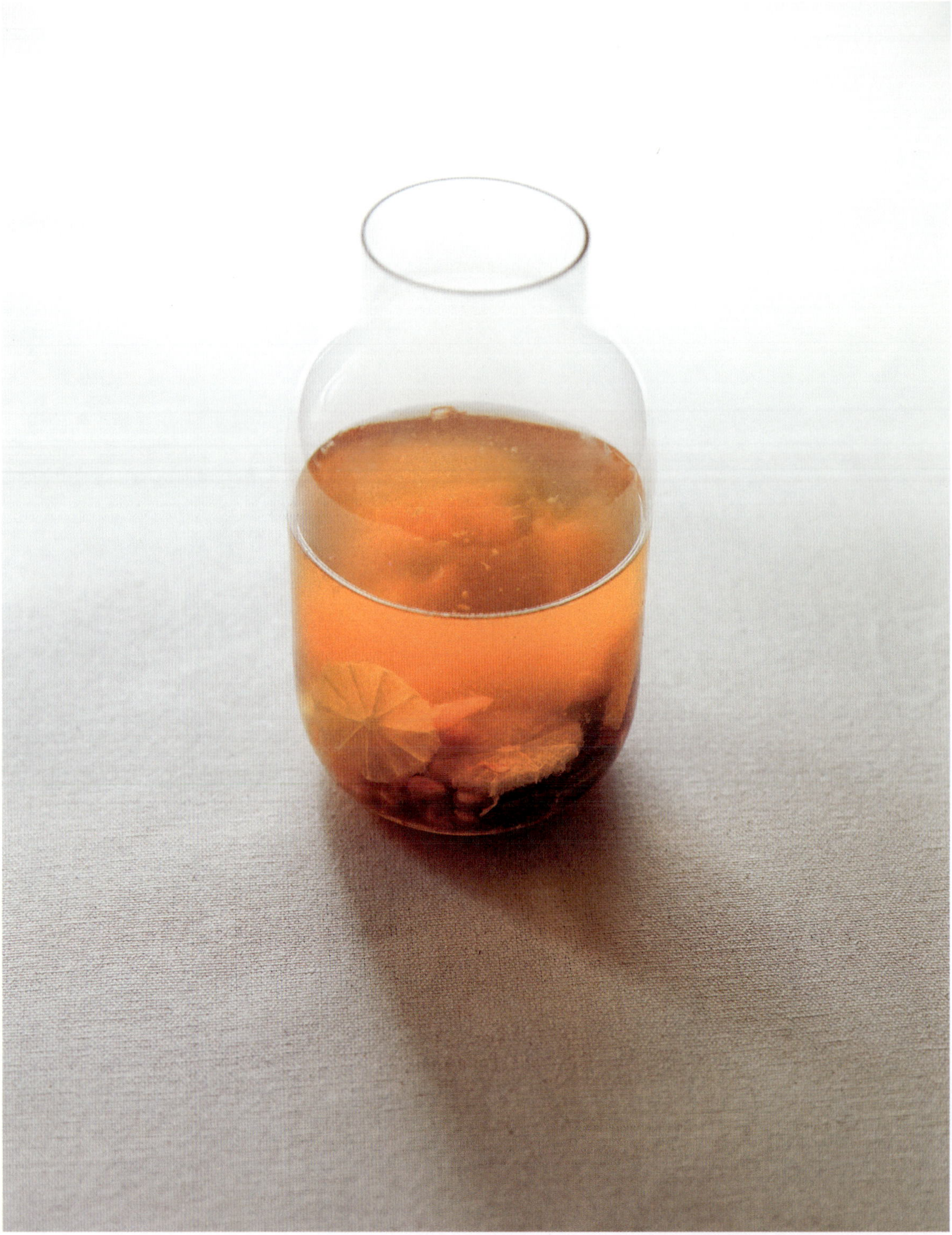

Kombucha punch

This is a refreshing drink for a hot summer afternoon using kombucha P90.

Serves 4

Ice cubes
1 lime, sliced
1 orange, peeled, quartered and sliced
Seeds of 1 pomegranate
60ml/2¼fl oz/¼ cup vermouth
40ml/1½fl oz/8 tsp vodka
300ml/10fl oz/1¼ cups green tea kombucha P90
200ml/7fl oz/scant 1 cup elderflower pressé
200ml/7fl oz/scant 1 cup sparkling water

— Place ice cubes, sliced lime, orange and pomegranate seeds into a large jug or bowl.
— Add the vermouth, vodka, kombucha, elderflower pressé and sparkling water and mix together.
— Serve straight away.

Amazake

Amazake is an uplifting, sweet and thick rice drink from Japan. The name means 'sweet sake', as the fermentation process has converted the starch in the rice to sugars by fungus Aspergillus oryzae (commonly known as koji). Koji is a wonder mould which has been used in China for over two thousand years in the production of alcoholic drinks. It also provides the basis for the production of miso, soy sauce and rice vinegar. This is almost worth making alone for the sublimely sweet aroma it creates as it ferments.

Prep 1 hour + cooling
Ready 1 day
Makes approx 700ml/24fl oz jar

150g/5½oz/¾ cup rice
450ml/16fl oz/2 cups water
150g/5½oz/¾ cup koji rice
Grated ginger or other spices, to serve (optional)

— Place the rice and water in a pan and bring to the boil. Reduce the heat and simmer for about 40 minutes until the rice is soft.
— Remove from the heat, but do not drain. Leave the rice cool to 60°C/140°F, then add the koji rice and mix well.
— Pour the rice mixture into a large clean jar and place the jar in a position where a temperature of between 50–60°C/122–140°F can be maintained. Leave for 2 hours, stir.
— Leave for another 4 hours, then stir again. The amazake should be ready after about 10 hours, but it might be longer if the heat hasn't been maintained above 50°C/122°F.
— Transfer to a sterilised 1 litre/34fl oz jar P12 and leave to cool to room temperature, then store in the fridge for up to a week.
— To make the final sweet drink, add 1 part amazake base to 1 part water and heat up. This recipe should make enough for four people at least. It can be served at any temperature. Serve with a little grated ginger or other spices, if you like.

There are different methods of maintaining an incubation temperature of 50–60°C/122–140°F. The easiest method is to use a rice steamer and set it to 'keep warm'. An insulated picnic box partly filled with warm water and regularly topped up can also work.

We have had success by putting the jar on a thin book on top of a dehydrator, but make sure it doesn't dry out.

Amazake can be used to make the natural seasoning shio-koji, which is used in Japan to bring out the umami flavours in different foods.

Drunken rice pudding

As a student Simon learned that during World War II the SAS would put a tot of whisky into their porridge to keep out the early morning cold while sleeping in the North African desert. He too would eat porridge every morning, but alas only had vodka to hand and the result was somewhat disappointing. Years later, reading about how the Korean public voted for the name 'drunken rice' for their rice wine, it was time to return to the quest of boozy breakfasts and desserts, this time with amazake P94.

Serves 2

160g/5¾oz amazake P94
4 tbsp sake
100g/3½oz/scant 1 cup raspberries, fresh or frozen (if using frozen, thaw before using)
4-6 tbsp sour cream or crème fraîche
4 tbsp gintopf fruit P166

— Fill a large pan with about 2.5cm/1in water and bring to the boil over a medium heat.
— Mix the amazake with the sake in a heatproof bowl that will comfortably fit over the large pan and place on top making sure the bowl doesn't touch the water below.
— Stir frequently until very warm.
— Add the raspberries and stir gently.
— Remove from the heat and divide between 2 serving bowls.
— Top with sour cream and gintopf fruit and serve.

Cocoffins

English yeast-leavened muffins were sold door-to-door in the Victorian era in Britain, but have since become eclipsed by the American sweet, baked muffin. Simon came across a sourdough version of the English classic in Australian baker Yoke Mardewi's book, which inspired experiments with different flours. It also provided the opportunity to come up with silly names. At the Growing Communities Farmers Market in Stoke Newington we sold chuffins (chestnut muffins), kaffins (kamut muffins) and spuffins (spelt muffins), but the favourite was these coconut muffins.

Prep 40 minutes + 1 hour standing
Ready 12 hours
Ready about 12–14

100g/3½oz white or wholemeal spelt production leaven P81
240ml/8fl oz/1 cup water
240ml/8½fl oz/1 cup milk kefir P32 or plain yoghurt P20 or shop bought
470g/17oz/scant 3⅔ cups white spelt flour
130g/4½oz/scant 1½ cups desiccated (dried shredded) coconut
10g/¼oz/2½ tsp sea salt
Rice flour, for dusting
Butter and jam, to serve

— Using a handheld blender, mix the production leaven, water and kefir or yoghurt together in a bowl.
— Add the flour and desiccated coconut and mix until there are no dry lumps.
— Leave for 20 minutes, then add the salt and knead for 5–10 minutes.
— Cover and chill in the fridge for 12 hours, or overnight.
— Sprinkle rice flour over a work surface and roll out the dough to a thickness of 1.5cm/⅝in.
— Using a round cutter or a crumpet hoop, cut the dough out into circles.
— Roll up the scraps, re-roll and cut out more circles, about 12–14 in total.
— Dip the circles in rice flour and place on a board, then cover and leave to rise for at least 1 hour.
— Heat a griddle or an unoiled frying pan over a medium heat. Add the cocoffins in batches and cook for 5–10 minutes, or until they are browned slightly underneath. Flip them over and cook for another 5 or so minutes until browned slightly on the other side.
— Leave to cool on a rack. To serve, split them in half horizontally and spread with butter and jam.

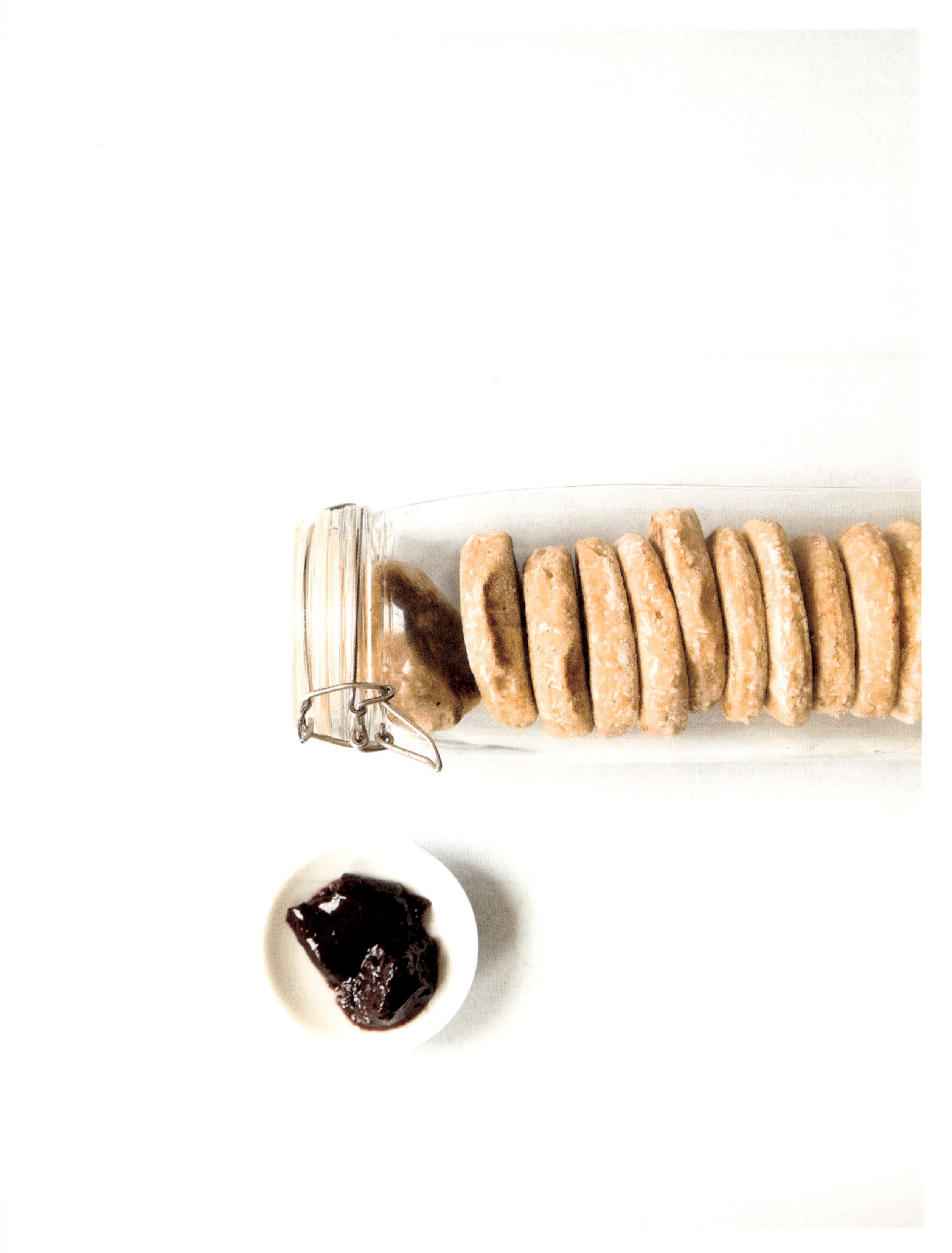

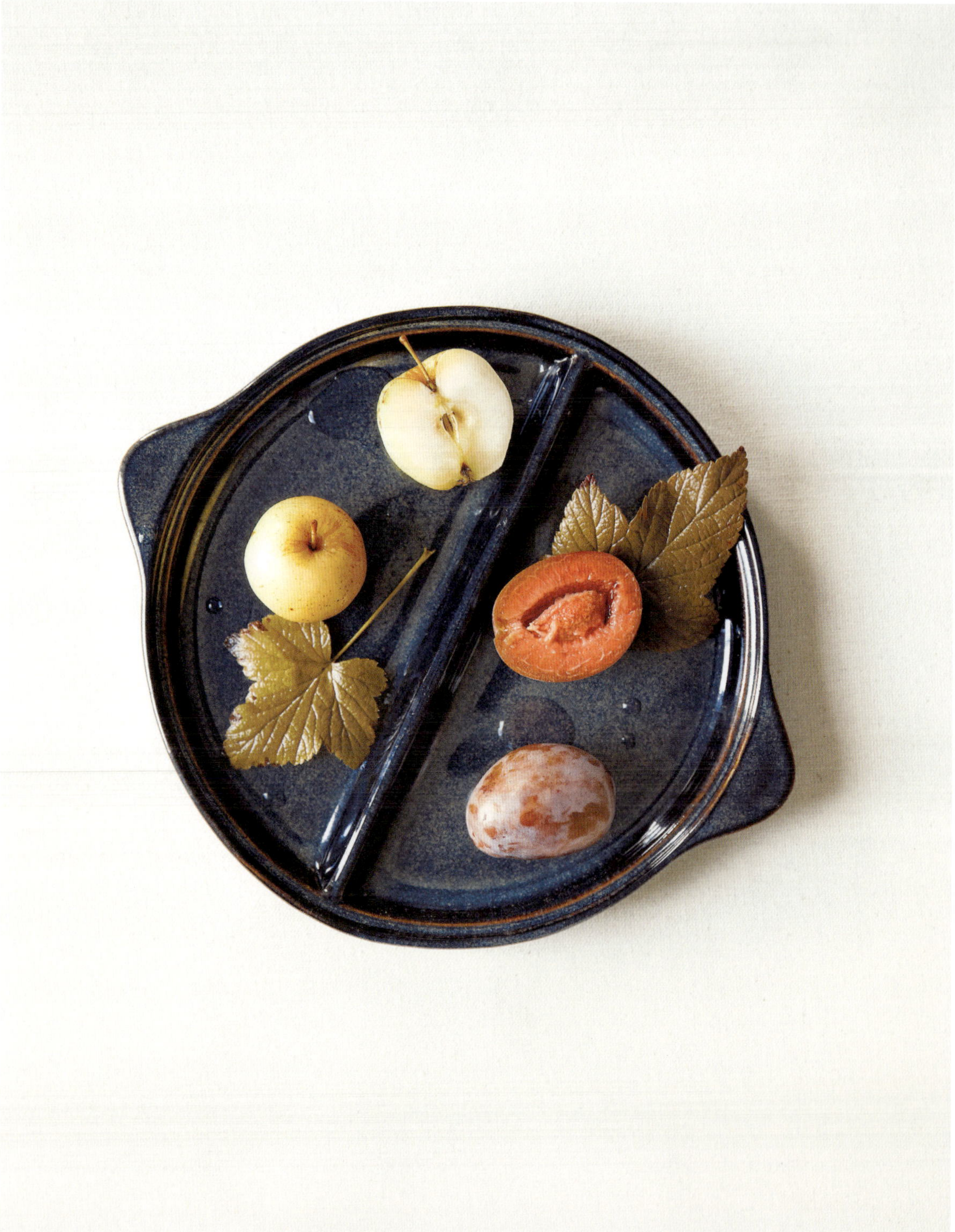

Fermented apples

Usually apples appear in a supporting role to cabbage in sauerkraut, but here they take centre stage. The apples become sour and slightly salty when fermented, but remain firm and add brilliant flavour to both savoury and sweet dishes. Add to fruit muffins P100.

Prep 20 minutes
Ready 4 weeks
Makes approx 2.5 litre/85fl oz jar

800g/1¾lb small apples (the best are hard, sharp-flavoured apples or large crabapples)
6–7 blackcurrant leaves (or vine or oak leaves)
1.5 litres/50fl oz/6¼ cups water
60g/2¼oz/¼ cup pink Himalayan salt (pure, without iodine or anti-caking agent)
60g/2¼oz/¼ cup raw honey

— Thoroughly wash the apples and blackcurrant leaves and place whole in a sterilised jar P12.
— Bring the water to the boil in a large saucepan, then carefully pour it into a large heatproof bowl. Add the salt and stir until it has dissolved. Leave to cool until warm, but no longer hot.
— Add the honey to the warm brine and stir until it has dissolved.
— Pour the brine into the jar to cover the apples and leave to ferment in a warm place for 4 weeks.
— Once ready keep in a cool place, such as the fridge or garden shed (if cold). Store for up to 3 months.

In order to keep the apples submerged under the brine, place a small plate, sterilised stone or sterilised jar filled with water on top of the apples.

Once ready to refrigerate, you can move the apples to 2 smaller sterilised jars, making sure that the apples remain covered in brine.

Fermented plums

Prep 20 minutes
Ready 4 weeks
Makes approx 2 litre/67fl oz jar

500g/1lb 2oz plums, Wegierka, Victoria or other ripe, firm variety
4–5 blackcurrant or vine leaves
1.25 litres/2 pints boiled water
50g/1¾oz salt (pure, without iodine or anti-caking agent)
50g/1¾oz sugar

— Wash the plums and blackcurrant or vine leaves and place in a sterilised jar P12.
— Bring the water to the boil in a saucepan, add the salt and sugar and stir until dissolved. Leave the brine to cool.
— Pour the brine over the plums and leave in a warm place to ferment for 4 weeks.
— Once ready keep in a cool place, such as the fridge or garden shed (if cold), and store for up to 5 months.

Fermented fruit muffins

These muffins combine a mixture of sweet and savoury flavours with the help of fermented apples and plums P99. The quantity of sugar could be reduced if you prefer a more savoury flavour.

Makes 24 cupcakes

4 eggs, separated
100g/3½oz/½ cup brown sugar
100g/3½oz/7 tbsp butter, melted and cooled
300g/10½oz/3 cups pumpkin, peeled, deseeded and grated
4 small fermented crab apples (or a raw cooking apple), chopped P99
2 fermented plums, chopped P99
80g/3oz/½ cup strong wholewheat flour
80g/3oz/½ cup roughly chopped walnuts
80g/3oz/½ cup roughly chopped hazelnuts
2 tsp ground cinnamon
1 tsp ground coriander
1 tsp ground ginger
½ tsp ground nutmeg
1 tsp ground allspice
3 tsp baking powder

— Preheat the oven to 180°C/350°F/gas mark 4. Line two 12-hole cupcake trays with silicone cupcake cases. Paper cases can be used instead, but they tend to stick a little more.
— Beat the egg whites until white and stiff, then slowly add the sugar and continue beating until all the sugar is mixed well with egg white.
— Slowly add the egg yolk and continue beating until mixed well.
— Slowly pour in the butter and gently mix together. Add the pumpkin and other fruit and mix gently.
— Sift the flour into another bowl, add the nuts, spices and baking powder and mix well. Add the egg/butter/pumpkin mixture to the bowl and very gently mix together.
— Divide the mixture between the cupcake cases until two-thirds of the height and gently spread out with a spoon or spatula. Bake the cupcakes for 25 minutes, or until a skewer or toothpick inserted into the middle comes out clean.
— Turn out onto a wire rack to cool.

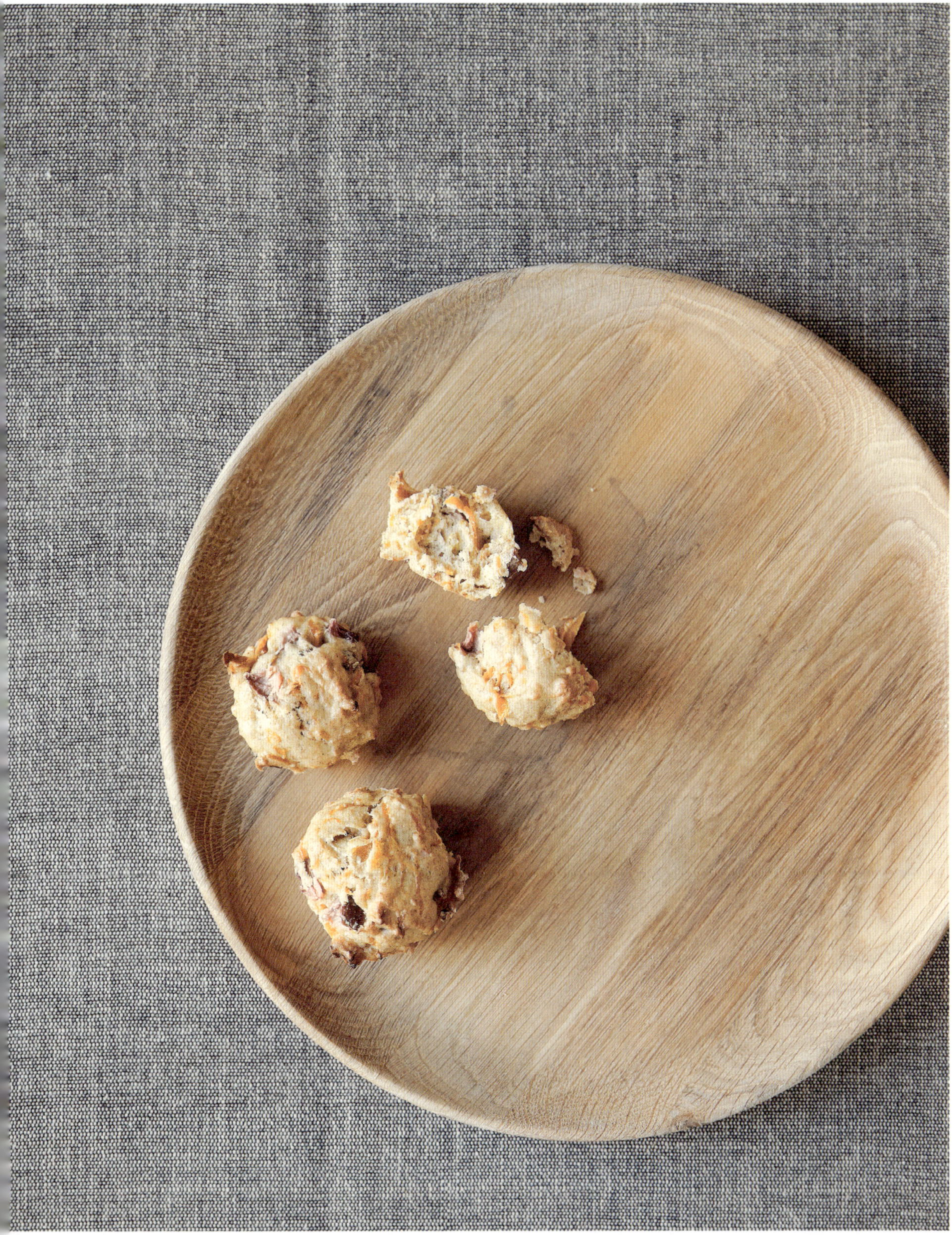

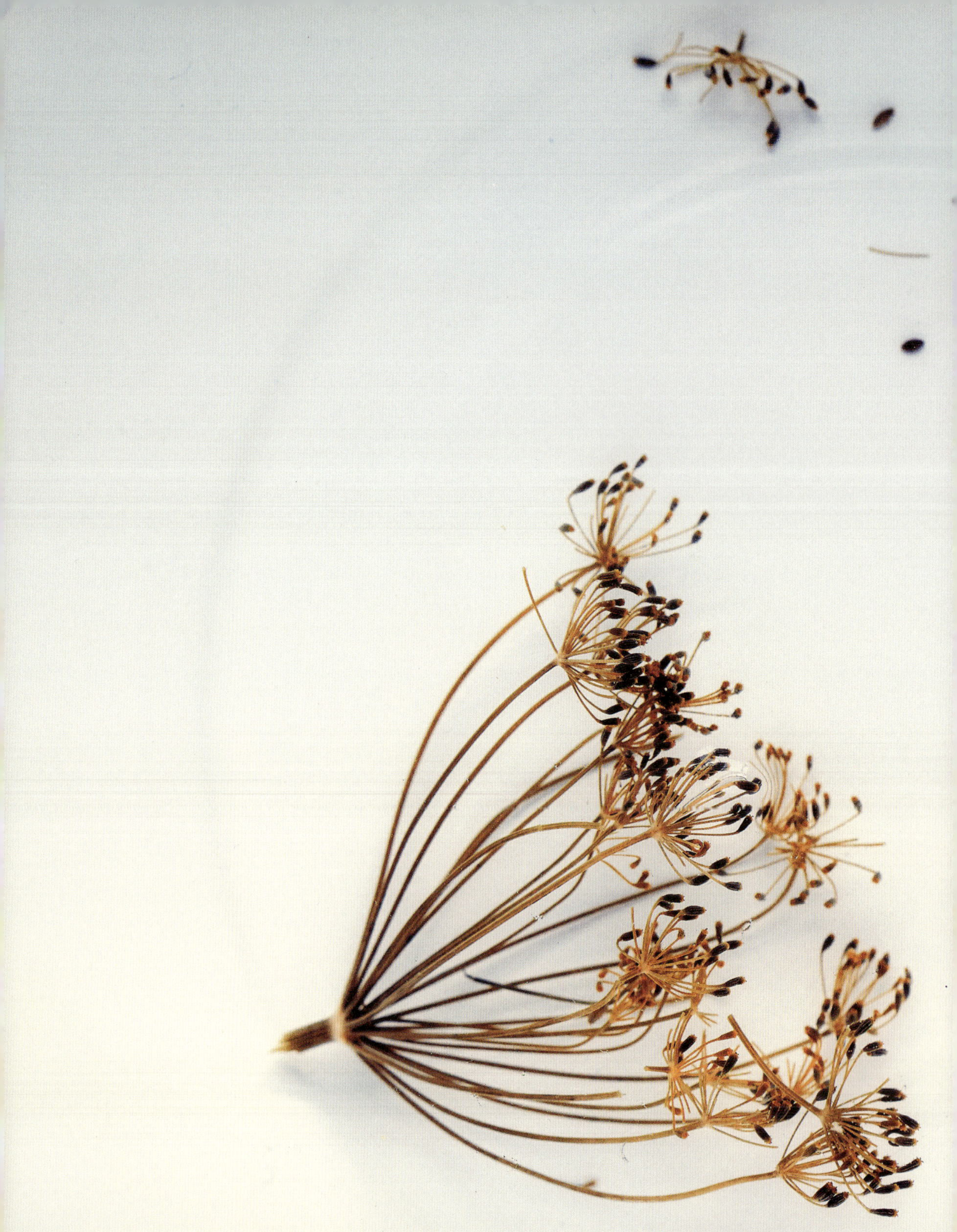

Pickle

Pickling is a preserving process that can be applied to vegetables, meat, fish, eggs, fruit and even nuts. It not only preserves, but creates new flavours – it's a gateway to fresh and exciting tastes, elevating ordinary vegetables and fruit into delicacies. They can be served as an accompaniment, and on occasion as main dishes in themselves, but they can also be incorporated into cooking with surprisingly good results.

The possibilities are endless, and the recipes and the pickling techniques in this book are here just to start you off on a journey of discovery. There is a spread of recipes – some involve strong pickling solutions and will preserve food for months, others are lighter and are intended to maximise the health benefits of raw ingredients such as apple cider vinegar and cold-pressed honey.

Pickling uses a vinegar solution or alcohol as a protective barrier against bacteria, yeast and oxygen. We often use distilled spirit vinegar at 10% strength. If that is not available then malt vinegar can be used, but the ratio of vinegar and water will need to be adjusted to take into account the lower-strength vinegar. For example, if a recipe requires 100ml/3½fl oz distilled spirit vinegar at 10% strength and 300ml/10fl oz water, the replacement quantities will need to be 200ml/7fl oz of distilled malt vinegar at 5% strength and 200ml/7fl oz water.

Pickle

Recipes that use cider or wine vinegar are also delicious, but it is not safe to keep them for as long as foods preserved in distilled vinegar or alcohol. Many recipes (and especially those that use raw cider vinegar) should be kept in the fridge and consumed in a relatively short time, but they are well worth trying.

If you're planning to store pickles in a cupboard for a prolonged period of time it is crucial to pasteurise them to ensure safety, even if the jars are sealed: otherwise you may risk botulism, a serious illness caused by the Clostridium botulinum bacteria. See P12 for more information on sealing and pasteurising food safely.

Once pickled, some fruit and vegetables change colour – the best example is garlic, which can turn blue or green. This is caused by an enzymatic reaction and is perfectly harmless.

Pickled ramiro peppers

Pickled peppers are very popular in Eastern Europe and the Balkans, where many different versions abound. Here we have two variations: the first comes from Gaba's mum in Poland and is stronger, more sour and has the warmth of allspice. The second, which comes from our Polish friend Edyta, is milder and uses garlic, mustard and bay leaves. You could try a Serbian-style pickle by roasting the peppers in the oven before you pickle them.

Prep 45 minutes
Ready 4 weeks
Makes approx 700ml/24fl oz jar

500g/1lb 2oz peppers (ramiro or mixed red, orange and yellow bell), cut in halves, quarters or smaller pieces depending on preference

Pickling solution
300ml/10fl oz/1¼ cups water
100ml/3½fl oz/scant ½ cup distilled spirit vinegar 10%
50g/1¾oz/¼ cup sugar
½ tsp salt
4–5 allspice berries
4 black peppercorns
4 dried chilli flakes
100ml/3½fl oz/scant ½ cup olive oil

Optional
2 tsp white mustard seeds
4 garlic cloves, sliced
1–3 bay leaves

— First make the pickling solution. Place the water, vinegar, sugar, salt, allspice berries, black peppercorns and chilli flakes in a medium saucepan and mix together. Bring to the boil over a medium heat.
— Add the peppers, return to the boil, then reduce the heat and simmer for a further 5 minutes.
— Carefully scoop the pepper pieces out with a slotted spoon and place in a sterilised 500–700ml/18–24fl oz jar or 2–3 smaller sterilised jars P12.
— Add mustard seeds, bay leaf and sliced garlic to each jar, if you like.
— Bring the remaining pickling solution to the boil and pour over the peppers, making sure they are covered, but leave 2cm/¾in space between the peppers and the rim of the jar. Top it with a layer of olive oil, about 1–1.5cm/½–⅝in. Cover the jar with a sterilised lid and once cool check the seal P12. If not sealed, pasteurise P13.
— You can try them after a week, but the flavour develops the longer they are left.
— Sealed and/or pasteurised jars can be kept in a cupboard for at least 6 months before opening. Once opened store in the fridge and use within 1 month. You can store unsealed ones in the fridge for up to 2 weeks.

If necessary, the distilled spirit vinegar 10% can be replaced with distilled malt vinegar, but the quantities of vinegar and water will need to be adjusted to take into account the strength of the vinegar. See P104 for instructions.

You can make a weaker pickling solution if you prefer a milder flavour: mix 100ml/3½fl oz/scant ½ cup distilled vinegar 10% with 400ml/14fl oz/1¾ cups water. You can also make it sweeter by increasing the amount of sugar.

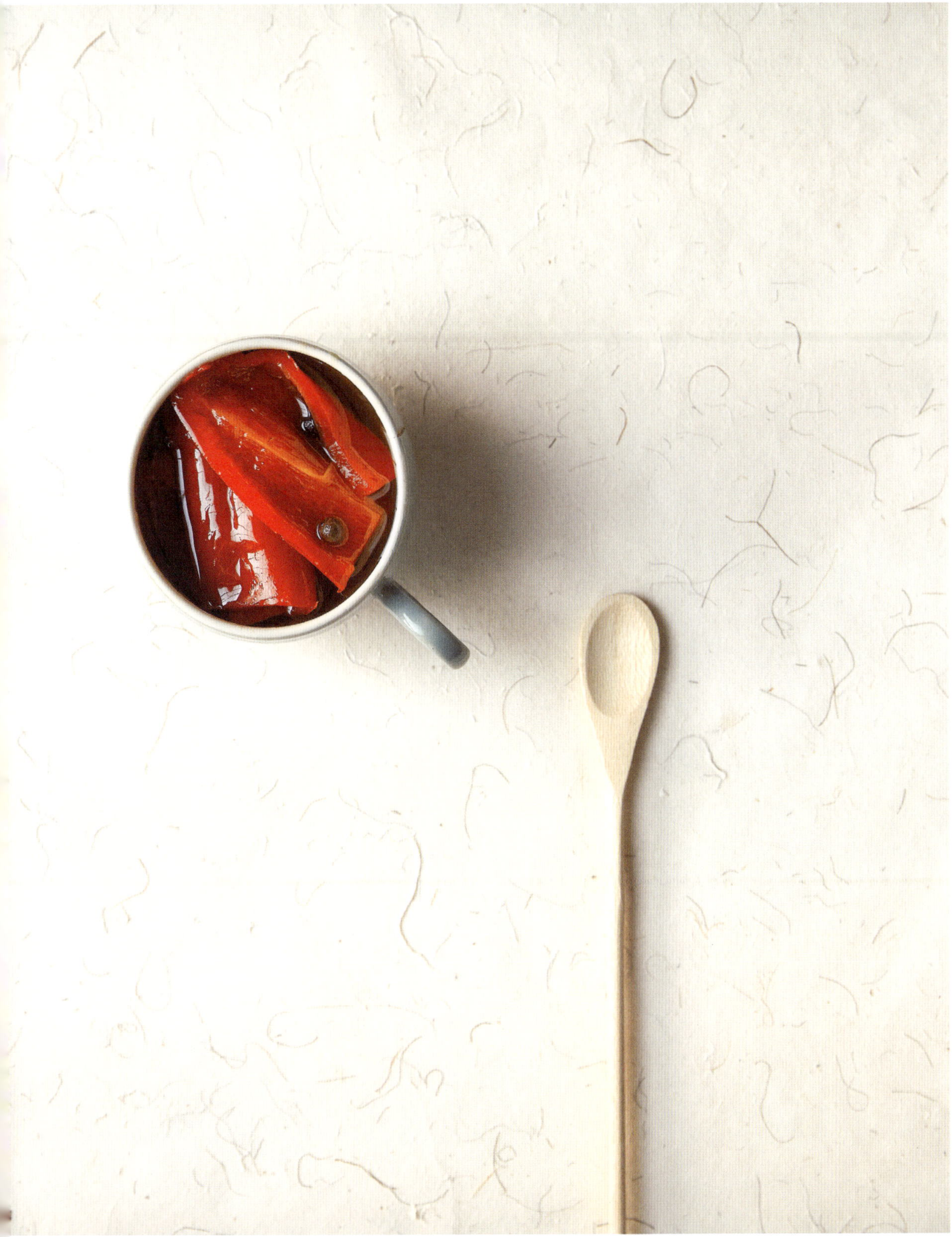

Nasturtium capers
Pickled porcini mushrooms P110

Pickled nasturtium capers

Our allotment has nasturtiums which produce an abundance of seeds each year, and if they remain on the soil we end up weeding masses of new plants in spring too. This recipe solves that problem and is a great substitute for capers. Pair with mackerel P110.

Prep 45 minutes + 2 days soaking
Ready 4 weeks
Makes approx 500ml/18fl oz jar

150g/5½oz/1 cup fresh green nasturtium seeds (or fresh capers)

Brine
300ml/10fl oz/1¼ cups water
45g/1½oz/3 tbsp salt (pure, without iodine or anti-caking agent)

Pickling solution
300ml/10fl oz/1¼ cups water
50ml/2fl oz/scant ¼ cup distilled spirit vinegar 10%
2-3 tsp sugar
2 whole cloves
1 small cinnamon stick
2-3 allspice berries

— For the brine, pour the water into a saucepan, add the salt and bring to the boil.
— Add the nasturtium seeds and return to the boil, then reduce the heat and simmer for 5-10 minutes.
— Take off the heat and leave the seeds in the brine for 24-48 hours.
— Wash the nasturtium seeds and place in sterilised jars P12.
— To make the pickling solution, combine the water, vinegar, sugar and spices in a small saucepan and bring to the boil.
— Cover the nasturtium seeds with the boiling pickling solution. Close the jars immediately and once cool check the seal P12. If not sealed, pasteurise P13.
— Try them after a week, but the flavour develops the longer you keep them. It is best to leave them for at least 4 weeks before eating.
— Sealed and/or pasteurised jars can be kept for 6 months. Store unsealed ones covered in vinegar in the fridge for up to 6 months. Once open, use within 1 month.

Pickled porcini mushrooms

We use this recipe to use the smaller porcini that we've foraged. Other wild mushrooms such as chanterelles can often be found at farmers' markets and are lovely too.

Prep 35 minutes
Ready 4 days
Makes approx 700ml/24fl oz jar

30g/1oz/1 cup small porcini mushrooms or other wild mushrooms or small cultivated mushrooms, rinsed
½ tsp salt

Pickling solution
100ml/3½fl oz/scant ½ cup distilled spirit vinegar 10%
300ml/10fl oz/1¼ cups water
1 small onion, cut in half then sliced
1 tsp sugar
2 bay leaves
½ tsp allspice berries
½ tsp black peppercorns
2 cloves

— Place mushrooms in a saucepan, cover with water, add the salt and bring to the boil. Reduce the heat and simmer for 20 minutes, then drain.
— Place all the pickling solution ingredients in a medium saucepan and bring to the boil. Reduce the heat and simmer for 5 minutes.
— Add the mushrooms and return to the boil, then transfer to sterilised jars P12.
— Close the jars immediately and once cool check the seal. If not sealed, pasteurise P13.
— Leave for at least 4 days before serving. Sealed and/or pasteurised jars can be kept in a cupboard for at least 6 months. Once opened store in the fridge and use within 3 months.

Mushroom hunting is a wonderful adventure in autumn, but it's advisable to learn how to identify mushrooms by going on guided walks. Never pick anything you are not 100% certain is safe.

Mackerel, Chinese cabbage and nasturtium caper salad

This makes a great light summer lunch. The nasturtium add a nice peppery bite. The leaves and the flowers of the nasturtium are also edible so could be washed and added if you have some growing nearby.

Serves 2

6 medium napa (Chinese) cabbage leaves, shredded
1 whole or 2 halves smoked mackerel, cut into large pieces
125ml/4fl oz/½ cup tartar sauce P27
Freshly ground black pepper
2 tbsp nasturtium capers P109
1 tbsp dried fermented pink turnip P191
1 tbsp dried carrot kimchi P188

— Divide the shredded cabbage between 2 plates.
— Place the mackerel pieces on top of the cabbage and drizzle with the tartar sauce. Season with black pepper and sprinkle with the nasturtium capers, dried fermented pink turnip and dried kimchi carrot.
— Serve with a light sourdough loaf P82 or ciabatta.

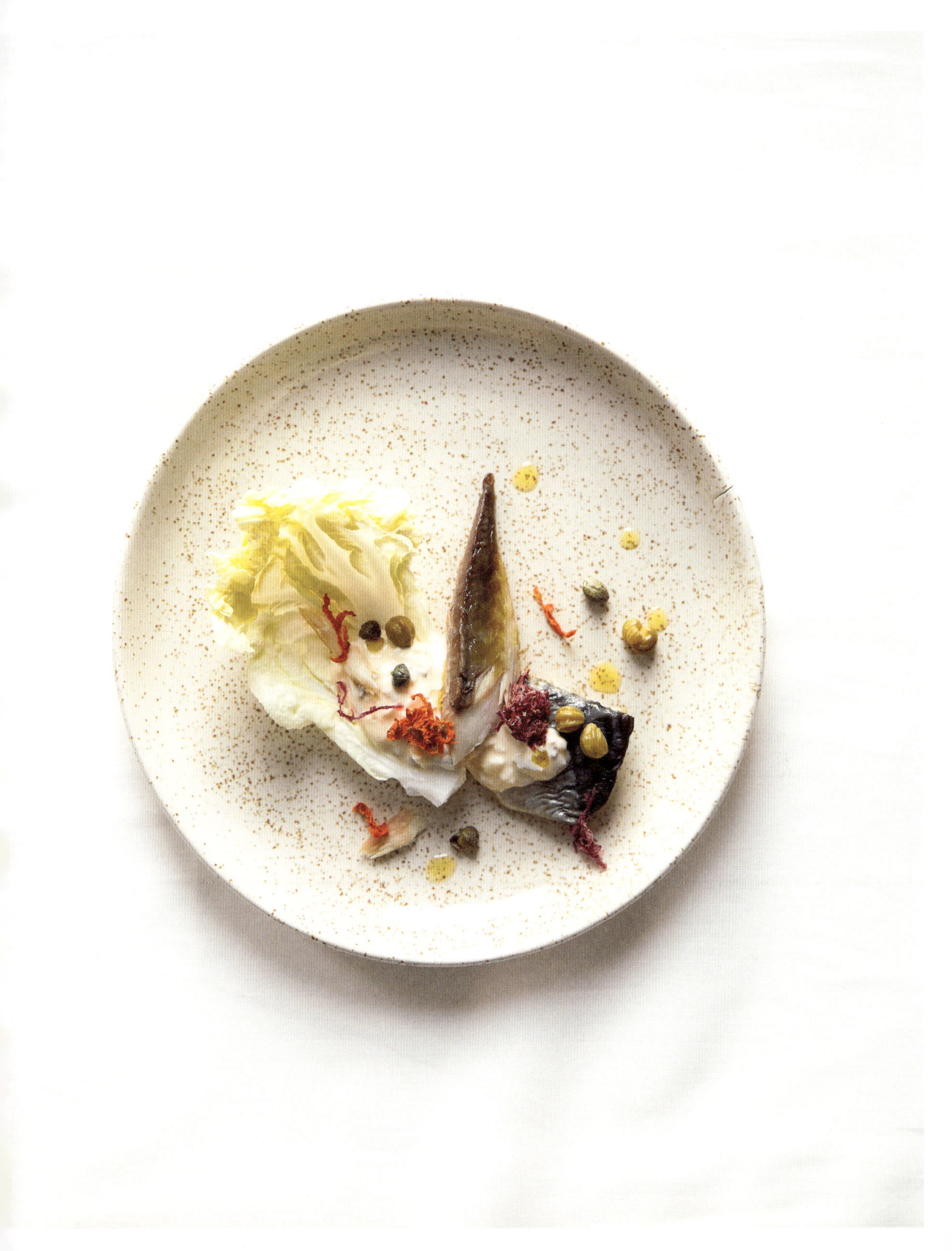

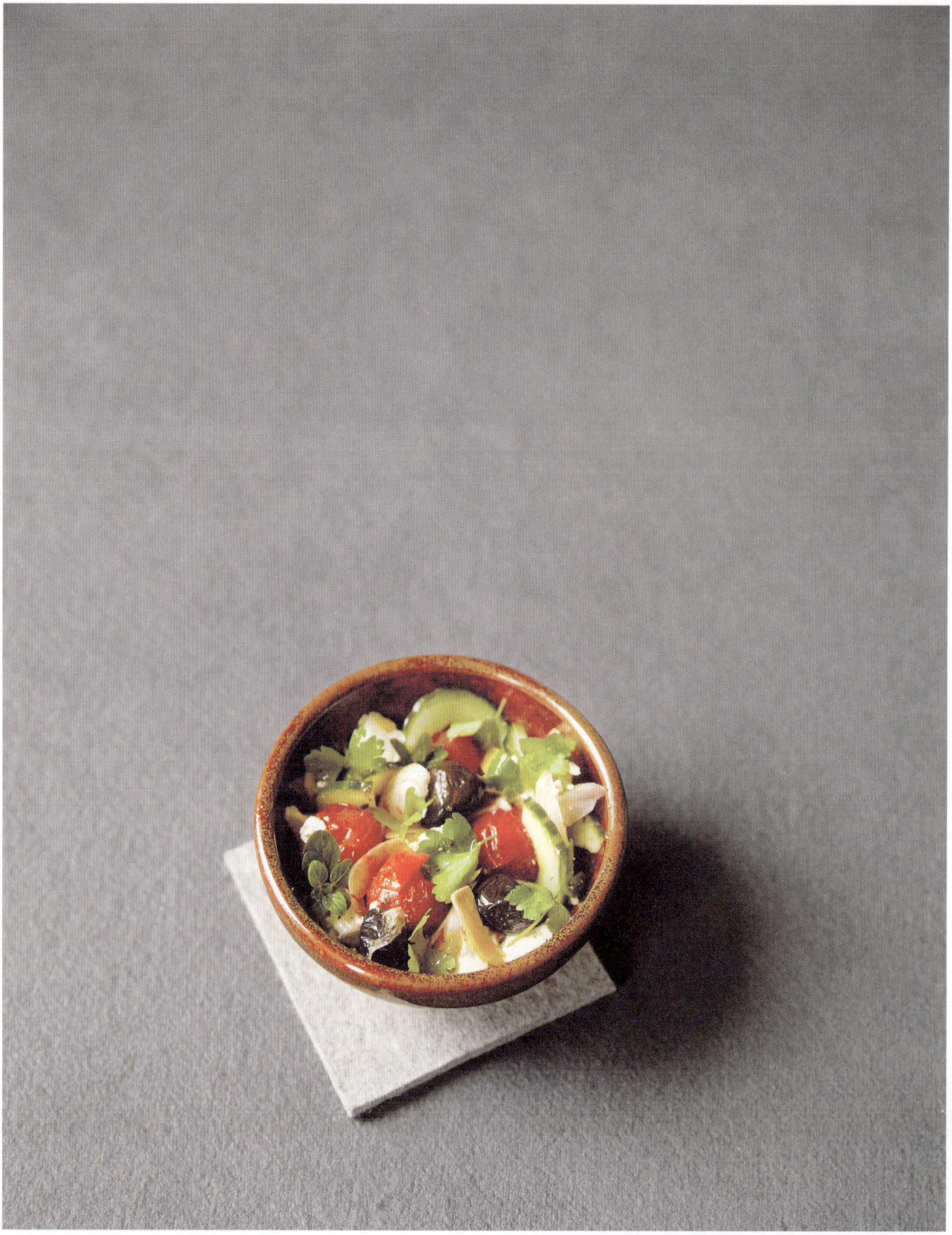

Pickled cherry tomatoes

Tomatoes pickle very well in brine, but this method using olive oil, allspice and pepper gives cherry tomatoes a special richness. Sprinkle into a Greek salad below.

Prep 40 minutes
Ready 1 week
Makes approx 1 litre/34fl oz jar

30 firm cherry tomatoes
6–9 garlic cloves, halved
3 thyme sprigs (optional)
3 rosemary sprigs (optional)

Brine
100ml/3½fl oz/scant ½ cup distilled spirit vinegar 10%
400ml/14fl oz/1¾ cups water
100ml/3½fl oz/scant ½ cup olive oil
6 peppercorns
6 allspice berries
½ tsp salt
¼ tsp dried chilli flakes (optional)

— Mix all the brine ingredients together in a medium saucepan and bring to the boil. Add the tomatoes and boil for 3 minutes.
— Remove the tomatoes from the brine and peel off the skins.
— Place tomatoes into sterilised jars P12 and add 2–3 garlic cloves to each jar and herbs, if liked.
— Return the brine to the boil, then carefully pour over the tomatoes making sure they are covered.
— Close the jars immediately and once cool check for the seal. If not sealed, pasteurise.
— Leave for at least a week before serving. Sealed and/or pasteurised jars can be kept in a cupboard for at least 6 months. Once opened, store in the fridge and eat within 2 weeks.

Greek salad

Serves 2

5–10 pickled cherry tomatoes above, depending on taste
Caster (superfine) sugar, for sprinkling
¼ red onion
½ cucumber
50g/1¾oz mixed salad leaves
15 kalamata olives
100g/3½oz feta cheese
Olive oil, for dressing salad
Salt and freshly ground black pepper

— Place the pickled cherry tomatoes in a large bowl and lightly sprinkle with sugar.
— Cut the onion in half, then cut each half thinly into half moons. Slice the cucumber lengthways and cut into thick half moons.
— Place the mixed salad leaves in a large salad bowl. Top with the onion, cucumber, olives and the pickled cherry tomatoes. Crumble the feta on top, then dress with olive oil and season to taste with salt and pepper.

Chilli and tomato paste

A spicy pickled paste that balances the sweetness of the tomatoes and peppers with a hefty dash of vinegar. Serve with a meat or cheese board, grilled meat, hard-boiled eggs, or with seafood as below.

Prep 50 minutes
Ready 2 hours
Makes approx 1 litre/34fl oz jar

350g/12oz red (bell) peppers, sliced
500g/1lb 2oz tomatoes, chopped
500g/1lb 2oz onions, sliced
1–2 chillies, sliced
45ml/1½fl oz/3 tbsp olive oil
45ml/1½fl oz/3 tbsp white wine vinegar
45g/1½oz/scant ¼ cup honey
½ tsp black peppercorns
½ tsp allspice berries
2 whole cloves
Pinch of salt
¼ tsp ground ginger
⅓ tsp ground cinnamon

— Mix all the ingredients together except the cinnamon in a medium saucepan. Bring to the boil, then reduce the heat and simmer for 30 minutes.
— Transfer the mixture to a food processor (or use a handblender) and blitz until smooth, then return to the rinsed-out saucepan and add the cinnamon.
— Return to the boil, then reduce the heat and simmer, stirring constantly until it thickens to the consistency of thick ketchup.

— While still very hot, carefully pour the mixture into sterilised jars P12. Close the jars immediately and once cool check the seal P12. If sealed, it will keep in the fridge for up to 5 days. If not sealed, pasteurise P13.
— Sealed and/or pasteurised jars can be kept in a cupboard for at least 6 months. Once opened, store in the fridge and use within 1 month.

Avocado and smoked prawns with chilli and tomato sauce

The smokiness of the prawns melds with the creaminess of the avocado and is fortified by the richness of rum. If you cannot find smoked prawns try grilling some tiger prawns instead.

Serves 2

2 tbsp mayonnaise
2 tbsp plain live yoghurt P20
3 tbsp chilli and tomato paste above
2 tablespoons rum
½ tsp salt
Freshly ground black pepper
2 ripe avocados
6–8 smoked prawns (shrimp) or grilled tiger prawns

— Combine mayonnaise, yoghurt, chilli and tomato paste and rum together in a small bowl. Season with the salt and pepper to taste, and set aside.
— Prepare the avocados by cutting in half and removing the stones. Using a large spoon, remove the avocado flesh from the skins and cut into thick slices. Arrange on 2 plates.

— Remove the shells from the prawns and arrange them on top of the avocado slices.
— Drizzle the chilli and tomato sauce over the top and serve with toasted sourdough P82.
— The chilli and tomato sauce will keep in the fridge for up to 5 days.

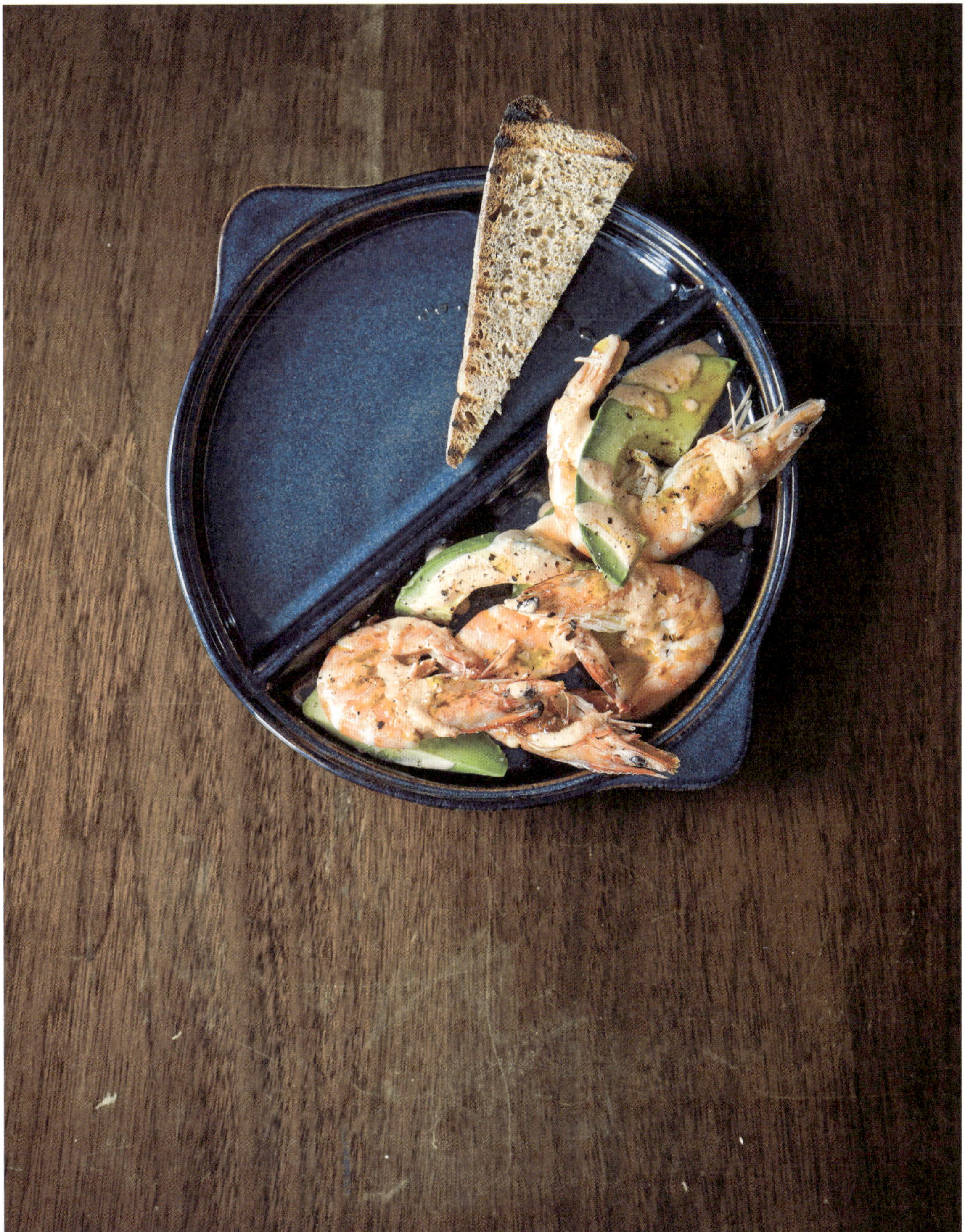

Sweet and spicy gherkins

The usual way to eat gherkins is in brine, but this combination of sugar and chilli makes something sublime. It will even be appreciated by people who wouldn't normally touch a gherkin. Serve with a sourdough cheese sandwich, or use as a pizza topping P61.

Prep 30 minutes + 6 hours standing
Ready 15 hours
Makes approx 500ml/18fl oz jar

- 6 long, thin cucumbers/gherkins (it's best to use Chinese, Persian or Armenian varieties of cucumber for this recipe)
- 3 tbsp salt (pure, without iodine or anti-caking agent)
- 1 garlic head, cloves thinly sliced
- 2 tsp chilli powder
- 8 tbsp rapeseed (canola) oil
- 250ml/9fl oz/generous 1 cup distilled spirit vinegar 10%
- 10 tbsp sugar

— Slice the cucumbers either thickly into 5mm/¼in slices for a crunchy effect or very thinly for a softer result.
— Place the sliced cucumbers in a large bowl, add the salt and mix until coated. Cover and leave for 6 hours.
— Drain the water from the cucumbers, then squeeze them gently and return to the bowl. Add the garlic and chilli powder and mix.
— Heat the oil in a small saucepan, then pour over the cucumber, do not stir.

— Mix the vinegar and sugar together in a small saucepan and bring to the boil. Pour over the cucumbers, then leave to cool before chilling in the fridge overnight.
— Serve or transfer to small sterilised jars P12 and pasteurise P13.
— The pickled cucumbers will keep in the fridge for up to 3 weeks or if pasteurised in jars they will keep in the cupboard for at least 6 months. Once opened store in the fridge and use within 3 weeks.

Pickled green tomato

We make this to deal with a glut of green tomatoes when our plants get hit by blight. It's a great sandwich energiser.

Prep 3 hours + 24 hours standing
Ready 28 hours
Makes approx 2.5 litre/85fl oz

- 2.5kg/5½lb green tomatoes, chopped
- 6 onions (about 600g/1¼lb), chopped
- 180g/6½oz/½ cup salt (pure, without iodine or anti-caking agent)

Pickling solution
- 500g/1lb 2oz/2½ cups sugar
- 500ml/18fl oz/2 cups vinegar
- 2½ tsp white mustard seeds
- 4 allspice berries; 4 black peppercorns
- 6 bay leaves

— Mix the tomatoes and onions together in a large bowl. Cover with the salt and leave for 24 hours.
— Squeeze the tomatoes and onions well to remove any excess liquid.
— To make the pickling solution, combine all the ingredients in a large saucepan and bring to the boil. Add the tomatoes and onions, then reduce the heat and simmer, stirring frequently, for at least 1½ hours until thickened, soft and golden in colour. The cooking time will depending on personal preference. You can stop

cooking once the tomatoes are golden green and soft, but we prefer to cook them for about 3 hours until it is golden brown and thick.
— While still very hot carefully decant into sterilised jars P12. Close the jars immediately and once cool check the seal P12. If not sealed, pasteurise P13.
— Sealed and/or pasteurised) jars can kept in a cupboard for at least 6 months. Once opened, store in the fridge and use within 1 month.

Pickled plums

A bowl of these was passed around the table in Poland once and we were hooked. The spiciness and sharpness are simply stunning – can this be the same fruit that spawned tins of prunes in syrup? You can serve it as an accompaniment to cold meats or a cheese board.

Prep 15 minutes + 4-day process
Ready 4 weeks
Makes approx 2 litre/67fl oz jar

1kg/2¼lb plums, purple such as Victoria or Polish Wegierki plums, ripe but still firm
250ml/9fl oz/generous 1 cup water
250ml/9fl oz/generous 1 cup vinegar
500g/1lb 2oz/2½ cups sugar
5 allspice berries
5 whole cloves

— Pierce the plums a few times with a fork and place in a bowl.
— To make the pickling solution, combine the water, vinegar, sugar and spices in a medium saucepan and bring to the boil.
— Pour the boiling pickling solution over the plums, cover and leave for 24 hours.
— Repeat this step over the next 2 days. Pour the pickling solution into a saucepan, bring to the boil, then pour back over the plums and cover.
— On day 4 place the plums in a saucepan, cover with the pickling solution and bring to the boil, then carefully transfer the hot plums to sterilised jars P12 with a slotted spoon and cover with the hot pickling solution.
— Close the jars immediately and once cool check the seal P12. If not sealed, pasteurise P13.
— You can try them after a week but the flavour develops the longer you keep them. It is best to leave them for 4 weeks before eating.
— Sealed and/or pasteurised jars can be kept in a cupboard for at least 6 months. Once opened store in the fridge and use within 1 month.

Beetroot and red pepper pickle

Prep 1 hour
Ready 2 hours
Makes approx 2 litre/67fl oz jar

1kg/2¼lb beetroot (beets)
300g/10½oz/2 large red (bell) peppers, finely chopped
1 large onion, chopped
2 garlic cloves, chopped

Pickling solution
200ml/7fl oz/scant 1 cup water
200ml/7fl oz/scant 1 cup distilled spirit vinegar 10%
150g/5½oz/¾ cup sugar
1 tbsp salt
6 black peppercorns
1 star anise
2 bay leaves
1 tsp allspice berries
¼ tsp dried chilli flakes
4 whole cloves

— Boil the beetroot until soft, then cool, peel and grate.
— To make the pickling solution, combine all the ingredients in a large saucepan. Bring to the boil, then add the peppers and onion. Return to the boil, then simmer for 10 minutes.
— Add the beetroot, return to the boil, then simmer for a further 15 minutes.
— Add the garlic, boil again and simmer for 5 more minutes.
— While still very hot decant into sterilised jars P12.
— Close the jars immediately and once cool check the seal P12. If not sealed, pasteurise P13.
— Sealed and/or pasteurised jars can be kept for 6 months. Once opened, chill and use within 1 month.

Pickled green tomato P116
Pickled plums P117
Beetroot and red pepper pickle P117

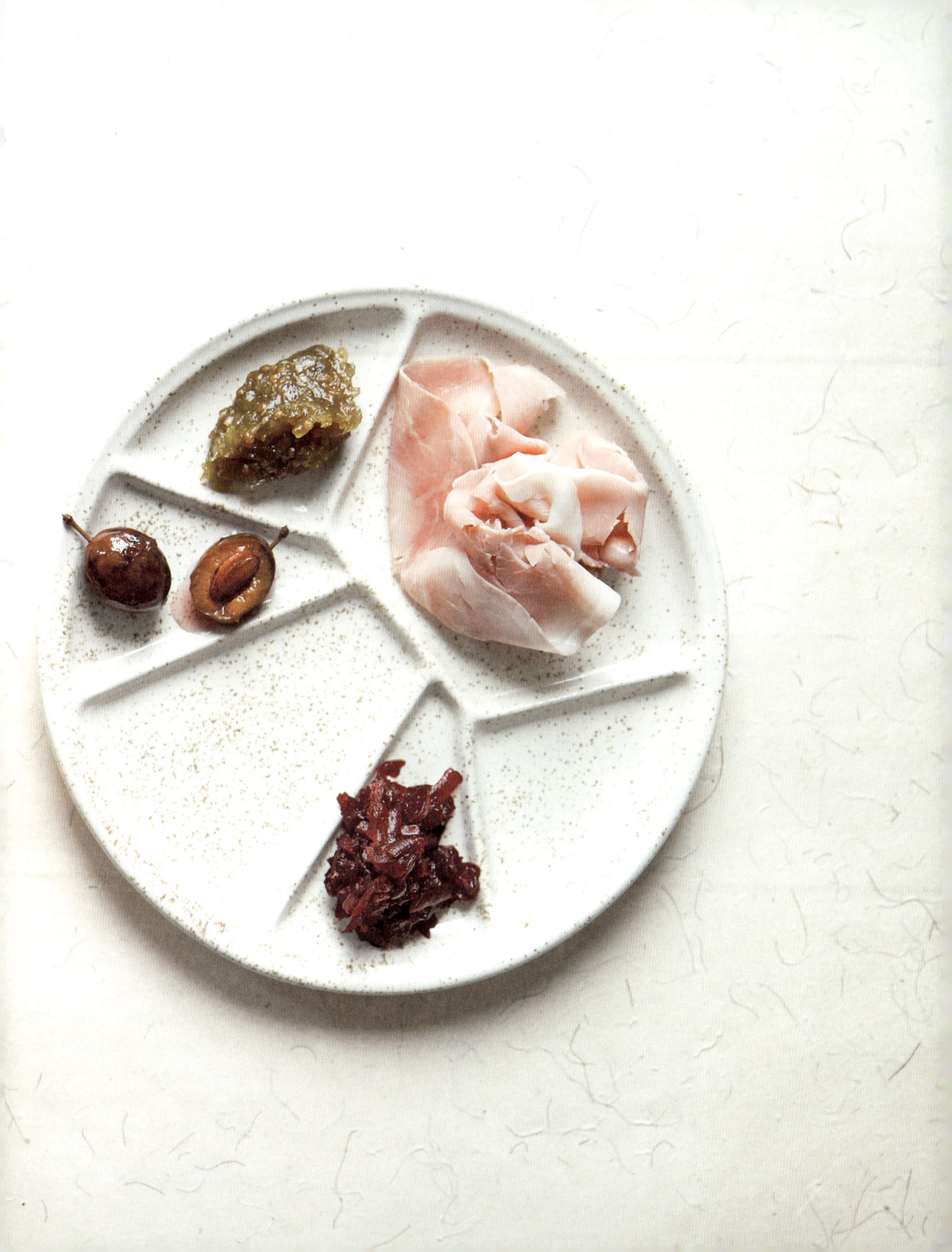

Spicy pineapple and mango pickle

This is inspired by Indian sweet mango pickles and can be served as a part of a thali P200 or as a condiment on a cheese board.

Prep 1 hour 20 minutes
Ready 2 hours
Makes approx 1 litre/34fl oz jar

1 tsp coriander seeds
1 tsp white mustard seeds
10 black peppercorns
3 tbsp rapeseed (canola) oil
½ tsp hot pepper flakes
1 tsp ground cumin
2 small onions, finely chopped
1 large pineapple, peeled, tough core removed, cut into 1.5cm/⅝in cubes
2 large mangoes, peeled, stoned and cut into 1.5 x 1.5cm/⅝ x ⅝in cubes
1 long red chilli, chopped
2cm/¾in piece of ginger, skin scraped off and very finely chopped
50g/1¾oz/⅓ cup raisins
10 dried apricots, chopped into raisin-sized pieces
100g/3½oz/½ cup brown sugar
1 tbsp pink Himalayan salt
150ml/5fl oz/⅔ cup distilled spirit vinegar 10%

— Crush the coriander seeds, mustard seeds and black peppercorns in a mortar with a pestle.
— Heat the oil in a large saucepan, add all the spices and fry, stirring constantly for 2 minutes.
— Add the onions, pineapple, mangoes, chilli and ginger and bring to the boil, stirring frequently.
— Add the raisins, apricots, sugar, salt and vinegar. Return to the boil, then reduce the heat and simmer, stirring frequently for 35–40 minutes until thick.
— While still hot decant into sterilised jars P12. Close immediately and once cool check the seal P12. If not sealed pasteurise P13.
— Sealed and/or pasteurised jars can be kept in a cupboard for at least 6 months. Once opened, store in the fridge and use within 1 month.

Green chilli and red onion pickle

This recipe is our version of an Indian-style chutney and can be served alongside a curry.

Prep 30 minutes + 4 hours standing
Ready 2 hours
Makes approx 500ml/18fl oz jar

2 medium red onions, halved and thinly sliced
1 large courgette (zucchini), cut on a mandolin into thin matchsticks
1 turnip, peeled and cut on a mandolin into thin matchsticks
5 small thin green chillies, halved
1 tsp salt

Pickling solution
½ tsp black peppercorns
1 tsp coriander seeds
1 tsp caraway seeds
1 tsp mustard seeds
150ml/5fl oz/⅔ cup distilled spirit vinegar 10%
80g/3oz/scant ½ cup sugar
2 bay leaves
1 tsp allspice berries

— Place all the vegetables and chillies in a large bowl and sprinkle with the salt. Mix well and leave to stand for 1–3 hours.
— Squeeze all the liquid out of the vegetables and return to the bowl.
— To make the pickling solution, heat a medium frying pan and dry-toast the peppercorns, coriander, caraway and mustard seeds for about 30 seconds.
— Transfer the toasted seeds to a medium saucepan with the remaining pickling solution ingredients and bring to the boil. Pour over the vegetables and mix well.
— Leave to stand for 1 hour, then transfer to sterilised jars P12.
— Chill and use within 3 weeks. Alternatively, pasteurise P13 and store for up to 3 months.

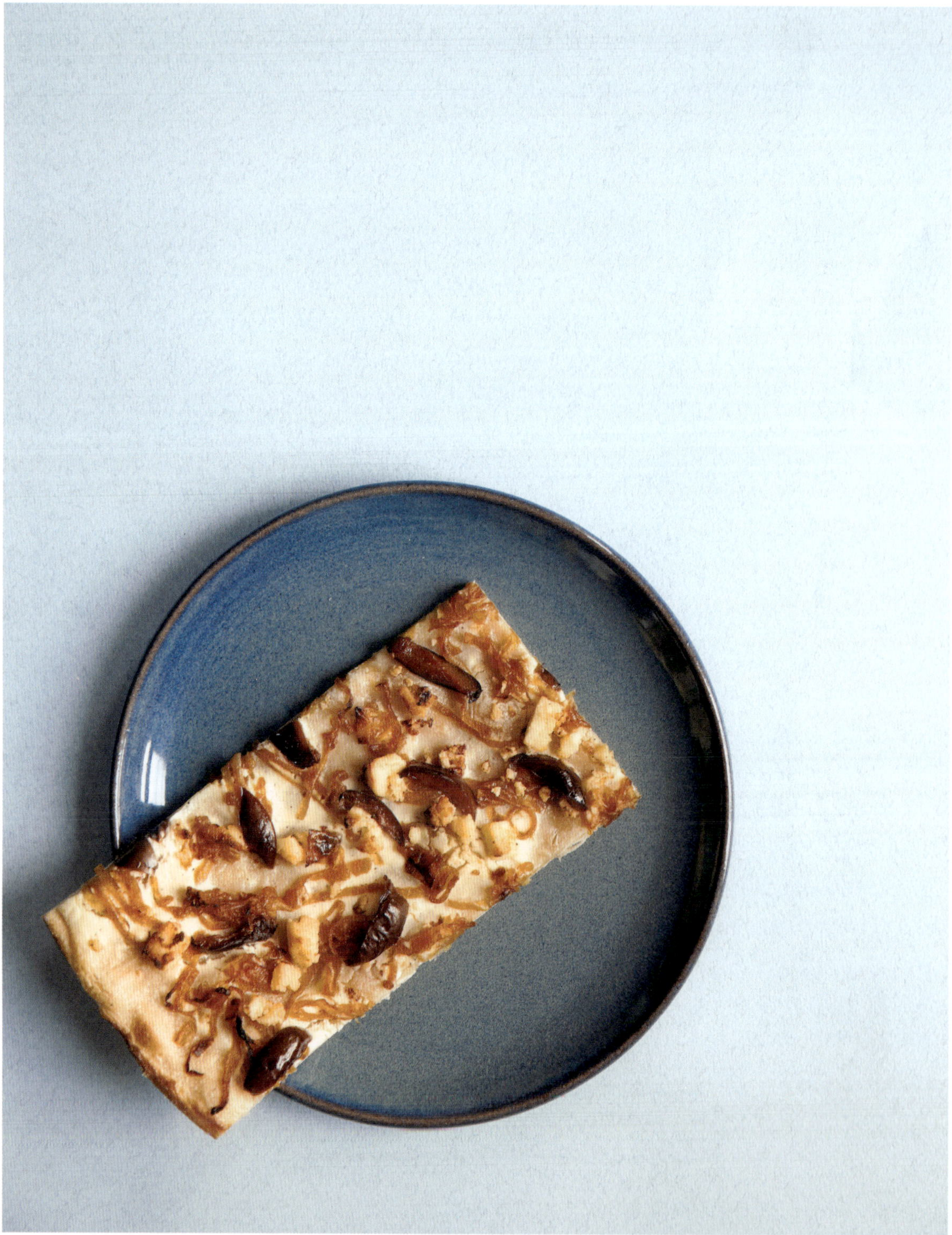

Pickled plum flammekueche

We first discovered this at a brewpub in Lille in northern France, but it originates in the Alsace region and is a bit like a pizza. The dough isn't as leavened as pizza dough, so the base remains thin and crispy.

Makes 4, larger than a dinner plate

Dough
500g/1lb 2oz/3½ cups strong white flour
Pinch of salt
250ml/9fl oz/generous 1 cup bottle conditioned beer (with yeast)
4 tbsp olive oil
Coarse semolina, for sprinkling

Toppings
1 medium sweet potato, peeled and cut into 2cm/¾in cubes
1 hokkaido pumpkin, peeled and cut into 2cm/¾in cubes
Salt and freshly ground black pepper
Pinch of korma curry spice
Olive oil, to season
2 knobs of butter, for frying
4 onions, sliced
½–1 tsp smoked paprika
220g/8oz paneer cheese, cut into 1.5cm/⅝in cubes
300ml/10fl oz/1¼ cups sour cream
8 pickled plums, each pitted and sliced into 6–8 strips P117
4 honey-pickled garlic cloves, sliced P133
3 tbsp pickled nuts, chopped P42
1 tbsp olive oil

— To make the dough, put the flour in a large bowl with the salt.
— Pour the last part of a bottle of live beer into a measuring jug. Add the olive oil and mix into the flour to form a stiff dough.
— Leave for 20 minutes, then knead for 5–10 minutes.
— Wrap the dough in a plastic bag or clingfilm and chill in the fridge for at least 8 hours, preferably overnight.
— When ready to bake, preheat the oven to 230°C/450°F/gas mark 8 and place a roasting tin in the oven to heat up.
— To make the toppings, mix the sweet potato and pumpkin together in a bowl. Season with salt, black pepper, curry spice and a little olive oil, then place into the heated roasting tin and roast for 15–20 minutes, or until soft. Turn the vegetables a couple of times during cooking.
— Melt half the butter in a frying pan, add the onions (or 1 if you prefer to work with a smaller portion) and fry over a low heat until soft and golden brown. Season with salt, pepper and half the smoked paprika and fry for another minute.
— Divide the onions into 4 equal portions and set aside.
— Melt the remaining butter in another frying pan and fry the paneer, turning frequently until it starts to turn golden. Season with pepper, the remaining smoked paprika and a little salt, then fry for a further 1–2 minutes. Divide the cheese into 4 equal portions and set aside.

— Meanwhile, remove the dough from the fridge and cut into quarters.
— Sprinkle coarse semolina over a piece of baking parchment.
— Roll the first quarter of dough into a very thin circle or rectangle on to the baking parchment. z with the remaining dough.
— Season the sour cream with a little salt and pepper and spread evenly all over each piece of rolled out dough, then sprinkle each with a portion of onion and a portion of cheese. Scatter the pickled plums over 2 flammekueche and scatter the roasted sweet vegetables, sliced pickled garlic and chopped pickled nuts over the remaining 2.
— Preheat a baking tray in the oven. Slide the first flammekueche together with the baking parchment on to a second baking tray and slide it on to the preheated tray. Bake for 10–15 minutes, or until the crust is golden brown. Remove from the oven and bake the remaining 3 flammekueche separately in the same way. Serve.

Lightly pickled cucumbers

This recipe is based on a very popular side dish from Lithuania. Our friend Ona makes lightly pickled cucumbers with distilled spirit vinegar. We wanted to achieve something mellower, hence the addition of honey and apple cider vinegar. They go very well with fish below.

Prep 10 minutes
Ready 24–72 hours
Makes 1 large bowl

2 tbsp vegetable oil
1 large onion, halved and sliced
1 tsp salt
2 tsp raw/cold-pressed honey
350g/12oz cucumbers, peeled, halved and sliced 5mm/¼in thick
5 tsp raw cider vinegar with mother
½ tsp ground black pepper

— Heat the oil in a frying pan, add the onion and fry until soft and golden.
— Remove from the heat, add the salt and honey and mix well.
— Mix the onion, cucumber and vinegar together in a bowl, then chill for 24 hours before serving.
— Do not pasteurise this recipe. The flavour develops over the first few days and is at its best after 2–3 days. Store in the fridge and use within 10 days.

White fish in tempura batter

Serves 2

150g/5½oz/scant ¾ cup shortgrain brown rice
2 tbsp black sesame seeds
200g/7oz Sussex huss fillets (or any other firm white fish), cut into portions, about 4 x 4cm/ 1½ x 1½in thick
1 tsp salt
500ml/18fl oz/2 cups sunflower oil
200g/7oz/1½ cups gluten-free self-raising flour (or regular flour, but texture is much nicer with gluten-free)
150ml/5fl oz/⅔ cup soda water
2 tbsp seaweed flakes
50g/1¾oz lightly pickled cucumbers above
Soy sauce, to taste

— Cook the rice according to the packet instructions, then drain and keep warm in the pan while you prepare the other ingredients.
— Toast the black sesame seeds in a dry frying pan over a medium heat until fragrant, then remove from the heat and set aside.
— Season the fish with a little of the salt and set aside.
— Heat the sunflower oil in a deep, heavy-based pan over a high heat. You can judge how hot the oil is with your hand. Hold your hand carefully just above the pan and if the heat in the air tingles your hand, then it is hot enough. If it feels very hot then the temperature of your oil should be reduced slightly.

— To make the batter, mix the flour, soda water, remaining salt and seaweed flakes together in a bowl. Use the batter immediately (otherwise it will lose its potency and its texture).
— Coat the fish pieces in the batter.
— Carefully lower the battered fish in batches into the hot oil, and once it starts to float and is golden brown on all sides remove it with a slotted spoon and drain on kitchen paper.
— To serve, add a few spoonfuls of cooked rice to a bowl, then top with the tempura battered fish, the pickled cucumber, toasted sesame seeds and soy sauce and serve.

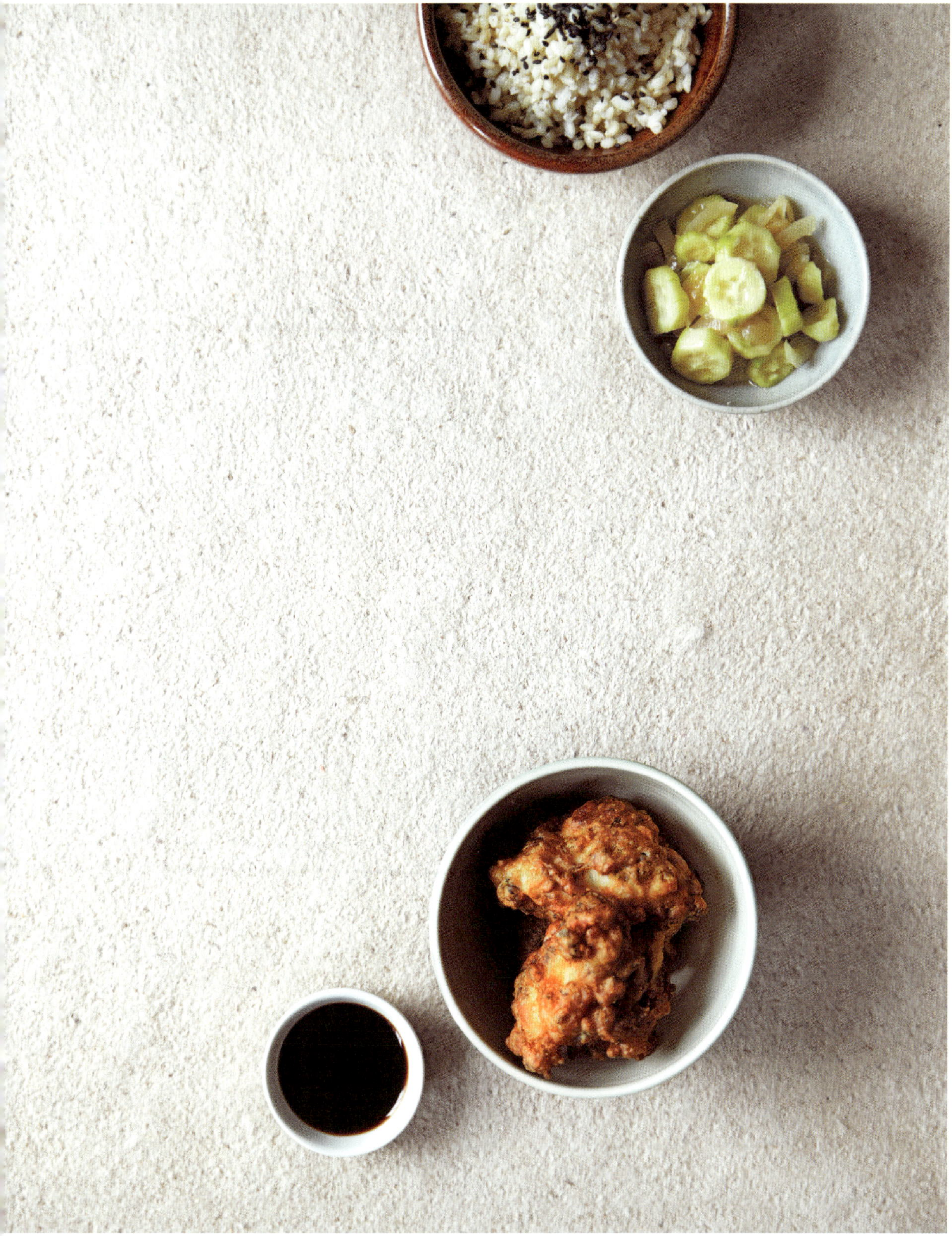

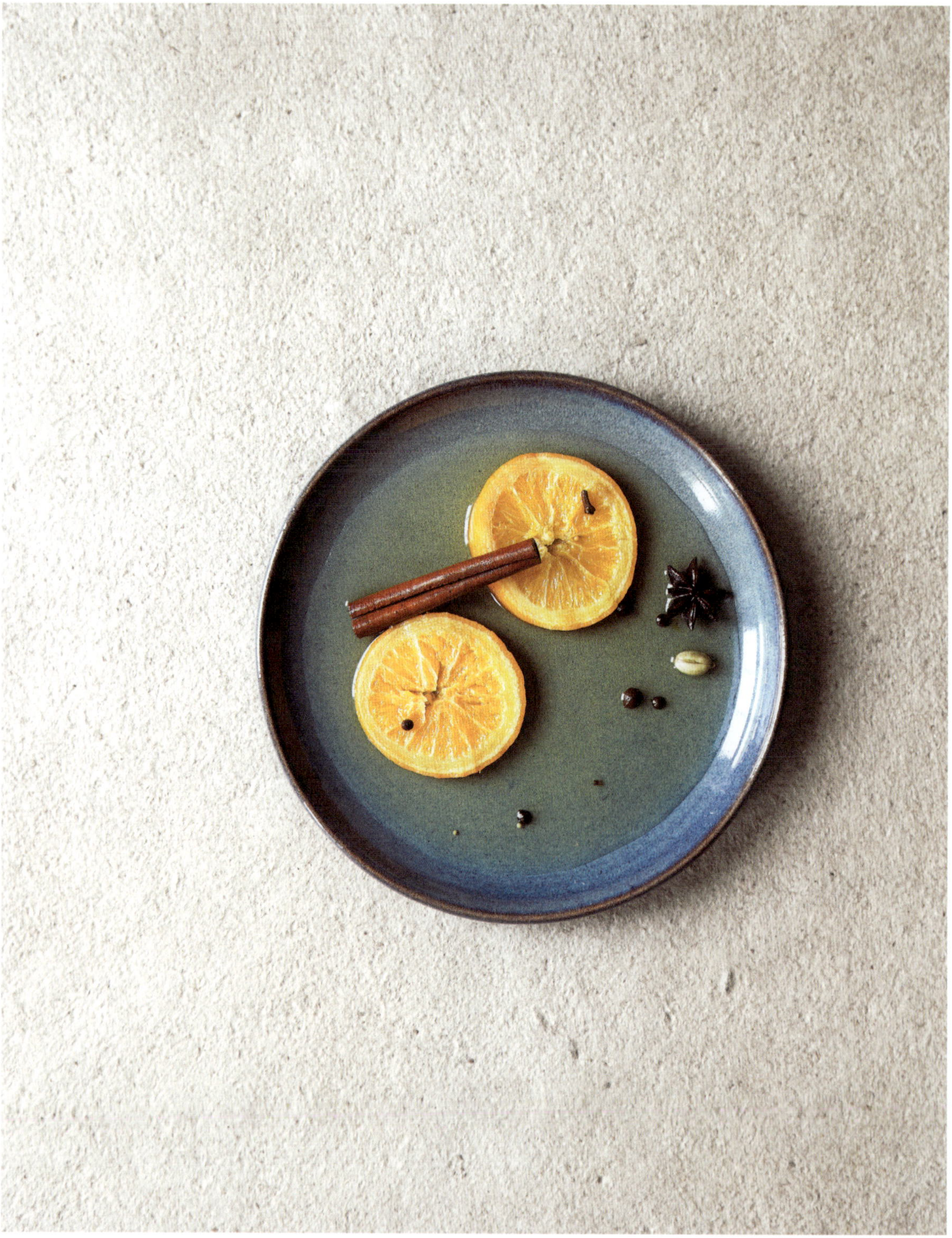

Pickled oranges

These pickled oranges go really well with mature white cheese, as well as with seafood P128.

Prep 40 minutes + cooling
Ready 1 week
Makes approx 1 litre / 34fl oz jar

4 oranges, unwaxed
½ tsp salt

Pickling solution
250ml / 9fl oz / generous 1 cup water
250ml / 9fl oz / generous 1 cup cider vinegar
50g / 1¾oz / 3 tbsp honey
100g / 3½oz / ½ cup sugar
1 cinnamon stick
1 tsp allspice berries
8 cloves
4 cardamom pods
2 star anise

— Place the whole oranges in a medium saucepan, pour in enough water to cover and add the salt. Bring to the boil, then reduce the heat and simmer for 25 minutes. Remove from the heat and leave to cool.
— Cut the oranges into thick slices and place them into a sterilised jar P12.
— To make the pickling solution, mix all the ingredients together in a saucepan. Bring to the boil, then reduce the heat and simmer for 5 minutes. Pour the hot pickling solution over the orange and leave to cool, then cover with and chill in the fridge.
— Leave the oranges for a week or so before using. No need to seal or pasteurise. Store in the fridge and use within 3 months.

Pickled pears

Gaba's mum makes these in summer and opens the first jar at Christmas. They are a fine accompaniment to cold turkey on Boxing Day, or with roast duck P131.

Prep 10 minutes + 4-day process
Ready 4 weeks
Makes approx 2 litre / 67fl oz jar

1kg / 2¼lb pears (choose the smallest pears you can find, ripe but still firm)

Pickling solution
250ml / 9fl oz / generous 1 cup water
250ml / 9fl oz / generous 1 cup distilled spirit vinegar 10%
500g / 1lb 2oz / 2½ cups sugar
1 tsp allspice berries
1 tsp whole cloves

— Peel the pears but leave the stalks on, then place in a heatproof bowl.
— To make the pickling solution, mix all the ingredients together in a saucepan and bring to the boil.
— Pour the boiling pickling solution over the pears, then cover and leave for 24 hours.
— Repeat this step over the next 2 days. Pour the pickling solution into a saucepan, bring to the boil, then pour back over the pears and cover.
— On day 4 place the pears in a saucepan, cover with the pickling solution and bring to the boil, then transfer the hot pears to sterilised jars P12 and cover with the hot pickling solution.
— Close the jars immediately and once cool check the seal. If not sealed, pasteurise P13.
— You can try them after a week but the flavour develops the longer you keep them. It is best to leave them for 4 weeks before eating.
— Sealed and/or pasteurised jars can be kept in a cupboard for at least 6 months. Once opened store in the fridge and use within 1 month.

Pickled oranges, spiced cuttlefish and squid ink linguini

Serves 4

1 whole cuttlefish (ask your fishmonger to clean it for you)
500g/1lb 2oz squid ink linguini
Olive oil, for drizzling and frying
3 slices stale bread, made into breadcrumbs
3 garlic cloves, sliced
200g/7oz pickled oranges P127
Salt and freshly ground black pepper
20g/¾oz parsley leaves

Marinade
1 tsp ground Aleppo pepper, or paprika
1 tsp Urfa chilli, or other chilli flakes
2 tsp fennel seeds, toasted and ground
Grated zest and juice of 1 orange
Juice of 1 lemon
4 tsp olive oil
1 tsp dried oregano

— With a blunt kitchen knife, deeply score the cuttlefish into small rectangles and slice the inside diagonally and in both directions to create a diamond pattern. The scoring will need to be deep enough to help cook the fish faster, and give it the nice 'spiral effect' you're looking for. Don't cut all the way through the cuttlefish. Set aside.

— For the marinade, mix the Aleppo pepper, Urfa chilli, fennel seeds, half the orange zest (you can save the rest of the orange peel in a little tub with a little of the juice, so it doesn't dry out), and all the juice, lemon juice, oregano and olive oil together in a shallow glass dish. Add the cuttlefish and marinate at least for 1 hour, preferably overnight. This marinade contains lemon juice so will partly cook the fish due to the citric acid in the juice, so you can just finish off the cooking process on a very hot griddle.

— Cook the pasta according to the packet instructions until al dente. Drain, keeping a little of the cooking liquid to the side. Drizzle a little olive oil over the pasta and set aside.

— Preheat a griddle until hot. Remove the cuttlefish from the marinade, reserving the rest of the marinade, and place on the griddle. Cook the fish on both sides until it has some nice grill marks.

— At the same time, heat a little olive oil in a frying pan, add the breadcrumbs and the sliced garlic and fry until they are golden brown. Set aside.

— Place the pasta, cuttlefish, pickled oranges and the leftover marinade in the frying pan and heat, stirring, until everything is warm. Season to taste. If it looks too dry then use some of the reserved pasta cooking liquid.

— Place generous portions of the pasta mix on each plate and top with the parsley leaves, fried breadcrumbs and garlic, remaining orange zest, and a drizzle of olive oil.

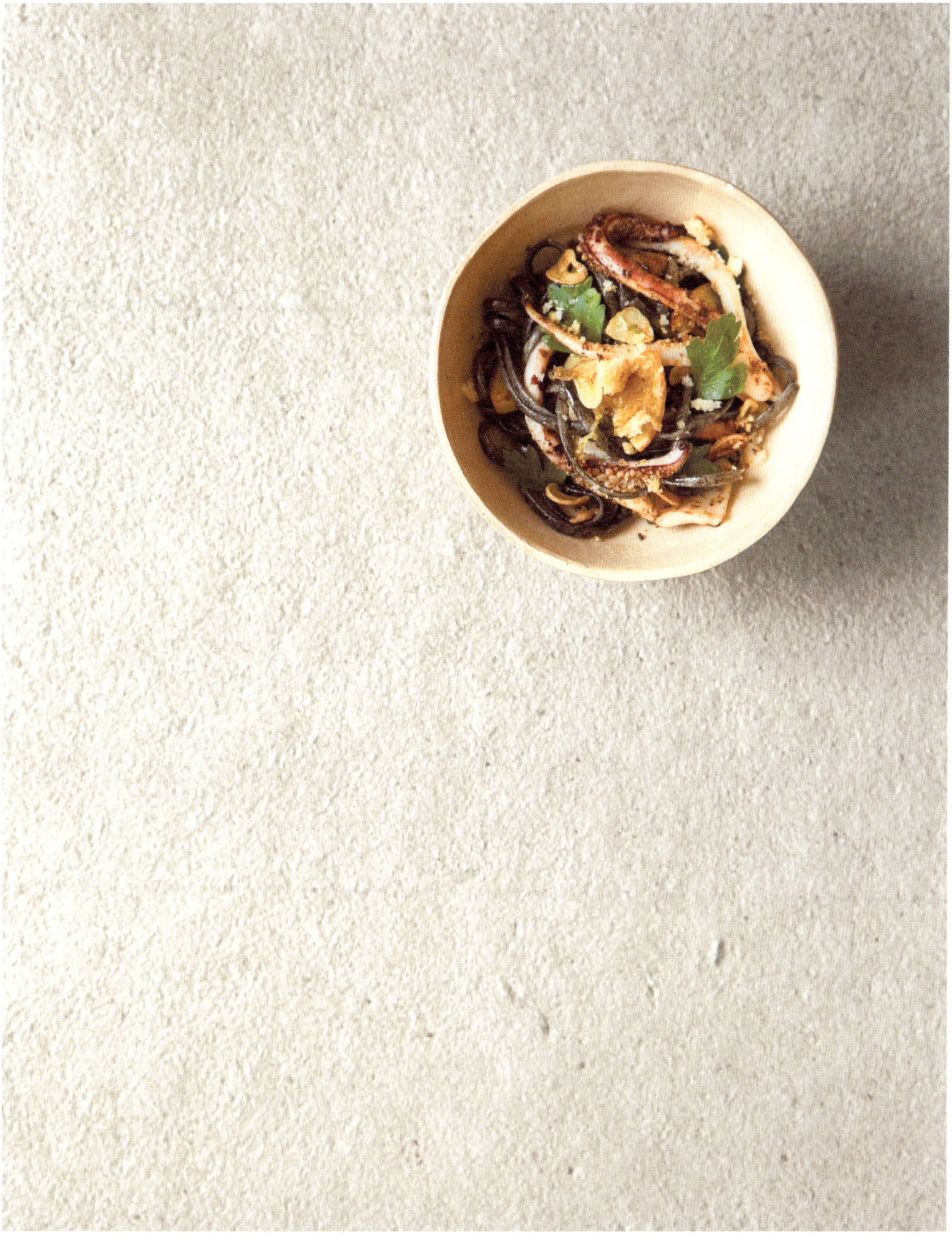

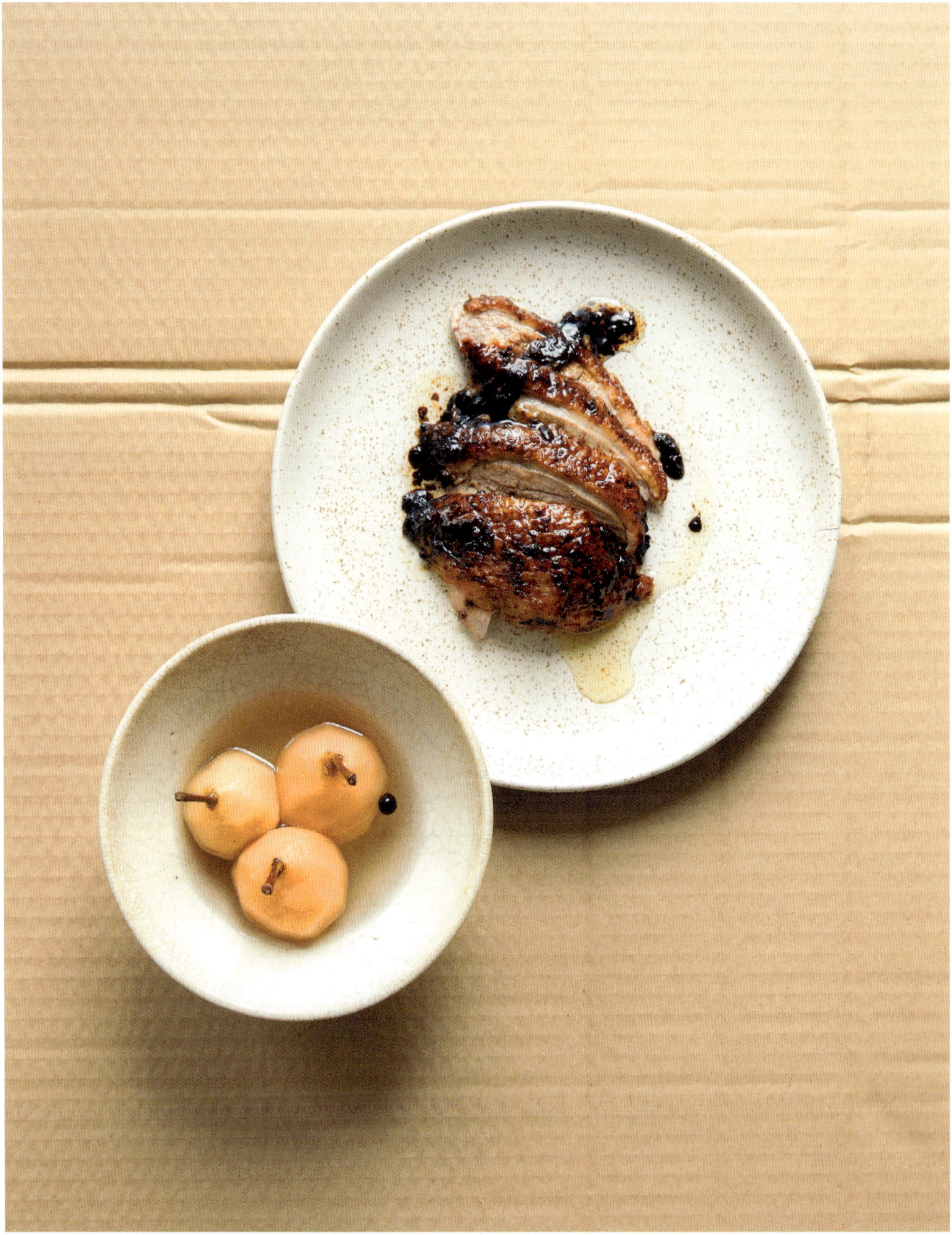

Duck with pickled pears

Serves 4

1 whole free range duck
200g/7oz shallots, halved, and skin left on
120g/4oz pickled pears P127

Brine
(this is an optional step, but it will make the duck more tender and juicy, as well as better seasoned)
2 litres/67fl oz/8 cups water
150g/5½oz/scant ⅔ cup sea salt (pure, without iodine or anti-caking agent)
4 bay leaves
2 tbsp coriander seeds
2 tsp mustard seeds
10 garlic cloves, crushed
5 star anise pods
10 cloves
10g/¼oz piece of ginger, skin scraped off and finely chopped

Marinade
1 tsp nutmeg, freshly grated
40ml/1½fl oz sweet soy sauce
20g/¾oz ginger, skin scraped off and grated
Grated zest of 1 orange
2 star anise, ground
1½ tsp salt
1 tsp ground black pepper
1 tsp ground Szechuan pepper

— Make the brine (if using) by mixing all the ingredients together. Add the duck to the brine and leave in the fridge for 3–8 hours. Discard the brine afterwards.

— For the marinade, mix all the ingredients together and rub it all over the duck skin until it is completely covered. Leave in the fridge for at least 1 hour, preferably overnight to marinate.

— When ready to cook, preheat the oven to 200°C/400°F/gas mark 6. Use a roasting tray that will just fit the duck and line the bottom with the shallots. The marinade should give the shallots enough flavour so there is no need for seasoning, but do so if you think
they need it.

— Place the duck and remaining marinade in the tray and roast in the oven for 30 minutes, then baste it with all the juices. Return it to the oven and turn the oven temperature down to 120°C/250°F/gas mark ½. Roast for another hour, or until it reaches an internal cooking temperature of 70°C/158°F.

— Let the duck rest for 20 minutes before carving. Serve slices of the duck with a generous amount of pickled pears.

Pickled celery

After a few weeks this spicy, crunchy pickled celery will become quite fiery. If you prefer a milder flavour you can reduce the amount of chilli or leave it out altogether. Cut a few longer celery sticks as garnish for a bloody mary below or add to a stir-fry P187.

Prep 15 minutes
Ready 24-72 hours
Makes approx 750ml/25fl oz jar

400g/14oz celery sticks
2 garlic cloves, thickly sliced
1 red chilli, sliced

Pickling solution
250ml/9fl oz/generous 1 cup apple cider vinegar
250ml/9fl oz/generous 1 cup water
100g/3½oz/½ cup sugar
5 whole cloves
½ tsp sea salt
2 tsp white mustard seeds

— Cut the celery sticks diagonally into 1cm/½in wide chunks, then put them into sterilised jars P12 with the garlic and chilli.
— To make the pickling solution, mix all the ingredients together in a small saucepan and bring to the boil.
— Pour the boiling pickling solution over the celery. Leave to cool, then chill in the fridge.
— Do not pasteurise. The flavour develops over several days. Leave for at least 24 hours before trying. We recommend keeping them for at least 2-3 days before serving. They will keep in the fridge for at least 2 months.

Bloody mary

Pickled? Why not? Vodka and pickles are the closest of companions.

Serves 2

1-2 tsp dried sour gherkin salt P190
½ lemon
Ice cubes
100ml/3½fl oz/scant ½ cup vodka
300ml/10fl oz/1¼ cups tomato juice
1 tsp Tabasco
2 tsp Worcestershire sauce (optional)
Freshly ground black pepper
2 pickled celery sticks above

— Pour the dried sour gherkin salt on to a small plate.
— Rub the juicy side of the lemon along the lip of a large glass, then roll the outer edge of the glass in the salt until the rim is completely coated. Repeat with another glass.
— Fill the glasses with ice cubes and set aside.
— Squeeze the juice from the lemon into a cocktail shaker. Add the remaining ingredients, except the pickled celery sticks, and shake gently. Strain into the prepared glasses.
— Garnish with the pickled celery sticks and serve.

Honey-pickled garlic

These are pleasingly sweet and tender and complement many a dish including pulled pork P134. While we can't guarantee that they will cure a cold, we certainly feel better munching them if we feel something coming on.

Prep 15 minutes
Ready 1 week
Makes approx 500ml/18fl oz jar

5 garlic heads

Pickling solution
100ml/3½fl oz/scant ½ cup apple cider vinegar
50ml/2fl oz/scant ¼ cup water
10 tbsp honey
Juice of 1 lemon
2 star anise
5 black peppercorns
½ tsp salt
5 whole cloves

— To make the pickling solution, mix all the ingredients together in a small saucepan. Bring to the boil and add the garlic. Boil for a minute, then remove the garlic heads and put them into sterilised jars P12.
— Bring the pickling solution to the boil and pour over the garlic.
— Close the jars immediately and once cool check the seal P12. If not sealed, pasteurise P13.
— Leave them for at least a week before using.
— Sealed and/or pasteurised jars can be kept in a cupboard for at least 6 months. Once opened, store in the fridge and use within 1 month.

Pulled pork with swede mash, grilled nectarines and honey-pickled garlic

Serves 4

1.5kg/3¼lb pork belly or shoulder (ask your butcher to score it for you, and to leave it on the bone. The bones add more flavour to the meat when you cook it and it will keep more of the juices in)
1 tsp ground sea salt
50ml/2fl oz/scant ¼ cup red wine vinegar
50g/1¾oz honey-pickled garlic, plus extra to serve P133
100g/3½oz shallots, sliced
A couple of thyme sprigs
500g/1lb 2oz swede (rutabaga)
2 nectarines, sliced in wedges
40g/1½oz alfalfa sprouts (or any other sprouts)

Marinade
1 tsp Urfa chilli, or other chilli flakes
2 tsp dill seeds, toasted and ground
2 tsp aniseed, toasted and ground
1 tsp dried lavender (optional)
1 tsp sumac

— Mix all the marinade ingredients together in a large dish, add the pork, skin-side up, with 1 teaspoon of salt. Make sure the skin doesn't have any marinade on, so that it forms good crackling. Leave to marinate in the fridge for at least 1 hour, preferably overnight. You can even leave the pork uncovered in the fridge, so it dries out a little.

— Take the pork out the fridge an hour prior to roasting to let it return to room temperature, so it will be tender when cooked. Rub the skin with 1 teaspoon salt.

— Preheat the oven to 200°C/400°F/gas mark 6.

— Place the pork in an oven tray and roast for 30 minutes, then turn the oven temperature down to 160°C/325°F/gas mark 3 and roast for a further 2 hours. Increase the oven temperature again to 200°C/400°F/gas mark 6 and roast for another 30 minutes to finish the crackling.

— Once the pork is cooked, remove from the oven and leave to rest for 20 minutes. Slice the crackling off the meat and set aside, and remove the bones and cartilage. Reserve the cooking juices in the tray.

— Place the meat in a heavy-based pan, add the vinegar, cooking juices, pickled garlic, shallots and thyme and cook over a very low heat for about 2 hours. It is done when the meat falls apart in tender strings. If it gets too dry, then just add a little hot water or white wine to the pan.

— When the meat is nearly done, peel the swede, cut it into small cubes and boil it in a pan of water with a little salt until very tender. (Swede is quite watery, so use a small pan and add about 2cm/¾in water). Drain any excess water into a cup and mash the swede with a little of the pork juice, if you like, until it is a creamy and smooth mash. Keep warm in the pan.

— Preheat the oven on 160°C/325°F/gas mark 3. Place the crackling on a baking tray, put in the oven and gently reheat for about 15 minutes.

— Meanwhile, preheat a griddle pan until very hot. Add the nectarine wedges and sear both sides until you see the desired grill marks.

— Place the mash, pulled pork, crackling, grilled nectarines and alfalfa sprouts on a plate, adding some more pickled garlic, if you like.

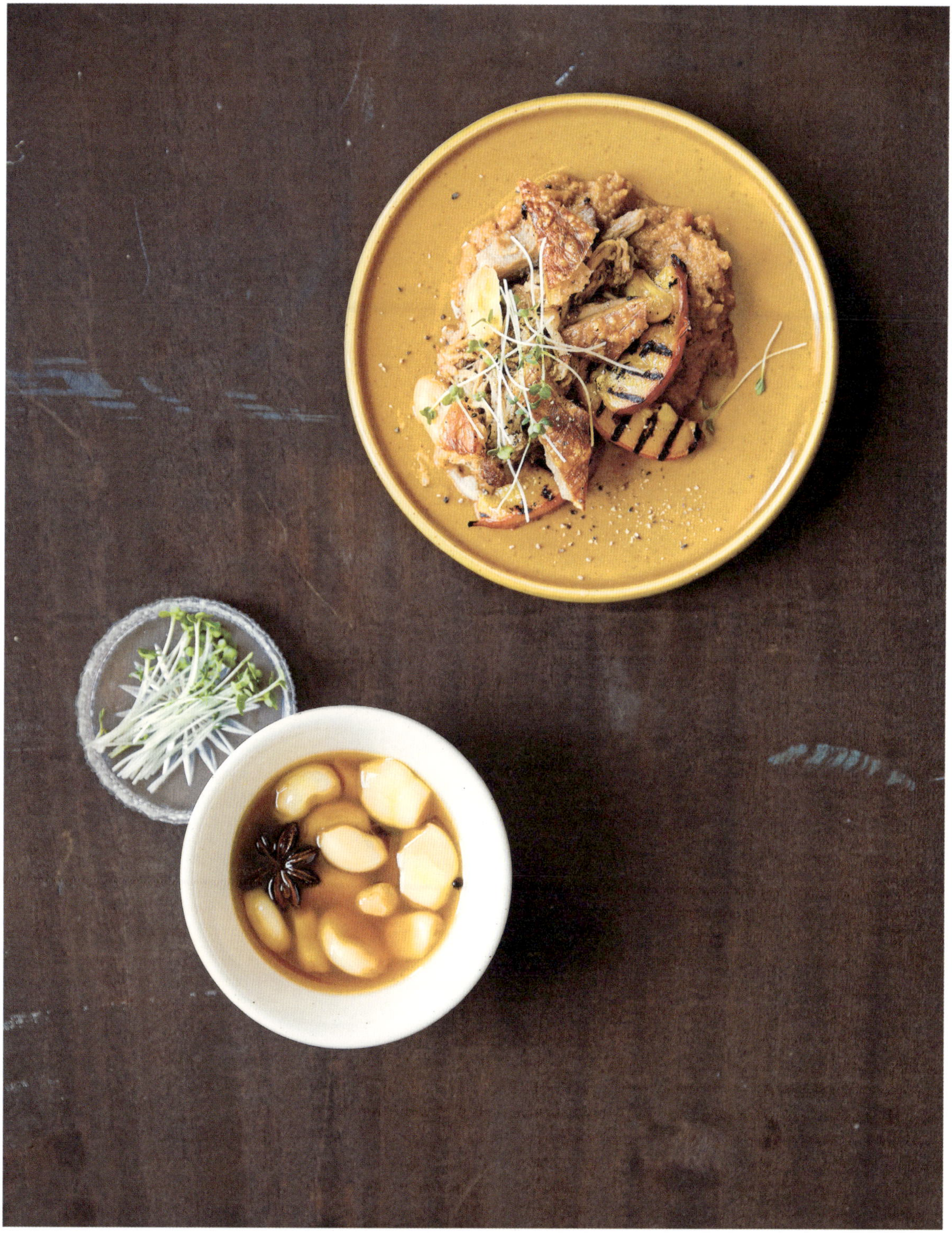

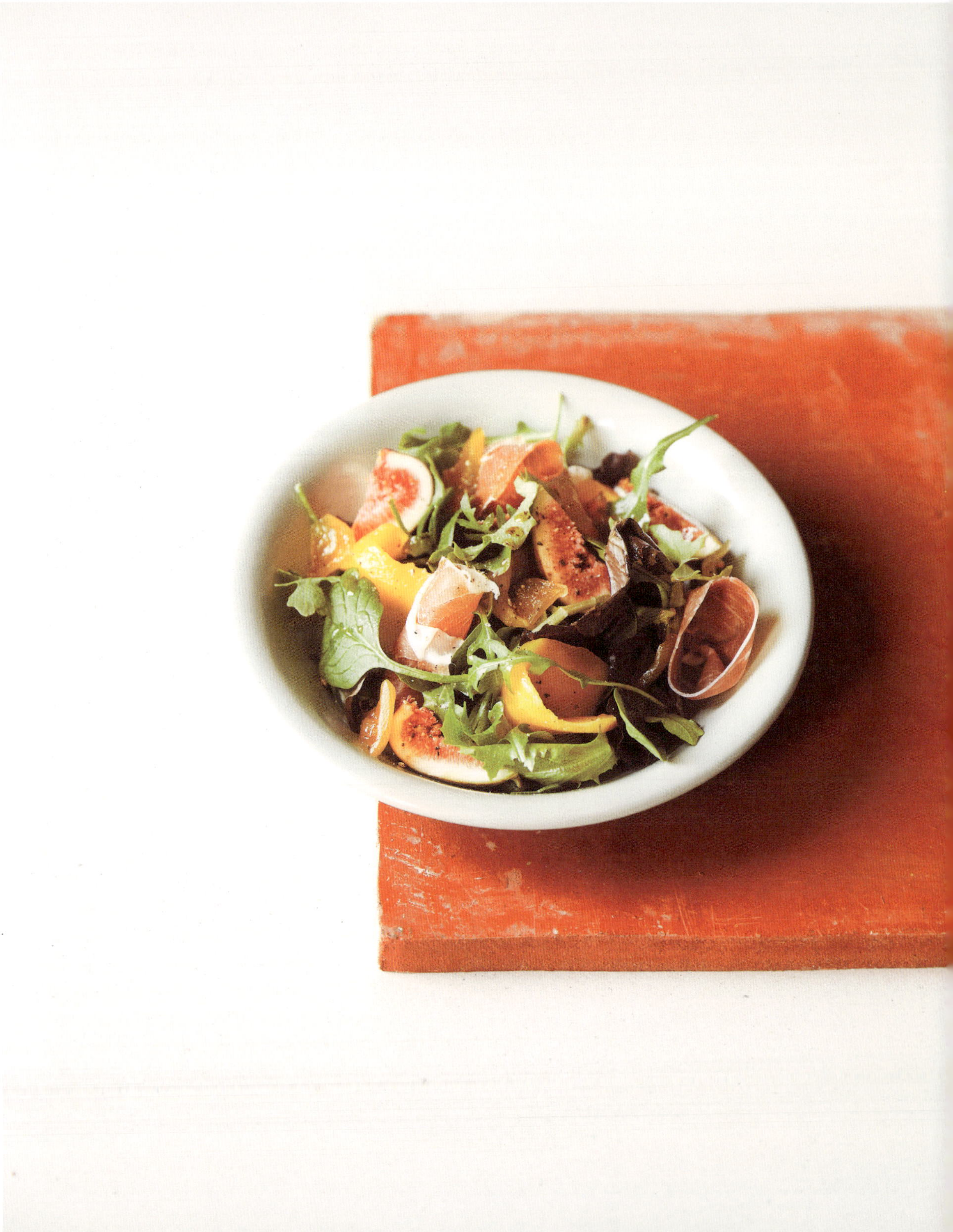

Pickled watermelon rind

Prep 30 minutes + overnight chilling,
 + 4-day process
Ready 11 days
Makes approx 750ml/25fl oz jar

1 small watermelon to give 450g/1lb watermelon rind

Brine
1.5 litres/50fl oz/6¼ cups water
50g/1¾oz/5 tbsp salt, plus 1 tsp (pure, without iodine or anti-caking agent)

Pickling solution
250g/9oz/1¼ cups sugar
100ml/3½fl oz/scant ½ cup water
100ml/3½fl oz/scant ½ cup apple cider vinegar
1 cinnamon stick
5 cloves
1 tsp allspice berries
1 tsp white mustard seeds
1 star anise

— Using a vegetable peeler, remove the tough green rind from the watermelon and discard.
— Cut the watermelon into quarters and cut the pulp from the rind. You can leave a thin layer of pink on the rind (you can reserve the pulp for dried candied watermelon P240).
— To make the brine, mix 500ml/18fl oz water and 50g/1¾oz salt together.
— Cut the rind into 1.5 x 2cm/⅝ x ¾in strips, cover with the brine and chill in the fridge overnight.
— Next day, rinse the watermelon rind, place in a saucepan and cover with 1 litre/34 fl oz/4 cups water and 1 teaspoon salt. Bring to the boil, then reduce the heat and simmer for 5 minutes, or until soft.
— Strain and put the rind into a bowl.
— Mix all the pickling solution ingredients together in a saucepan. Bring to the boil, then reduce the heat and simmer for 5 minutes.
— Pour the hot pickling solution over the watermelon rind, then place a plate on top of the rind to keep it submerged in the pickling solution. Cover, leave to cool, then chill in the fridge overnight.
— Next day, strain the liquid from the rind into a saucepan. Bring to the boil and pour back over the rind. Cover and chill in the fridge overnight. Repeat once more on the next day.
— On day 4 strain the liquid from the rind into a saucepan and put the watermelon rind into hot sterilised jars P12.
— Bring the pickling solution to the boil, then pour over the watermelon rind and close the lid immediately. There's no need to seal or pasteurise.
— Leave for at least a week before serving. This will keep unopened in the fridge for at least 3 months. Once opened store in the fridge and use within 2 months.

Pickled watermelon rind salad

This tastes as good as it looks. Try to use rocket leaves as they really enhance the flavour of the salad.

Serves 2

Mixed salad leaves
1 fresh fig, sliced
½ mango, peeled and sliced
4 slices of Parma ham (prosciutto), torn into large pieces
2 tbsp pickled watermelon rind above

Dressing
Juice of 1 mandarin
4 tbsp soy sauce
½ tbsp honey
4 tbsp olive oil
1 tbsp lemon juice

— Combine all the dressing ingredients together in a small screw-top jar, seal with a lid and shake a few times to emulsify.
— Wash and dry the salad leaves and assemble on 2 plates.
— Arrange the sliced fig, mango, Parma ham and pickled watermelon rind on top of the salad leaves.
— Drizzle with the dressing and serve.

Ajvar

This is a mighty fine Balkan speciality that creates a rich red paste out of red peppers and aubergines. The recipe came to us from our friend Dada, who got it from her mum who lives in Novi Sad on the banks of the Danube.

Prep 1 hour 30 minutes
Ready 2 hours
Makes approx 2 litre/67fl oz jar

1.8kg/4lb red (bell) peppers (about 9 peppers), deseeded and quartered
550g/1lb 4oz aubergine (eggplant; about 2 medium aubergines)
500ml/18fl oz/2 cups water
50ml/2fl oz/scant ¼ cup vinegar
1½ tbsp salt
40g/1½oz/scant ¼ cup sugar
1 onion, thinly sliced
1 chilli, roughly chopped (optional)
½ bulb garlic, chopped
125ml/4fl oz/½ cup oil

— Place the peppers, aubergine and chilli in a large saucepan. Add the water, vinegar, 1 tablespoon salt and 2 tablespoons of the sugar. Bring to the boil, then reduce the heat and simmer for about 40-60 minutes until the peppers and aubergines are soft.
— When cooked, transfer to a food processor and blend until smooth.
— Add the onion, chilli (if using) and garlic and mix well. Place the mixture in a saucepan, add the oil and cook for 30 minutes. Taste and add more salt or sugar if needed.

— Transfer the mixture to sterilised jars P12. Close the jars immediately and turn them upside down for 5-10 minutes, then turn them over again and leave to cool.
— Once cool check the seal P12. If not sealed, pasteurise P13.
— Sealed (pasteurised) jars can be kept in a cupboard for at least 6 months. Once opened, store in the fridge and use within 1 week.

Grilled sirloin steak with ajvar and leaves

Serves 2

300g/10½oz sirloin steak (or another cut if you'd prefer)
Salt and freshly ground black pepper
50g/1¾oz lamb's lettuce
30g/1oz ajvar above
30g/1oz broccoli sprouts (or any other type of sprouts)
Olive oil, for drizzling

— Preheat a griddle pan or barbecue to a smoking-hot temperature. Season the sirloin on both sides and lay on the griddle (no oil or butter needed). Depending on how rare you like your steak, and how thick the cut of meat is, grill the steak for about 2-4 minutes on each side. You can judge how done it is by testing the firmness with your finger – really firm equals really cooked.

— Let the steak rest for about 10 minutes, then cut it thinly against the grain with a very sharp knife.
— Place a handful of lamb's lettuce on 2 serving plates. Put the sliced sirloin on top. Sprinkle a good amount of ajvar over the plate, then add the broccoli sprouts and a drizzle of olive oil. Finish with some freshly ground pepper and sea salt.

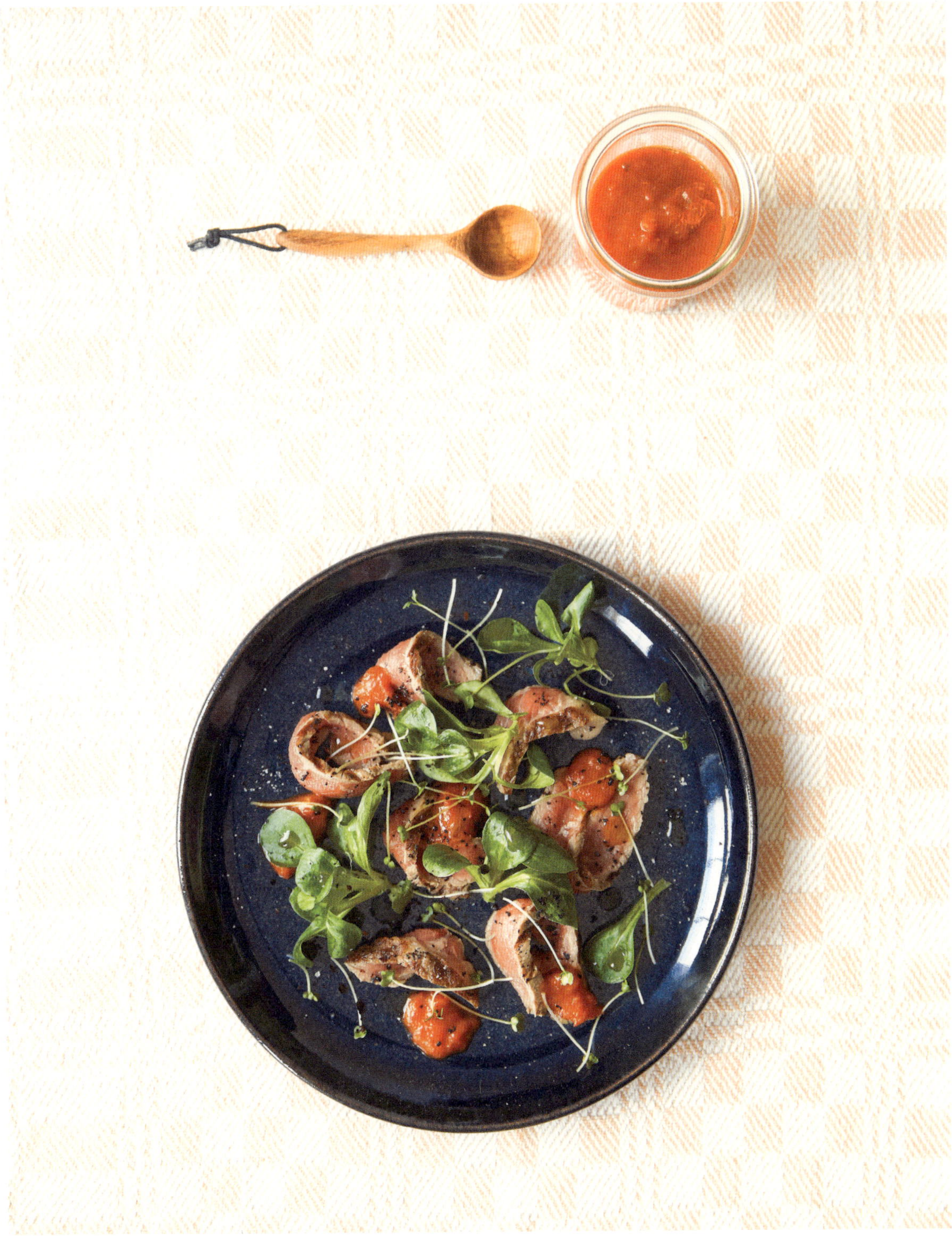

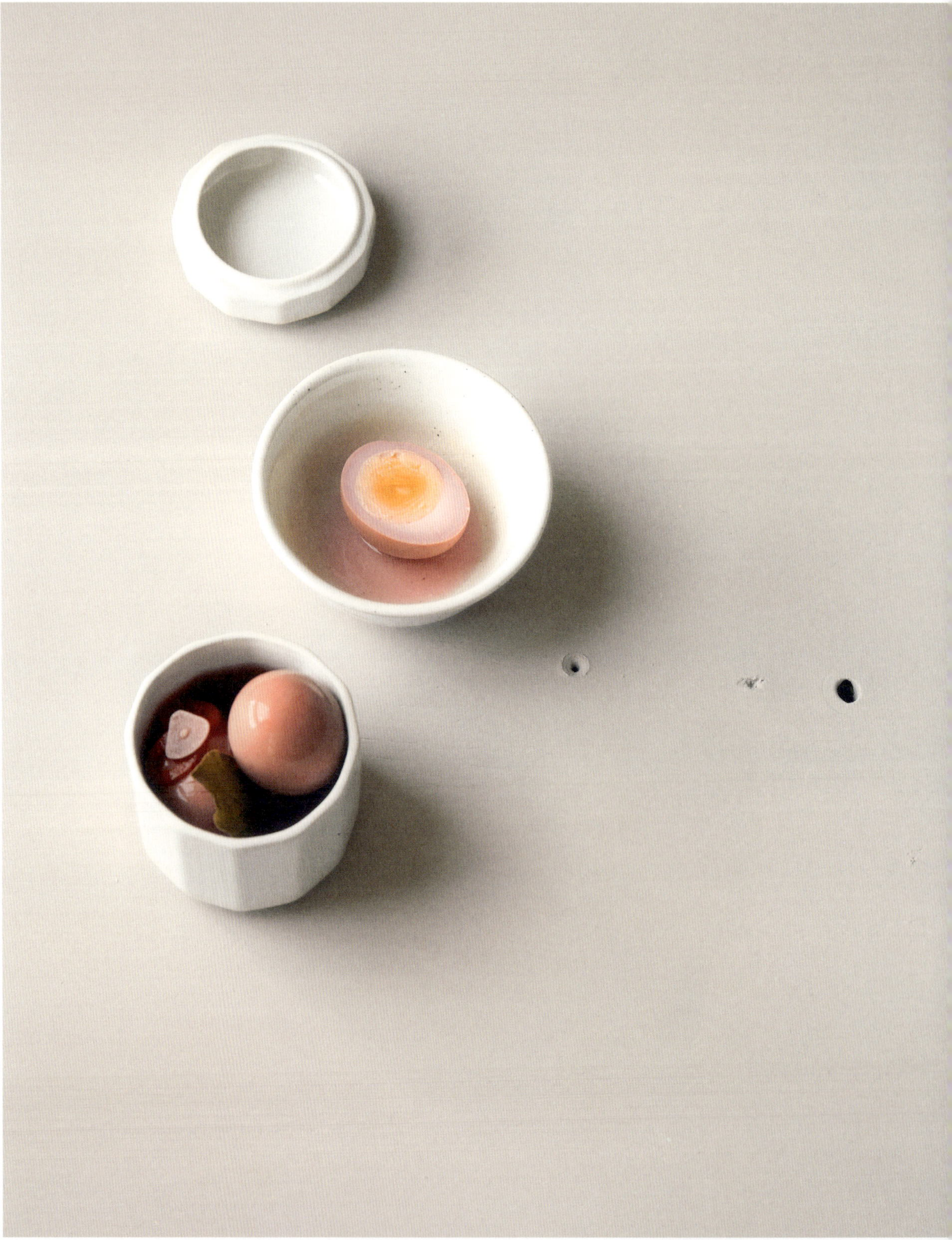

Hot pink pickled eggs

Ordinary pickled eggs can look a bit clinical – these are much more fun. The pink colour should penetrate through the egg white after a few days along with the spicy flavour.

Prep 30 minutes
Ready 7 days
Makes approx 500ml/18fl oz jar

4 hard-boiled eggs
1 large red chilli, sliced
1 garlic clove, sliced

Pickling solution
100ml/3½fl oz/scant ½ cup distilled spirit vinegar 10%
200ml/7fl oz/scant 1 cup water
1 tbsp honey
1 tbsp white mustard seeds
1 tsp allspice berries
1 tsp hot pepper flakes

— Place the eggs, chilli and garlic in a sterilised jar P12.
— Mix all the pickling solution ingredients together in a saucepan and bring to the boil, then pour over the eggs.
— Leave to cool, then chill in the fridge. Keep for at least 3 days before eating. The flavour will get stronger over time. Store in the fridge and use within 3 weeks (there's no need to seal or pasteurise).

Pickled shallots

This is a back-to-basics classic. In the past we've tried pickling with beer, but we decided it's more fun to drink a beer while making this recipe. Pair with a Thali P201.

Prep 20 minutes + overnight soaking
Ready 7 days
Makes approx 600ml/20fl oz jar

500g/1lb 2oz shallots or pickling onions, chopped
50g/1¾oz/5 tbsp sea salt (pure, without iodine or anti-caking agent)

Pickling solution
500ml/18fl oz/2 cups distilled malt vinegar
150g/5½oz/¾ cup sugar
½ tsp dried chilli flakes
½ tsp mustard seeds
½ tsp coriander seeds
10 allspice berries
5 cloves

— In a bowl, sprinkle the salt on the chopped shallots and leave overnight.
— Next day, rinse the shallots, dry and place into sterilised jars P12.
— Mix all the pickling solution ingredients in a small saucepan. Bring to boil, then pour over shallots.
— Close the jars immediately and once cool check the seal P12. If not sealed, pasteurise P13.
— You can try them after a month.
— Sealed and/or pasteurised jars can be kept in a cupboard for at least 6 months. Once opened, store in the fridge and use within 2 months.

Easy pickled nuts

Pickled nuts are usually made using unripe walnuts, which are hard to source. Here we use shelled nuts for ease. Sprinkle into a salad, like the one on P145.

Prep 10 minutes + 6-day process
Ready 1 month
Makes approx 500ml/18fl oz jar

40g/1½oz walnuts
30g/1oz almonds
30g/1oz hazelnuts

Pickling solution
200g/7oz sugar
100ml/3½fl oz water
100ml/3½fl oz/scant ½ cup distilled spirit vinegar 10%
1 cinnamon stick
5 cloves
1 tsp allspice berries
1 tsp white mustard seeds
1 star anise

— Place the nuts in a sterilised jar P12.
— Mix all the pickling solution ingredients together in a small saucepan, bring to the boil, then pour over the nuts and leave overnight.
— Next day, strain the pickling solution into a small saucepan. Bring the pickling solution to the boil and pour over the nuts.
— Repeat this step for a further 3 days. Strain the pickling solution into a saucepan, bring to the boil, then pour back over the nuts and cover.
— On day 6, transfer the jar to the fridge and keep for at least 4 weeks before eating (no need to seal or pasteurise). Once opened, store in the fridge and use within 3 months.

Pickled baby courgettes

While gherkins have hit it big in the pickling sphere, their cousins courgettes are often overlooked. It's a shame, as they have a robust texture which can keep its crunch.

Prep 10 minutes + cooling
Ready 48 hours
Makes approx 500ml/18fl oz jar

2 garlic cloves
1 red chilli
200g/7oz (about 5) baby courgettes (zucchini)

Pickling solution
130ml/4½fl oz/½ cup water
130ml/4½fl oz/½ cup cider vinegar
60g/2¼oz/⅓ cup sugar
1 tsp mustard seeds
1 tsp allspice berries
½ tsp salt and 5 black peppercorns

— Place the garlic, chilli and baby courgettes upright in a sterilised 500ml/18fl oz jar P12.
— Mix all the pickling solution ingredients together in a small saucepan and bring to the boil, then pour over the courgettes. Carefully pour the boiling liquid into the jars and leave to cool.
— Once cool cover with lids and chill in the fridge. Leave for 48 hours before using to allow the flavours to infuse (there's no need to seal or pasteurise).
— Store in the fridge and use within 4 weeks.

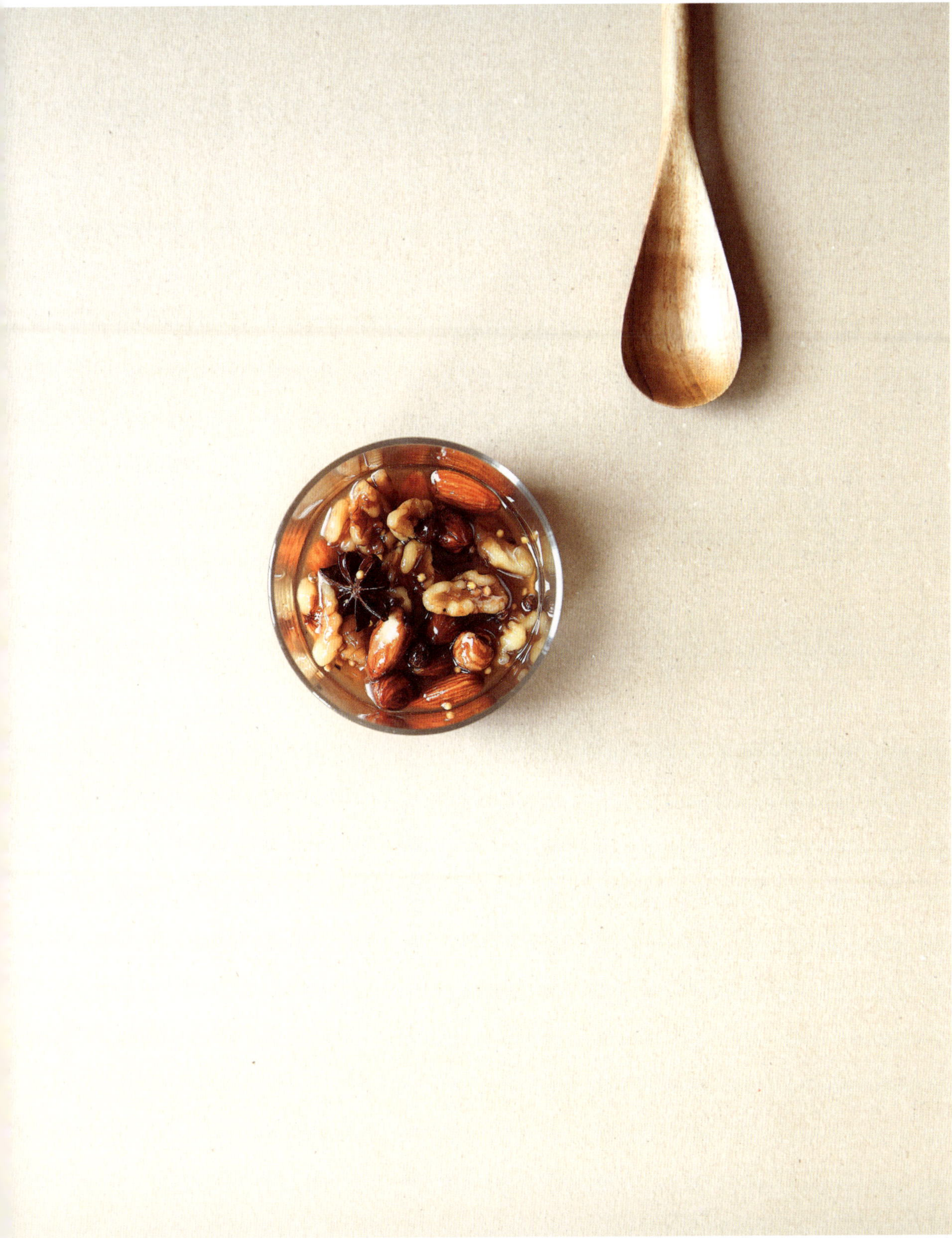

Roasted vegetable and buckwheat salad
Pickled baby courgette P142

Roasted vegetable and buckwheat salad

Other pickled vegetables such as gherkins P116, celery P132 and nasturtium capers P109 are also wonderful with this recipe. Hokkaido pumpkins are ideal, as they don't need peeling, but any pumpkin will do.

Serves 3-4

1 hokkaido pumpkin, cut into 1.5 x 1.5cm/⅝ x ⅝in pieces
2 small sweet potatoes, cut into 1.5 x 1.5cm/⅝ x ⅝in
2 small carrots, sliced into thick slices
1 parsnip, thickly sliced
1 large aubergine (eggplant), cut into 2cm/¾in cubes
Splash of olive oil
1 tsp coarse sea salt
300g/10½oz/scant 2 cups roasted buckwheat groats, cooked according to packet instructions
8-10 pickled shallots P141, cut in half or quarters
Pickled baby courgettes P142
Easy pickled nuts P142
15g/½oz/½ cup chopped fresh herbs (coriander/cilantro, mint, parsley)
Salt and freshly ground black pepper

Spice blend
1 tsp ground cinnamon
1 tsp ground cumin
1 tsp coriander
1 tsp paprika
1 tsp honey
2 tbsp soy sauce
2 tbsp lemon juice
1 tsp freshly ground nutmeg

— Preheat the oven to 230°C/450°F/gas mark 8. Place a baking tray in the oven to heat up.
— Combine all the spice blend ingredients together.
— Place all the fresh vegetables in a large bowl, add the spice blend and mix together well. Add a splash of olive oil and the coarse sea salt, then spread them out on the preheated baking tray and roast for 15-20 minutes, or until soft, turning a couple of times, until cooked.
— Place the cooked buckwheat groats in a large serving bowl, add the roasted vegetables, pickled shallots, pickled baby courgettes, pickled nuts and chopped herbs, and mix to combine.
— Taste and season with salt and black pepper, if needed.

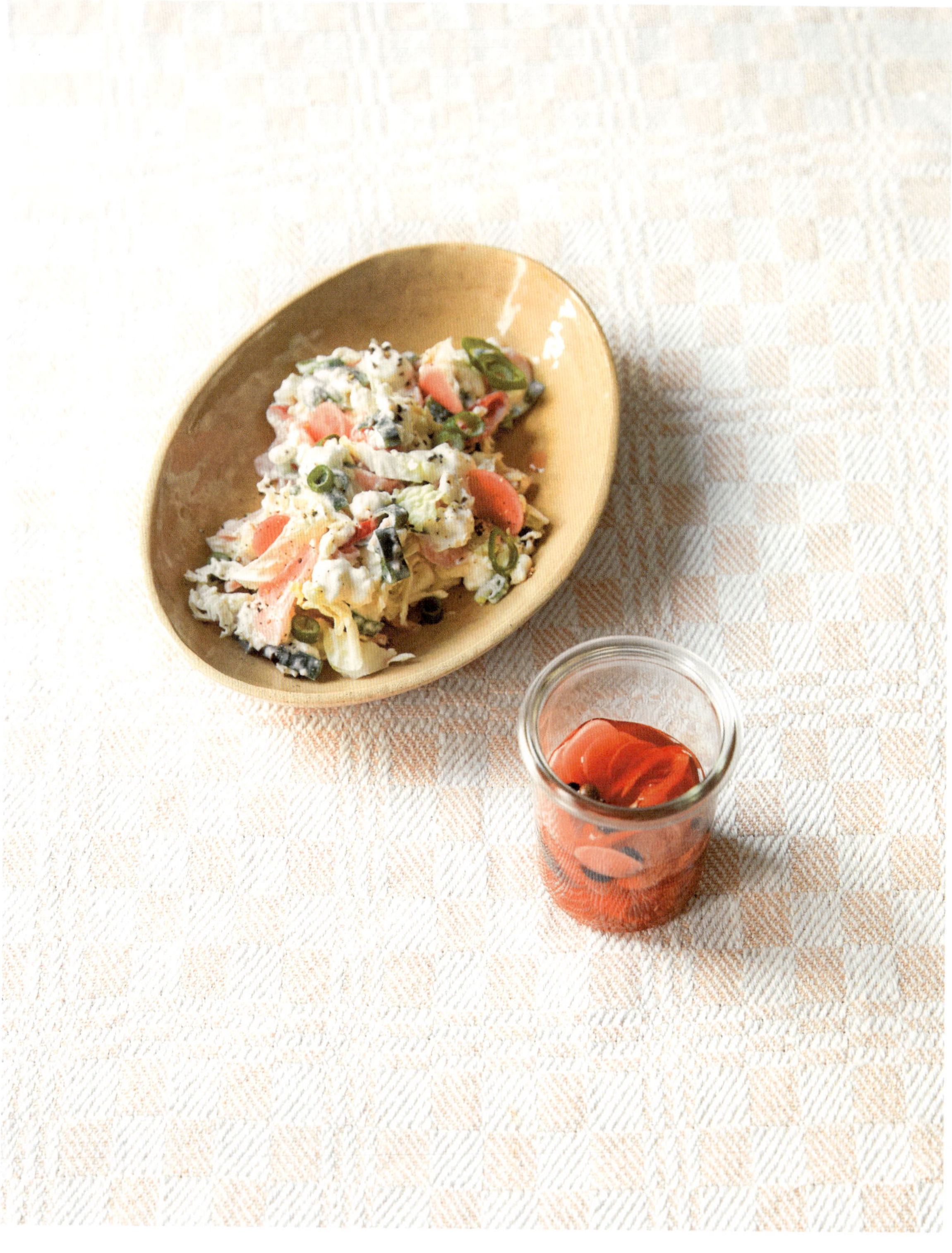

Chilli-pickled radish

This is a beautiful pickle due to the red colour that the radishes infuse into the pickling solution.

Prep 20 minutes
Ready 2 days
Makes approx 500ml/18fl oz jar

1 bunch radishes, about 10 bulbs, trimmed and very thinly sliced
2 garlic cloves, sliced
1 long red chilli, sliced
3cm/1¼in piece of fresh ginger, skin scraped off and cut into short matchsticks

Pickling solution
150ml/5fl oz/⅔ cup rice vinegar
100ml/3½fl oz/scant ½ cup water
3 tbsp honey
2 tbsp brown sugar
1 tsp mustard seeds
½ tsp allspice berries
1 tsp black peppercorns

— Place the radishes, garlic, chilli and ginger into a sterilised jar P12.
— Mix all the pickling solution ingredients together in a saucepan and bring to the boil. Carefully pour the boiling liquid into the jars and leave to cool.
— Once cool cover with lids and chill in the fridge. Leave for 48 hours before using to allow the flavours to infuse (there's no need to seal or pasteurise).
— Store in the fridge and use within 4 weeks.

Chilli-pickled radish and cottage cheese salad

Cottage cheese can be a bit bland, but not here: there can be no blandness where a chilli-pickled radish is involved.

Serves 1

3 tbsp chilli-pickled radish, above
3 tbsp cottage cheese
2 tbsp green part of 1 spring onion (scallion), sliced
1 leaf napa (Chinese) cabbage
Salt and freshly ground black pepper

— Mix all the salad ingredients together in a bowl, then season with salt and black pepper.
— This salad can be prepared up to 1 hour before serving.

Herring pickled many ways

A few years ago we went to a food market in Gothenburg in Sweden where we saw herring being pickled and marinated using a variety of methods. Gaba's love for herring turned into an obsession. Ever since, she has been trying to recreate it. Choose firm thick fishes, as thin and flaky ones will disintegrate when you pickle them.

Herring in black tea

Prep 10 minutes + 4 hours standing
Ready 2 days

Black tea
12 salted herring halves
   (about 1kg/2¼lb)

— Brew a large pot of black tea and leave to cool.
— Place the herrings in a large bowl and cover with the cooled tea (if there is not enough, top up with water).
— Leave to soak for 3–4 hours.
— Remove the herrings and divide into 3 equal portions, then cut each herring into 2.5cm/1in pieces.
— Use the herrings in the following recipes, or eat simply with sour cream.

Sweet and spicy pickled herring

This is pickled herring in the classic Swedish style.

Prep 10 minutes + cooling
Ready 2 days
Makes approx 1 litre/34fl oz jar

4 salted herring halves, soaked in tea and cut into 2.5cm/1in pieces above
1 onion, chopped

Pickling solution
300ml/10fl oz/1¼ cups white wine vinegar
250ml/9fl oz/generous 1 cup water
50ml/2fl oz/scant ¼ cup dark rum
150g/5½oz/¾ cup muscovado sugar
1 tbsp honey
1 tsp salt
½ tsp allspice berries
6 juniper berries
1 tsp white mustard seeds
6 cloves
1 tsp coriander
½ tsp freshly ground nutmeg
5 star anise
1 cinnamon stick

— Mix all the pickling solution ingredients together in a small saucepan and bring to the boil. Reduce the heat and simmer for 5 minutes, then leave to cool.
— Layer the herring, onion and spices from the pickling solution in a sterilised jar P12. Cover with the warm pickling solution and leave to cool.
— When it has cooled completely chill in the fridge for at least 2 days before using.
— Do not pasteurise. Store in the fridge and use within 1 month.

Carrot and onion pickled herring

This is a popular Polish way of pickling herring.

Prep 10 minutes + cooling
Ready 2 days
Makes approx 1 litre/34fl oz jar

½ onion, sliced
4 salted herring halves, soaked in tea and cut into 2.5 cm/1in pieces P148
1 medium carrot, sliced

Pickling solution
400ml/14fl oz/1¾ cups water
100ml/3½fl oz/scant ½ cup distilled spirit vinegar 10%
1 bay leaf
1 tbsp brown sugar
1 tbsp salt
1 tbsp black peppercorns
1 tbsp mustard seeds
1 tbsp allspice berries
½ tsp dried dill

— Mix all the pickling solution ingredients together in a saucepan and bring to the boil. Reduce the heat and simmer for 3 minutes.
— Add the onion and simmer for a further 2 minutes, then leave to cool a little. Remove the onion and reserve.
— Layer the herring, carrot and onion in a sterilised jar P12. Cover with the warm pickling solution and leave to cool. When it has cooled completely chill in the fridge for at least 2 days before using.
— Do not pasteurise. Store in the fridge and use within 1 month.

Orange and lemon pickled herring

Prep 10 minutes + cooling
Ready 2 days
Makes approx 1 litre/34fl oz jar

4 salted herring halves, soaked in tea and cut into 2.5cm/1in pieces P148
1 onion, sliced
4 slices of orange
4 slices of lemon

Pickling solution
100ml/3½fl oz/scant ½ cup distilled spirit vinegar 10%
200ml/7fl oz/scant 1 cup water
1 tsp salt
5 allspice berries
1 tsp white mustard seeds
5 cloves
1 tsp coriander seeds
1 cinnamon stick
1 bay leaf

— Mix all the pickling solution ingredients together in a saucepan and bring to the boil. Reduce the heat and simmer for 5 minutes, then leave to cool a little.
— Layer the herring, onion, orange and lemon slices in a sterilised jar P12. Cover with the warm pickling solution and leave to cool.
— When it has cooled completely chill in the fridge for at least 2 days before using.
— Do not pasteurise. Store in the fridge and use within 1 month.

Sweet and spicy pickled herring P148
Carrot and onion pickled herring P149
Apple and yoghurt herring salad P152

Herring in dill and mustard sauce P152
Orange and lemon pickled herring P149

Herring in dill and mustard sauce

Serves 4

1 portion (4 salted herring halves) of orange and lemon pickled herring P149
6 tbsp fermented mustard P54
2 tbsp dark muscovado (brown) sugar
2 tbsp apple cider vinegar
50ml/2fl oz/scant ¼ cup sunflower oil
2–3 tbsp chopped fresh dill
Salt and freshly ground black pepper

— To prepare the dill sauce, mix the mustard and sugar together, then add the vinegar and mix well. Slowly add the sunflower oil, stirring constantly. Add the dill and mix well. Season with salt and black pepper.
— Layer the herring pieces and dill sauce in a large bowl or jar, making sure that the herring is well covered with the sauce.
— Chill in the fridge for at least 12 hours before serving.

Apple and yoghurt herring salad

Serves 4

1 portion (4 salted herring halves) of orange and lemon pickled herring P149
2–3 tbsp raisins, soaked in hot water for 1 hour, drained
1 small apple (Cox), peeled, cored and chopped into small cubes
½ small onion, thinly chopped
150ml/5fl oz/⅔ cup plain live yoghurt P20
2–3 tbsp mayonnaise
Salt and freshly ground black pepper

— To make the yoghurt sauce, mix the yoghurt, mayonnaise, onion, raisins and apple together. Season with salt and black pepper.
— Layer the herring pieces and yoghurt sauce in a large bowl or jar, making sure that the herring is well covered with the sauce.
— Chill in the fridge for at least 12 hours before serving.

Balkan in a pickle

This was influenced by a Balkan tradition of preserving shredded vegetables for winter. We have provided two versions: one using a strong spirit vinegar which can be pasteurised and kept in the cupboard, as well as a healthier raw version which needs to be refrigerated.

Prep 30 minutes + 13 hours standing
Ready 1 month
Makes approx 1 litre/34fl oz jar

¼ cabbage, thinly shredded
1 carrot, use a mandolin to cut into thin matchsticks
½ small celeriac (celery root), use a mandolin to cut into thin matchsticks
½ onion, sliced
1 celery stick, thinly sliced
1 large red chilli, thinly sliced
1 courgette (zucchini), use a mandolin to cut into thin matchsticks
1 tbsp pink Himalayan salt

Pickling solution version 1
100ml/3½fl oz/scant ½ cup distilled spirit vinegar
60g/2¼oz/scant ⅓ cup brown sugar
2 tsp white mustard seeds
1 tsp black peppercorns
10 allspice berries
2 bay leaves
1 tsp coriander seeds

Pickling solution version 2
100ml/3½fl oz/scant ½ cup raw apple cider vinegar
2 tbsp raw/cold-pressed honey
2 tsp white mustard seeds
1 tsp black peppercorns
10 allspice berries
2 bay leaves
1 tsp coriander seeds

— If using pickling solution version 1, mix all the ingredients in a saucepan and bring to the boil. Reduce the heat and simmer for 2 minutes.

— For version 2, mix all ingredients in a saucepan and heat gently to dissolve the honey. Don't heat too much or the beneficial properties of the raw ingredients will be destroyed.

Method for both versions
— Mix the vegetables and salt together in a large bowl and leave for at least 1 hour, or preferably 5 hours.
— Drain the vegetables and squeeze out any excess moisture, then place in a sterilised jar P12.
— Pour the pickling solution of your choice into the jar and leave at room temperature overnight.
— Next day, transfer to the fridge. Consume within a month.
— Vegetables pickled using version 1 can be pasteurised in jars P13 and kept in a cool, dark place for up to 6 months. Once opened, store in the fridge and use within 2 weeks.
— Vegetables pickled using version 2 should not be pasteurised. Store in the fridge and use within 1 month.

Pickled French beans
Pickled bean falafel
Sourdough pitta bread P87
Balkan in a pickle P153

Pickled French beans

Prep 20 minutes
Ready 2 days
Makes approx 500ml/18fl oz jar

150g/5½oz French (green) beans, cut into 3cm/1¼in lengths
2 garlic cloves, chopped

Pickling solution
100ml/3½fl oz/scant ½ cup distilled spirit vinegar 10%
200ml/7fl oz/scant 1 cup water
4 tbsp brown sugar
1 tsp mustard seeds
1 tsp allspice berries
½ long red chilli, sliced
2 bay leaves
½ tsp black peppercorns

— Mix all the pickling solution ingredients together in a medium saucepan and bring to the boil.
— Add the French beans, return to the boil, then reduce the heat and simmer for 5 minutes.
— Remove from the heat, add the chopped garlic, stir and transfer to a sterilised jar P12.
— Close the jars immediately and once cool check the seal P12. If not sealed, pasteurise P13.
— You can try the beans after 2–3 days.
— Sealed and/or pasteurised jars can be kept in a cupboard for at least 6 months. Once opened, store in the fridge and use within 1 month.

Pickled bean falafel

We used to have problems making falafel – they would fall to bits in the frying pan – until our friend Nel brought this recipe back from Egypt. The secret is to use uncooked chickpeas. Tinned ones are no good as they have been boiled. The pickled French beans above add another layer of flavour and texture to the falafel.

Serves 3 4

500g/1lb 2oz/3 cups dried chickpeas
2 medium onions, finely chopped
2–3 garlic cloves, very finely chopped
½ bunch of parsley, chopped
2 eggs, lightly beaten
1 tsp ground cumin
1 tsp ground coriander
½–1 tsp salt
½–1 tsp ground black pepper
1 baking powder
3–4 tbsp pickled French beans above
90–125ml/3–4fl oz/⅓–½ cup vegetable oil

— Soak the dried chickpeas in a large bowl of water for 8–48 hours, then drain.
— Blitz the chickpeas, onion, garlic and parsley in a blender or food processor to a rough paste.
— Place in a bowl, add the eggs, cumin, coriander, salt, pepper, baking powder and pickled French beans, and mix well.
— Heat the oil in a large frying pan over a medium heat. Medium heat is best: if the heat is too high the falafels will burn on the outside but will not cook through.
— Using 2 tablespoons, form the mixture into oval shapes and place them carefully in the frying pan. Fry until golden. Once the bottom is golden brown turn over and fry on the other side until golden brown. Remove from the frying pan and drain on kitchen paper.
— If you would like to eat them warm place in a warm oven.
— Serve hot or cold with sourdough pitta bread P87 and Balkan pickles P153.

Miso pickled mushrooms

This recipe is a crossover between Japanese miso-pickling and European vinegar-pickling.

Prep 25 minutes
Ready 1 hour
Makes approx 500ml/18fl oz jar

500g/1lb 2oz small closed-cup chestnut (cremini) mushrooms, quartered

Pickling solution
2 small garlic cloves, finely chopped
1 tsp grated ginger
2 tsp hot pepper flakes
1 tbsp honey
2 tbsp soft brown sugar
2 tsp red miso
2 tbsp mirin
4 tbsp light soy sauce
4 cm/1½in piece of leek, quartered lengthways and thinly sliced
6 tbsp cider vinegar 5%

— Fill a medium saucepan with water, bring to the boil, add the mushrooms, then reduce the heat and simmer for 30 seconds, then drain them from the water.
— Mix all the pickling solution ingredients together, add the mushrooms and mix well.
— Do not pastuerise. Transfer to a sterilised jar P12 and leave to stand for 1 hour, then cover with a lid and transfer to the fridge. Use within a month.

Miso pickled eggs

These turn beige right through to the yolk and absorb the miso flavour with a hint of acidity from the rice vinegar.

Prep 15 minutes + cooling
Ready 4 days
Makes approx 500ml/18fl oz jar

3 eggs
100g/3½oz red miso paste
15g/½oz/1 tbsp sugar
2 tbsp mirin
100ml/3½fl oz/scant ½ cup rice vinegar

— Hard-boil the eggs, then peel them and place in a sterilised jar P12.
— Mix the miso, sugar and mirin together in a small heatproof bowl set over a saucepan of simmering water and heat, stirring frequently, until the sugar has dissolved.
— Add the vinegar, bring to the boil and pour over the eggs and leave to cool.
— Do not pasteurise. Once cool, cover and chill in the fridge. Leave for at least 4 days before eating and use within 4 weeks.

Miso pickled eggs
Miso pickled mushrooms
Misozuke carrots and cauliflower P158

Misozuke carrots and cauliflower

These Japanese pickles are made by using a pickling bed (miso-doko), which is very simple to make and can be reused several times. There are various kinds of miso and this will work with any or with a combination of different ones. If you don't have sake, sherry can be substituted; or leave out the mirin and the sake altogether if you prefer.

Prep 20 minutes
Ready 2–24 hours
Makes 1 small pickling bed

Pickling bed
300g / 10½oz miso paste
3 garlic cloves, crushed
4 tbsp mirin
4 tbsp sake
2 tsp ginger, skin scraped off and grated
1–2 tsp dried chilli flakes (optional)

Vegetables to be pickled
100g / 3½oz cauliflower florets
1 medium carrot, thickly sliced

— To make the pickling bed, mix all the ingredients together in a small jar or bowl.
— Push the cauliflower florets and the carrot slices down into the miso bed so that they are covered. Make sure each piece is well coated.
— Cover and leave the vegetables at room temperature for at least 2 hours. The flavour will be much more pronounced if it is left for up to 24 hours. Remove the vegetable pieces and scrape off the excess miso and return it to the container.
— Rinse the cauliflower and carrot pieces before using. Try adding them to a noodle salad P161.

Other vegetables such as turnip and kohlrabi can be pickled in this way, but softer vegetables like cucumber should be rubbed with salt and left to stand to extract water before pickling.

It is traditional to use tofu, but it should be pressed to remove as much moisture as possible first.

It is worthwhile to use the pickling bed a few times in succession, but it can also rest for a couple of days in the fridge. Excess water should be drained off the pickling bed otherwise the miso paste will not stick to the vegetables.

Lightly pickled baby spinach

This is inspired by a very gently pickled Korean spinach salad. Normally it wouldn't have vinegar, but we feel it's a pleasing addition and it lengthens the keeping time.

Prep 20 minutes
Ready 25 minutes
Makes 1 small bowl

200g/7oz baby spinach

Pickling solution
2 tsp sesame seeds, dry toasted
1 tsp red pepper flakes
3 tbsp onions, thinly sliced
5 tbsp light soy sauce
5 tbsp apple cider vinegar
2 tbsp honey
3 cm/1¼in piece of ginger, skin scraped off and grated

— Bring a large saucepan of water to the boil. Drop the spinach into the boiling water and boil, stirring constantly, for 30 seconds. Drain and cool under cold running water.
— Working in batches, using your hands, squeeze out all the moisture, then place the spinach in a bowl.
— Mix all the pickling solution ingredients together, then pour over the spinach and mix well.
— Do not pasteurise. Serve immediately or transfer to a sterilised jar P12. Store in the fridge and use within to 10 days.
— Try adding them to a noodle salad P161.

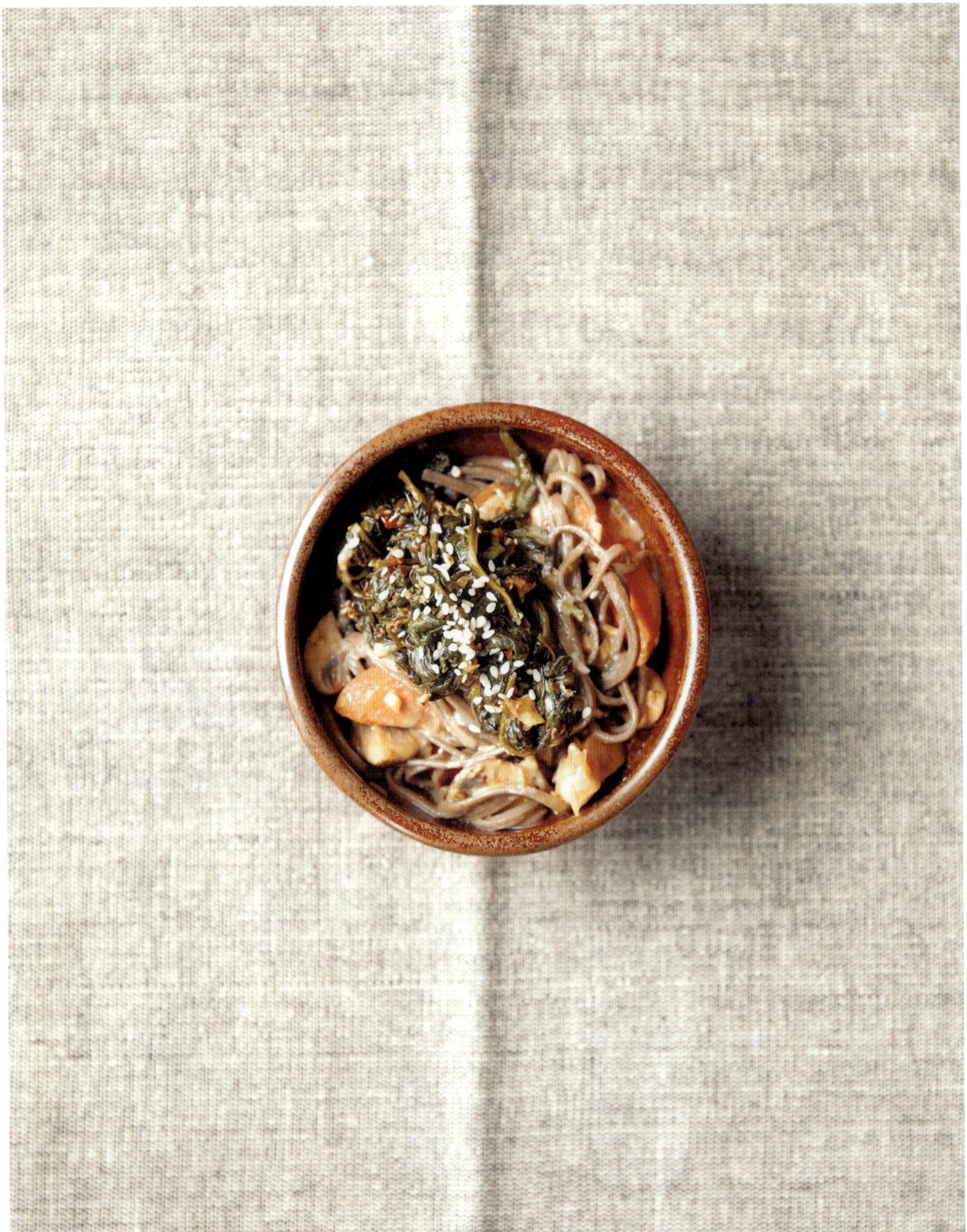

Misozuke and soba noodle salad

Serves 3

6 tbsp sesame seeds
4 tbsp white or red miso paste
1 tsp sugar
1 tbsp mirin
4 tbsp tahini
Juice of 1 lemon
Juice of 1 orange
250g/9oz soba noodles
6 tbsp sliced misozuke carrots P158
6–9 misozuke cauliflower florets P158
6 tbsp miso-pickled mushrooms P156
6 tbsp lightly pickled baby spinach P159
3 miso-pickled eggs, quartered or sliced P156

— Heat a frying pan over a medium heat, add the sesame seeds and dry-toast for about 2–3 minutes, or until golden brown. Set aside.
— For the sauce, mix the miso, sugar and mirin together in a small heatproof bowl set over a saucepan of gently simmering water. Stir until the sugar has dissolved, then remove from the heat, add the tahini and combine well. Add the lemon and orange juices and mix well. Set aside.
— Cook the soba noodles according to the packet instructions. Drain and mix with the miso and tahini sauce.
— Place the noodles in 3 serving bowls. In each bowl, place 2 tablespoons misozuke carrots, 2–3 misozuke cauliflower florets, 2 tablespoons miso-pickled mushrooms, 2 tablespoons lightly pickled baby spinach and 1 miso-pickled egg. Sprinkle with the toasted sesame seeds and serve.

Marrow and fennel chutney

Prep 1 hour + overnight standing
Ready 2 days
Makes approx 700ml/24fl oz jar

800g/1¾lb marrow, peeled, deseeded and cut into 1cm/½in cubes
400g/14oz (about 1 bulb) fennel, cut into 1cm/½in cubes
2 medium onions, chopped
5 tbsp salt
1 apple, peeled and chopped
3 tbsp raisins
6 tbsp dried cranberries

Pickling solution
250ml/9fl oz/generous 1 cup distilled spirit vinegar 10%
150g/5½oz/¾ cup brown sugar
2 star anise
10 black peppercorns
10 allspice berries
3 tsp yellow mustard seeds
3 bay leaves
¼ tsp dried chilli flakes

— Place the marrow, fennel and onions in a large bowl and sprinkle with the salt. Mix well and leave overnight.
— Next day, rinse the vegetables under cold running water, then drain and squeeze hard to remove the excess water. Work in batches.
— Place the vegetables in a large saucepan and add the apple, raisins and cranberries off the heat.
— Mix all the pickling solution ingredients together in a separate saucepan and bring to the boil. Stir until the sugar has dissolved.
— Pour the pickling solution over the vegetables and fruit, then bring to the boil. Reduce the heat and simmer, stirring frequently, for about 1 hour, or until light brown in colour and the marrow and fennel are very soft.
— Transfer immediately to 2 sterilised 330ml/10½fl oz jars P12.
— Close the jars immediately and once cool check the seal P12. If not sealed, pasteurise P13.
— Sealed and/or pasteurised jars can be kept in a cupboard for at least 6 months. Once opened, store in the fridge and use within 4 weeks.

Walnut and goat's cheese parcels

Soft goat's cheese, especially the cream cheese or camembert-style, is a perfect accompaniment to the marrow and fennel chutney.

Makes 24 parcels

50g/1¾oz/½ cup walnut halves
3 sheets (about 135g/4½oz) filo (phyllo) pastry
150g/5½oz/⅔ cup soft goat's cheese
4 tbsp marrow and fennel chutney above
Knob of butter

— Soak the walnuts in a bowl of water for 15 minutes, then drain.
— Preheat the oven to 200°C/400°F/gas mark 6. Line a baking tray with baking parchment.
— Cut each pastry sheet into about eight 10 x 12cm/4 x 5in rectangles.
— Place 1 teaspoon or small slice of goat's cheese in the middle of each pastry rectangle.
— Place ½ teaspoon of marrow and fennel chutney on top of the cheese and top it with a walnut half.
— Fold up the edges to create a parcel. Repeat with the remaining pastry pieces and place them on the baking tray.
— Melt the butter in a small saucepan and brush the top of each parcel with a little butter.
— Bake the parcels for about 10 minutes, or until golden brown.
— Remove from the oven and let them rest for 5 minutes before serving.

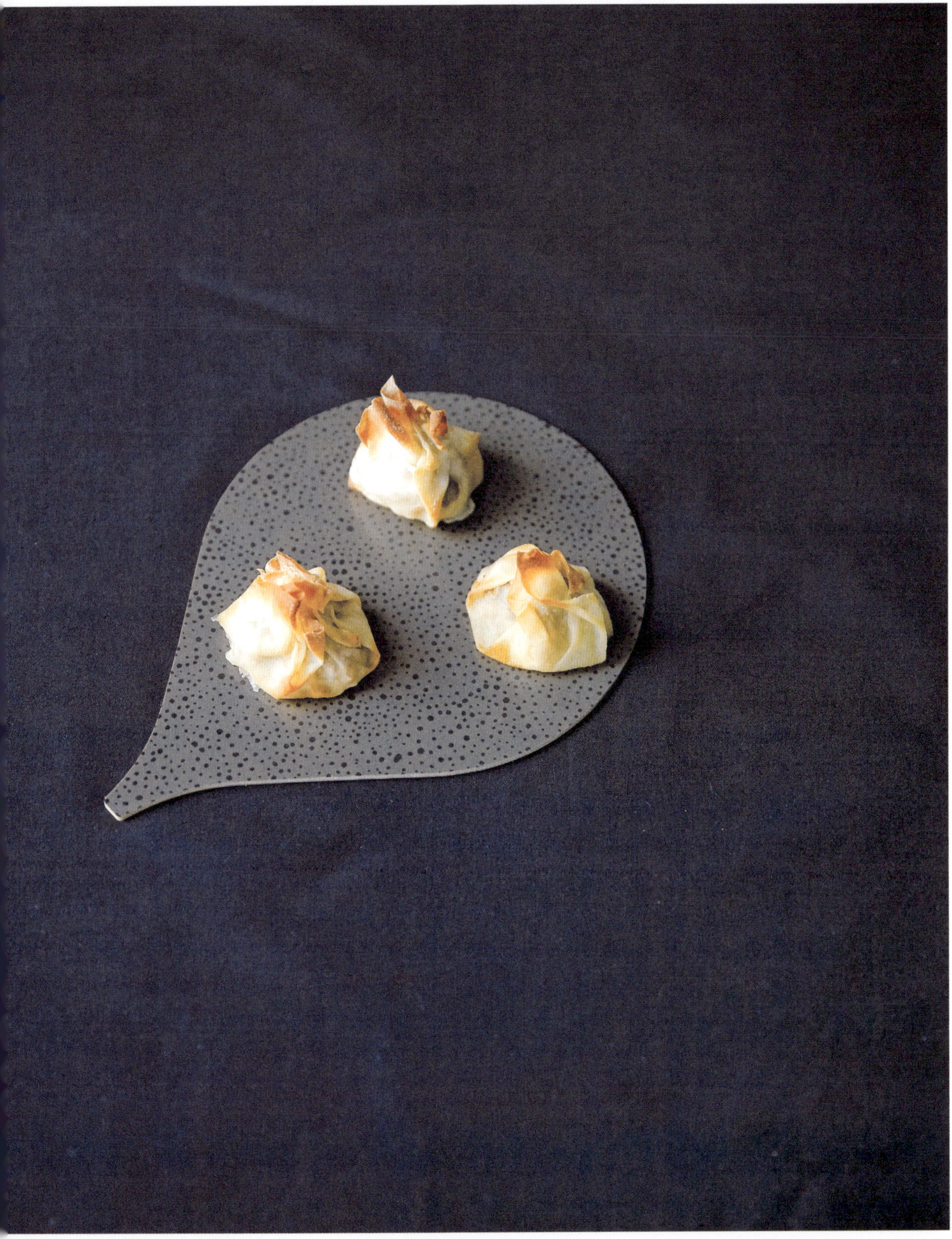

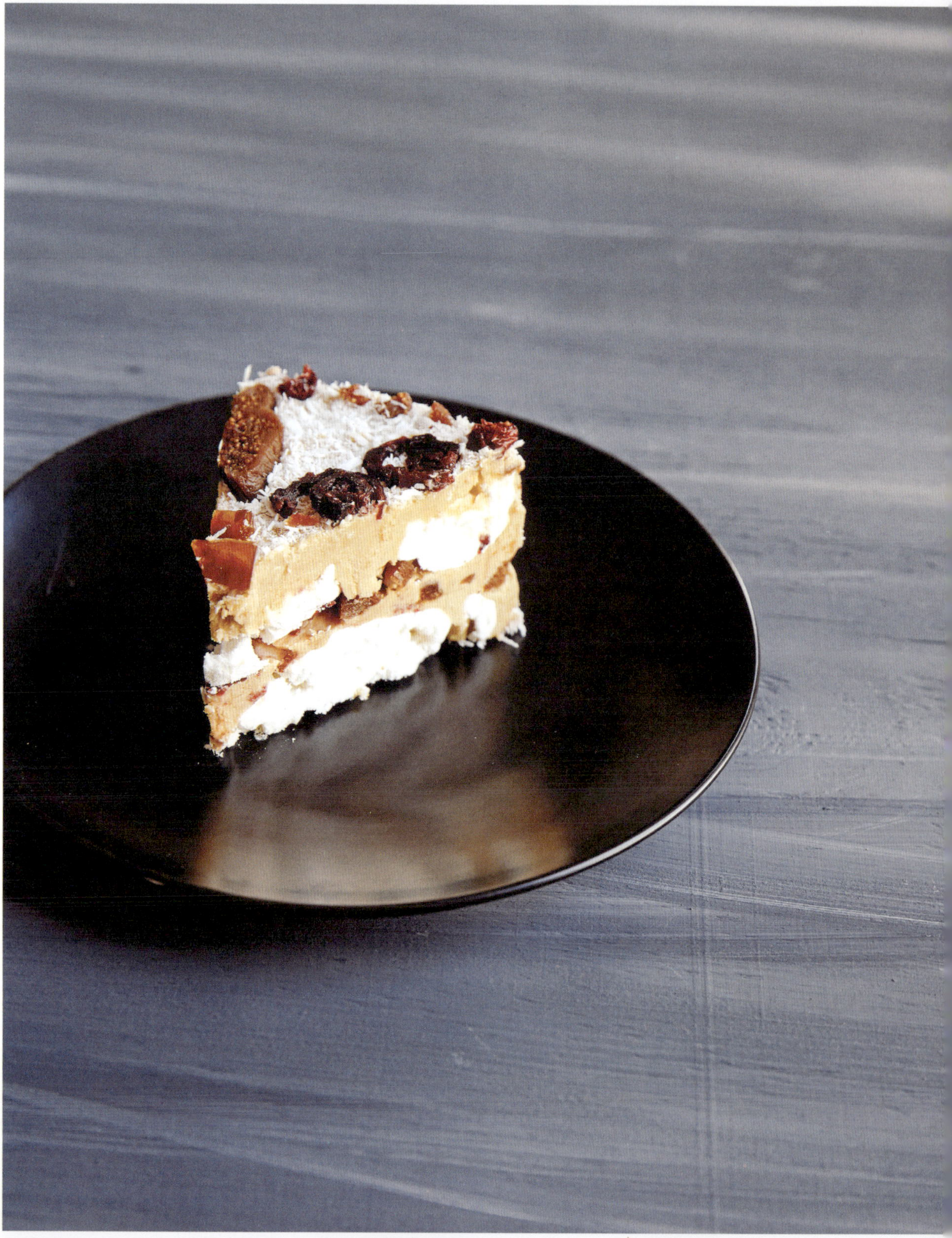

Dried fruit pickled in brandy

As with sloe gin, this benefits from a long maturation period: this improves the flavour and takes the edge off the alcohol (but it isn't unheard of to crack open a jar earlier). Delicious in the coffee meringue cake below.

Prep 20 minutes + cooling
Ready 3 months
Makes approx 1.5 litres/50fl oz jar

200g/7oz/1 cup dried apricots P231
200g/7oz dried figs P230
50g/1¾oz/1¼ cups raisins
30g/1oz/¼ cup dried cranberries P230
25ml/1fl oz/2 tbsp water
100g/3½oz/½ cup brown sugar
2 star anise
½ cinnamon stick
4 cardamom pods, crushed
3 cloves
700ml/24fl oz/3 cups brandy

— Place all the dried fruit in a large sterilised jar P12.
— Place the water, sugar and spices in a small saucepan and bring to the boil. Reduce the heat and simmer, stirring constantly until the sugar has dissolved. Leave to cool slightly
— Slowly add the brandy to the sugar mixture, stirring constantly, then pour over the fruit and close the jar.
— Leave to infuse for at least 3 months before serving. Shake well every few days. Both the fruit and the liquid can be used.

Coffee meringue cake

Makes one 21cm/8in cake

6 egg yolks
150g/5½oz/¾ cup sugar
60ml/2fl oz/¼ cup very strong coffee
500g/1lb 2oz/2¼ cups butter, softened at room temperature
20-24 small meringues (about 4cm/1½in)
8 dried figs pickled in brandy above, chopped, plus extra to decorate
8 dried apricots pickled in brandy above, chopped, plus extra to decorate
5-8 tsp rose petal paste (or morello cherry jam)
30g/1oz/⅓ cup desiccated (dried shredded) coconut
Fruit leathers P244-246, thinly sliced, to decorate

— Place the egg yolks in a medium heatproof bowl set over a pan of gently simmering water. The base of the bowl should not touch the water. Add the sugar and, using a handheld mixer, beat until the sugar has dissolved. Remove the bowl from the heat, add the coffee and mix using a whisk or mixer until the mixture thickens and drops in ribbons when the beater is lifted. Leave to cool to room temperature.
— Meanwhile, beat the butter in another bowl until soft.
— Add the butter to the egg mixture, a spoon at a time, mixing constantly. If the buttercream separates, keep mixing: it will come together.
— Place a 21cm/8in springform cake tin without the base on a serving plate or tray and place a few small dollops of buttercream on the plate to prevent the cake moving.

— Place the first layer of meringues flat-side down in the tin, then start to fill the gaps between the meringues with buttercream, adding some pickled dried fruit in between the meringues.
— Once the first layer is covered with buttercream start on the second layer. Spread some rose petal paste (or cherry jam) on each meringue and press it down on the bottom layer, flat-side up.
— Once all the meringues have been assembled, cover the top of the cake with a layer of buttercream, squeezing it into all the gaps. Remove the tin and coat the sides with a layer of buttercream, then coat the cake with coconut, by putting some coconut in a small dish and gently blowing at it to cover the top and side of the cake.
— Decorate with fruit leather spirals and brandy-pickled apricots and figs. Chill and eat within 3 days.

Gintopf

Instead of the high-proof rum that goes into the German/Danish rumtopf, this uses gin – it's not as strong, but it keeps the fruit pickled. Rumtopf's popularity has declined in recently and the pots it was made in can be found in junk shops, but demijohns or large jars are a good substitute.

Prep 10 minutes
Ready 3 months
Makes approx 2 litre / 67fl oz jar

150g/5½oz/1¼ cups raspberries + 75g/2¾oz/⅓ cup sugar
700ml/24fl oz/3 cups gin
200g/7oz sour cherries, stoned + 100g/3½oz/½ cup sugar
200g/7oz/1⅓ cups blackberries + 100g/3½oz/½ cup sugar
200g/7oz/1¾ cups blackcurrants + 100g/3½oz/½ cup sugar
150g/5½oz pears, peeled, cored and sliced + 75g/2¾oz/⅓ cup sugar

— Put the raspberries and 75g/2¾oz sugar/⅓ cup into a large glass sterilised jar (around 4 litre/7 pint/3.5 quart) or rumtopf pot P12 and pour in the gin.
— Repeat with the other fruits as they become available through the season (adding to the same jar).
— The gintopf will be ready about 3 months after the last fruit has been added. You can drink the gin, or eat the fruit (as below).

Gintopf fruit and ice cream

There is some great ice cream and gelato about these days – but this recipe isn't made for them. The gintopf fruit will elevate even the most mediocre of ice creams.

Serves 4

500ml/18fl oz/2 cups ice cream (vanilla, cream, coffee and chocolate flavours are good with this recipe)
8–12 tbsp gintopf fruit above

— Layer the ice cream with spoonfuls of the gintopf fruit in 4 small glasses and serve.

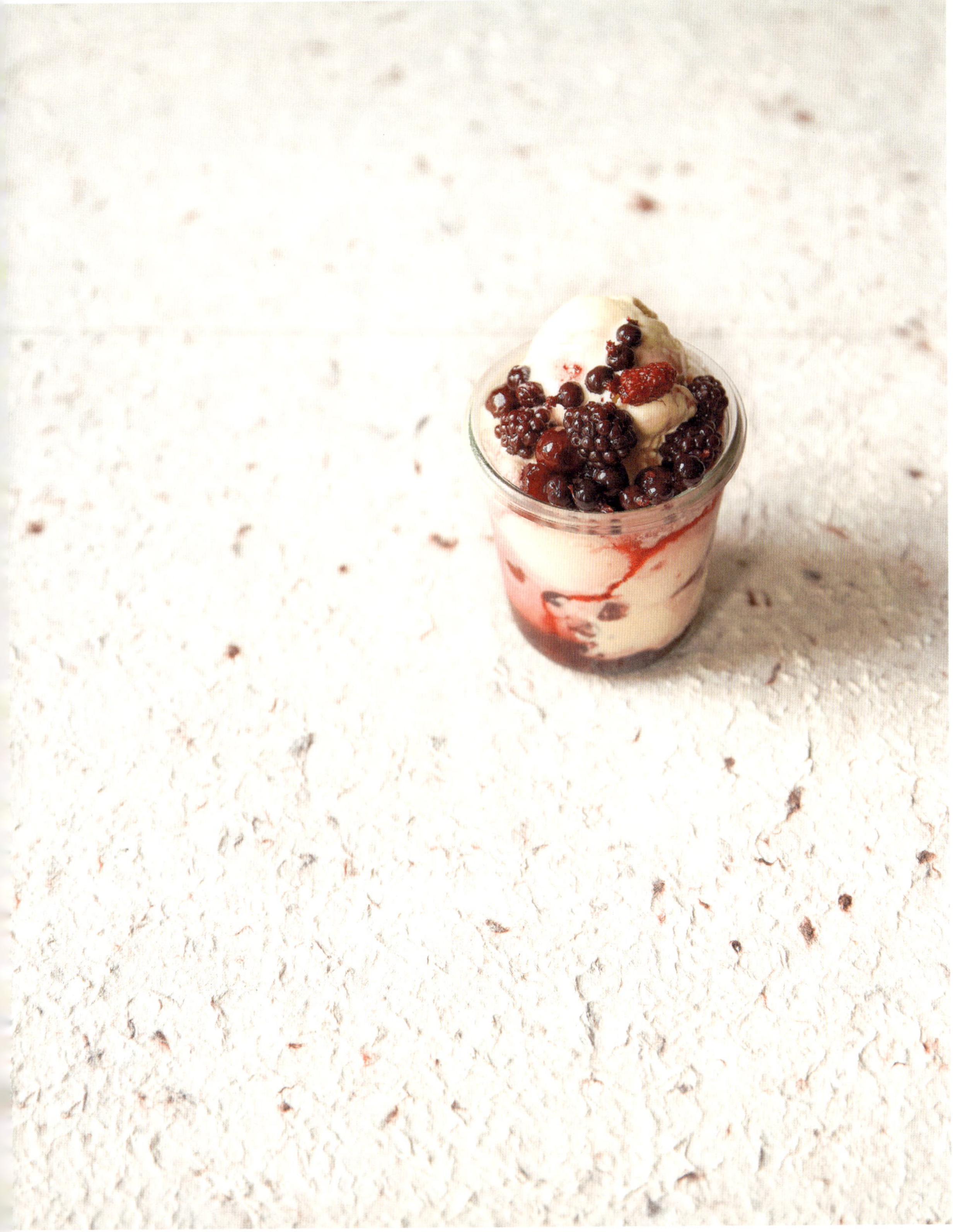

Dry

Drying or dehydrating is a very old and straightforward method which was traditionally used to preserve seasonal food for later use. In this process water or moisture is removed, which makes the food smaller and lighter. Dried foods do not require refrigeration and most do not require pasteurisation.

As with other food-preservation methods, whenever possible choose the best-quality fresh, ideally organic, fruit and vegetables. Drying is not a precise method, and the drying time will vary depending on the equipment used, moisture content of the vegetables and the humidity of the air.

To dry foods, one of three methods can be used. Firstly there is drying in the sun, which requires warm, dry days, so in Britain that leaves us with a choice between the oven or a dehydrator. In order to dry food three factors are needed: heat to force the water out (but not too much or the food will cook rather than dry); dry air to absorb the moisture, and air movement to carry it away. For most of the recipes in this book we used a basic dehydrator, with only high and low settings. We mainly keep it on the high setting and rotate the trays. The temperature tends to vary between 80°C/176°F on the bottom tray nearest to the fan and 60°C/140°F on the top tray.

Dry

If you do not have a dehydrator you can use a domestic oven instead. Just make sure that you can set it to a very low temperature, even the lowest. Our friends Steph and Sandy dry their fruit and vegetable crisps in an oven heated to 100°C/212°F. They place thinly sliced vegetables and fruit in a single layer on baking paper in the middle of the oven, keeping the door ajar, and dry for 1.5–2 hours turning once half way through.

Dried fruits retain more moisture than dried vegetables. If you intend to store them for longer than a few weeks then it is best to condition them first. Conditioning is the process of evenly distributing moisture present to prevent mould growth. Place the dried fruit in a plastic or glass container, seal and shake daily for 10 days to distribute the moisture. If condensation occurs, dry again for a while and repeat the conditioning process.

Dried foods should be stored in a cool, dry and dark place in an airtight container. They should keep for up to a year if stored correctly. The cooler the storage temperature, the longer they will last.

Dried foods are often rehydrated before cooking by soaking in water. The time needed will depend on the type and the size of the food. Most fruits can be rehydrated within 8 hours but most dried vegetables including mushrooms need only 2 hours. They should be cooked in the water in which they were soaked.

Dried wild mushrooms

Since childhood Gaba foraged for mushrooms with her family and introduced me to mushroom picking as soon as we met. We both love the serenity of the forest and the excitement of finding the next mushroom. The most precious is cep or penny bun (Boletus edulis), often known by its Italian name porcini. We are so fond of it that we keep records of how many we find each year. However, if you have never picked mushrooms before, don't pick your own without someone who is experienced. Many species are inedible or even poisonous, and they sometimes closely resemble edible fungi. You can find fresh wild mushrooms at farmers' markets or even in some greengrocers.

Prep 30 minutes
Dry 6–8 hours
Makes approx 100g/3½oz/3½ cups

1kg/2¼lb fresh porcini

— Wipe each mushroom clean with a damp cloth, then slice each head and stalk thinly.
— Examine each mushroom for signs of maggots. If you see small holes or the texture is similar to dry-rot (old decayed tree trunk) discard.
— Place the slices in a single layer on the dehydrator trays and dry for about 6–8 hours, or until completely dry. The drying time will vary depending how thickly you slice your mushrooms. Thinner mushroom slices will dry faster.
— Dried mushrooms can be stored in an airtight container for several months or even a year. They could even keep for longer, but it is best to make new batches every year to get the best flavour.

— Fresh mushrooms contain about 90 per cent water and dried mushrooms contain about 15 per cent water, so you will need a considerable amount of mushrooms to dry. About 850g/1lb 14oz fresh fungi is needed to get 100g/3½oz/3½ cups dried mushrooms.
— You can dry different types of mushrooms, but the best are porcini and other fungi from the Boletus family.
— The whole heads can be dried. The best are medium, about 3–4cm/1¼–1½in in diameter.
— You can use dried mushrooms to make stock, soup P174 or sauce P175, or add them to stews. If you dry whole heads you can make delicious 'cutlets' out of them. To do this, soak them for about 1 hour, then coat in flour, egg yolk and breadcrumbs and fry in butter.

— Fungi can also be sun-dried. On a hot sunny day, put sliced porcini or other fungi in a single layer on a kitchen paper-lined baking tray and place in full sun. The slices need to be turned every few hours. Once the sun goes down move the trays indoors to a dry warm place, then move back out into the sun the following day. Repeat until the mushrooms are completely dry.
— Alternatively, dry the mushrooms by simply stringing them up on a piece of thread and hanging them in a warm, dry place until dry.

Dried wild mushrooms
Wild porcini soup P174

Wild porcini soup

Dried wild mushrooms P172 make great stock but they are at their best when they take centre stage in sauces and soups. Wild mushrooms have a range of rich and earthy flavours that surpass many vegetables. The combination of dried wild mushrooms and fresh rosemary is inspired.

Serves 4

80g/3oz/⅓ cup dried wild mushrooms P172
1.25 litres/2 pints/5 cups water
4 tbsp flaked (slivered) almonds
30g/1oz/2 tbsp butter
1 medium onion, finely chopped
25g/1oz/scant ¼ cup ground hazelnuts
1 tsp finely chopped rosemary
60g/2¼oz chestnut (cremini) mushrooms, sliced
300ml/10fl oz/1¼ cups sour cream
Salt and freshly ground black pepper

— Soak the dried mushrooms in the water for 1 hour, then put on the heat and simmer them for another hour.
— Preheat the oven to 180°C/350°F/gas mark 4.
— Spread the flaked almonds out in a single layer on a baking tray and bake for about 4 minutes, checking and shaking or turning them frequently. Once they start to turn light brown remove them from the oven and immediately transfer them to a plate to prevent burning. Set aside.
— Melt half the butter in a small frying pan, add the onion and fry, stirring frequently until soft and golden.
— Remove the porcini from the stock and chop finely. Reserve the stock.
— Mix the chopped porcini and ground hazelnuts with the fried onion in the frying pan and fry for a further 3–4 minutes.
— Transfer the mixture to a saucepan and add the rosemary and mushroom stock and simmer for 15 minutes.
— Transfer to a blender and blend until smooth (or use a handheld blender), then return to the rinsed-out saucepan.
— Fry the chestnut mushrooms in the remaining butter in a frying pan for a few minutes until they are soft and start to turn golden. Add them to the blended mushroom soup.
— Add the sour cream to the soup and reheat gently. Be careful not to bring to the boil. Garnish the soup with the toasted almonds and serve with sourdough bread P82.
— This soup can be prepared the day before and kept in the fridge, if you like. Just be careful to reheat it gently.

Dried mushroom sauce

This can be used in a luxurious pasta dish with a sprinkle of hard cheese on top, or makes a brilliant accompaniment to steak or pan-roasted chicken supreme.

Serves 4-6

3 handfuls (about 70g/2½oz) of dried mushrooms P172
750ml/25fl oz/3 cups water
2 tbsp olive oil
1 large onion, chopped
1 tbsp chopped marjoram leaves
250ml/9fl oz/generous 1 cup double (heavy) cream
2-3 tsp plain (all-purpose) flour
Salt and freshly ground black pepper

— Place the mushrooms in a medium saucepan and pour in the water to cover. Leave to soak for 30 minutes.
— Bring the mushrooms and soaking water to the boil, then reduce the heat and simmer for 1 hour.
— Meanwhile, heat the oil in a frying pan, add the onions and sauté until golden. Add the marjoram and fry for another minute.
— Remove the mushrooms from the stock and chop finely, then return them to the stock in the pan. Add the fried onion mixture.
— Mix the cream with the flour in a bowl and add to the mushroom and stock. Season with salt and black pepper. Reheat gently for about 10 minutes before serving.

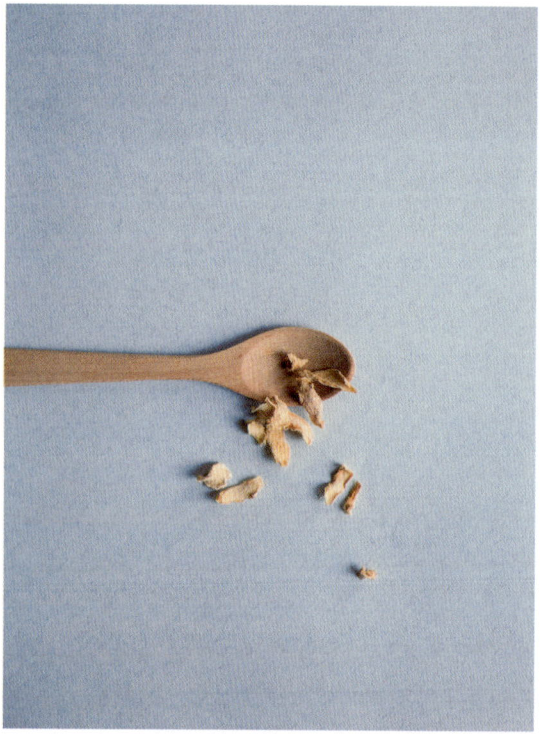

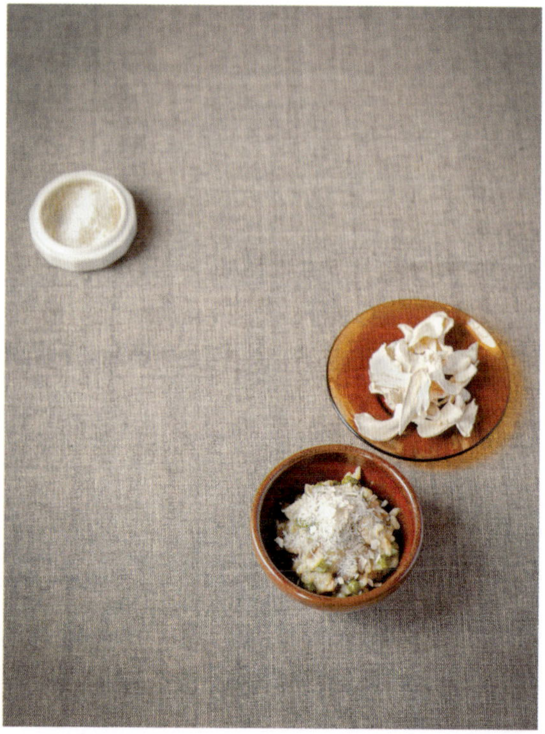

Dried horseradish and ginger

It's very useful to have a jar of dried root spices in your cupboard. Dried slices of horseradish can be added to ferments and pickles. The ginger can be sliced or ground.

Prep 20 minutes
Dry 6-8 hours

1 large fresh horseradish root, peeled and cut into thin slices
1 large piece of ginger, skin scraped off and cut into thin slices

— Spread the sliced roots out in a single layer on the dehydrator trays. If drying different roots at the same time, dry on separate trays
— Dry for 6-8 hours P170-1.
— Once completely dry store in separate airtight containers for several months.

For very thin chips, use a mandolin.

Horseradish can be sliced with a knife into 3mm/⅛in pieces or even cubed to be dried, before using in ferments.

Mushroom risotto topped with horseradish

Risotto depends on a good stock, so try making the one on P179. The dried horseradish above adds quite a kick, so add sparingly.

Serves 2

Butter, for frying
1 large onion, chopped
150g/5½oz chestnut (cremini) mushrooms, cut in half then sliced
Salt, to taste
1 tsp ground black pepper
4 garlic cloves, chopped
150g/5½oz/⅔ cup arborio rice
600-800ml/20-27fl oz/2½-3½ cups instant vegetable stock P179, or shop-bought
115g/4oz/1 cup green peas
50g/1¾oz/½ cup grated parmesan
2 handfuls of dried horseradish, broken into small pieces above

— Melt a knob of butter in a heavy-based saucepan over a low heat. Add the onion and fry gently until soft and golden. Add the mushrooms and fry for a further 5 minutes, stirring frequently. Season with salt and the black pepper. Add the garlic and fry for 2 minutes, then add the rice and fry, stirring, for 1-2 minutes.
— Add a ladleful of stock to the pan and stir. Once the rice has absorbed the liquid add another ladleful.
— Keep adding ladlefuls of stock and stir until it has all been absorbed and the rice is soft but still has a bit of a bite.
— Add the peas and cook for a further 4 minutes.
— Taste and add more salt and pepper if needed, then add half the parmesan and cook for 1 minute.
— Serve the risotto immediately sprinkled with extra parmesan and the horseradish chips. (Do not add dried horseradish when you cook the risotto. It will lose its strong flavour and the risotto will become bitter.)

Dried tomatoes

Home-dried tomatoes are very different to sundried. There are two results you can go for: either dry the tomatoes completely and store in airtight containers for 3-4 weeks, or dry to retain a bit of moisture and softness and store in a jar covered with olive oil in the fridge for 2–3 days.

Prep 30 minutes
Dry 28–35 hours

500g/1lb 2oz baby plum tomatoes or cherry tomatoes
1 tsp olive oil
1 tsp fresh or dried thyme
Pinch of pink Himalayan salt

— Cut a cross one-third of the way through each tomato.
— Using a dropper, place 1–2 drops of olive oil inside each tomato.
— Place a little thyme inside each tomato and sprinkle with salt (you can replace this with sugar if you want to bring out sweetness instead).
— Place on dehydrator trays and dry for 28–35 hours P170-1 depending on whether you want them completely dried or to leave them a bit soft.

Dried tomato pesto

This pesto makes a change from the traditional basil and pine nut combination. It goes well with pasta mixed with capers, puy lentils, olives and red pepper.

Makes approx 225ml/8fl oz jar

10g/¼oz/½ cup chopped coriander
2 tbsp dried basil P218, or shop bought
Pink Himalayan salt and freshly ground black pepper, to taste
50g/1¾oz dried tomatoes, chopped above
50g/1¾oz/⅓ cup cashew nuts
2 garlic cloves, chopped
150ml/5fl oz/⅔ cup mild olive oil
3 tbsp dried kale (optional) P187
50g/1¾oz/½ cup grated parmesan

— Blitz the coriander, basil and salt in a food processor until well combined and starting to turn into a smooth paste.
— Add the dried tomatoes, cashew nuts and garlic, and continue blitzing until the nuts have been chopped into very small pieces.
— While the machine is running, slowly pour in the olive oil and blend to a smooth paste.
— Add the dried kale (if using) and the parmesan and blitz until all the ingredients have been combined well. Season to taste with salt and black pepper.
— Leave to stand for at least 20 minutes before serving or store in an airtight jar in the fridge for up to 4 days.

Dried vegetables

This dried vegetable mix can be ground and made into a stock below or eaten as a snack.

Prep 30 minutes
Dry 6–8 hours each
Ready 2–3 days

This is a good way to use up leftover veg. This is just a suggested list of vegetables and flavours you could try.

1 small sweet potato, peeled and cut into small cubes or sliced
⅓ of a medium celeriac (celery root), peeled and cut into small cubes or sliced
2 medium carrots, sliced
1 medium leek, sliced
1 medium onion, cut in half and sliced
200g/7oz white cabbage, shredded
1 yellow or red (bell) pepper, sliced
⅓ of a fennel bulb, sliced
1 medium root parsley, peeled and sliced
4cm/1½in piece of ginger, skin scraped off and sliced
1 small piece of turmeric, peeled and sliced
1 garlic head, peeled and sliced

— Spread each vegetable and root out in a separate layer on a dehydrator tray.
— Dry for 6–8 hours P170-1. Depending of the size of the dehydrator and number of trays, it might take 2–3 days to dry all the vegetables.
— Once dried, transfer to a large airtight jar. They will keep for 3–4 weeks.

Instant vegetable stock

Make use of the dried vegetables above to make this homemade stock.

Makes approx 500ml/18fl oz stock

1 portion of dried mixed vegetables above (you will need 1 tbsp of this to make the stock)
1 tbsp fine pink Himalayan salt
500ml/18fl oz/2 cups boiling water

— Place a portion of the dried vegetables in a spice or coffee grinder and grind to a powder.
— Repeat with another portion of the dried vegetables. Work in batches until all the vegetables are ground.
— Once all the vegetables are ground add the salt and mix well.
— The dry stock can be stored in airtight containers for up to 6 months.

To make stock
— Put 1 tablespoon of the dried instant stock in a measuring jug, add the boiling water and mix well.
— Leave to stand for 5 minutes before using in your recipe.

Dried vegetables P179

Instant vegetable stock P179

Dried chilli beetroot

Root vegetables are very good for drying, but they benefit from some seasoning to enhance their flavour.

Prep 10 minutes + 10 minutes soaking
Dry about 7 hours

Juice of 1 lemon
150ml/5fl oz/⅔ cup water
500g/1lb 2oz beetroot (beets), peeled and thinly sliced
1 tsp coarse sea salt
2 tsp paprika
2 tsp dried chilli flakes

— Mix the lemon juice and water together in a large bowl.
— Add the beetroot and leave to soak for about 10 minutes, then drain.
— Sprinkle the beetroot with the salt, paprika and chilli and mix until the beetroot is coated all over.
— Place the beetroot on dehydrator trays in a single layer and dry for about 7 hours P170-1.
— They can be stored in airtight containers for several months.

Dried curried parsnip

Prep 10 minutes
Dry about 5 hours

1 large parsnip, cut into very thin slices
Juice of 1 lemon
Pinch of salt
Pinch of curry powder
Pinch of paprika
Pinch of dried chilli flakes

— Sprinkle the parsnip slices with lemon juice and salt.
— Sprinkle the curry powder over half the parsnip, then sprinkle the paprika and chilli flakes over the other half.
— Place the parsnip slices on dehydrator trays in a single layer and dry for about 5 hours P170-1.
— They can be stored in airtight containers for several months.

Dried carrot three ways

Carrots dry excellently and team up well with different seasonings: here are three versions to get you started.

Prep 10 minutes
Dry about 6–8 hours

100ml/3½fl oz/scant ½ cup water
2 tbsp cider vinegar
3 large carrots, cut into very thin slices (for best results use a mandolin)
1 tsp pink Himalayan salt
½ tsp dried dill
½ tsp smoked paprika
½ tsp dried chilli flakes

— Mix the water and cider vinegar together in a bowl.
— Dip the sliced carrots into the water, then divide the carrots into 3 portions.
— Sprinkle 1 portion of the carrots with a third of the salt and dill.
— Sprinkle the second portion of carrots with a third of the salt and the smoked paprika.
— Sprinkle the remaining portion of the carrots with the last third of the salt and the chilli flakes.
— Place the carrots in a single layer on dehydrator trays.
— Dry for about 6–8 hours P170-1, or until completely dry.
— They can be stored in airtight containers for several months.

Spiced courgette crisps

Courgettes can be a bit bland, but this spicy marinade turns them into a delicious snack.

Prep 10 minutes
Dry about 5 hours

1 medium courgette (zucchini), thinly sliced on a mandolin

Marinade
3 tbsp soy sauce
1 tbsp lemon juice
1 tsp dried chilli flakes
1 tbsp honey
½ tsp sea salt
½ tbsp very finely chopped ginger

— Combine all the marinade ingredients together in a bowl.
— Place the sliced courgette in a large bowl, add the marinade and mix until the courgettes are coated all over with the marinade.
— Remove the courgettes from the marinade and place in a single layer on dehydrator trays.
— Dry for 4–5 hours P170-1.
— They can be stored in an airtight container for up to a month.

Dried carrot (with smoked paprika) P183
Dried chilli beetroot P182
Dried carrot (with dill) P183
Dried curried parsnip P183

Spiced courgette crisps P183

Crispy kale and black rice stir-fry
Crispy dried kale
Pickled celery P132

Crispy dried kale

This makes a great snack, but also goes well in salads or sprinkled on a stir-fry below.

Prep 15 minutes
Dry 3-4 hours

200g/7oz curly kale, shredded with stalks removed
7 tbsp soy sauce
2 tbsp lemon juice
1 tbsp dried chilli flakes
2 tbsp honey
1 tsp sea salt
1 tbsp very finely chopped ginger

— Combine all the marinade ingredients together in a bowl.
— Place the shredded kale in a large bowl, add the marinade and mix until the kale is coated all over.
— Place the kale in a single layer on dehydrator trays.
— Dry for 3-4 hours P170-1 until crispy.
— Store in an airtight container for up to 2 weeks.

Crispy kale and black rice stir-fry

Serves 3

3 eggs
Salt, a pinch
1 tsp butter
2 tbsp rapeseed (canola) oil
5 spring onions (scallions), cut into 2cm/¾in pieces
2 shallots, sliced diagonally
1 red (bell) pepper, cut into 2cm/¾in pieces
2 carrots, cut into matchsticks
¼ napa (Chinese) cabbage, sliced
240g/8½oz/1 cup black Thai rice, cooked
2 garlic cloves, sliced
3 tbsp sliced pickled celery P132
9 tbsp crispy dried kale above

Sauce
3 tbsp cider vinegar
2 tbsp honey
6 tbsp soy sauce
Juice of ½ orange
Juice of ½ lime

— To make the sauce, mix all the sauce ingredients together in a bowl and set aside.
— Mix the eggs with a pinch of salt in a bowl.
— Melt the butter in a medium frying pan and fry the egg mixture for 2 minutes, then turn over and fry for a further 2 minutes.
— Place on a chopping board and cut into 2cm/¾in pieces. Set aside.
— Heat the oil in a wok, add the spring onions, shallots, pepper, carrots, cabbage and rice and stir-fry for about 4-5 minutes. Add the garlic and reserved egg and stir-fry for a further minute, or until everything is piping hot. Add the sauce and mix well to combine.
— Serve with the pickled celery and crispy kale sprinkled on top.

Dried carrot kimchi

Make use of kimchi P47 and turn into a topping for salads.

Prep 10 minutes
Dry about 7–8 hours

½ jar (about 200g/7oz) carrot kimchi P47

— Spread the carrot kimchi in a thin layer on 2–3 dehydrator trays and dry for about 2 hours P170-1.
— Divide into chunks and dry for a further 5 hours so the pieces of kimchi are separate.
— Turn off the dehydrator and leave to cool. Once cool check the carrot kimchi for dryness. If it is damp, continue drying.
— Once dried, store in an airtight container for up to 3 months.

Dried carrot kimchi salt

It's always good to have some seasoning salts to hand, and this is a fiery addition to soups and salads. This is also a good way of using up the last of a batch of kimchi P47.

Makes about 80g/3oz

60g/2¼oz dried carrot kimchi above
20g/¾oz/4 tsp pink Himalayan salt

— Place the dried carrot kimchi in a spice or clean coffee grinder and grind to a fine powder. Work in batches if making larger quantities.
— Mix the carrot kimchi powder with the salt and store in an airtight container for up to a year.

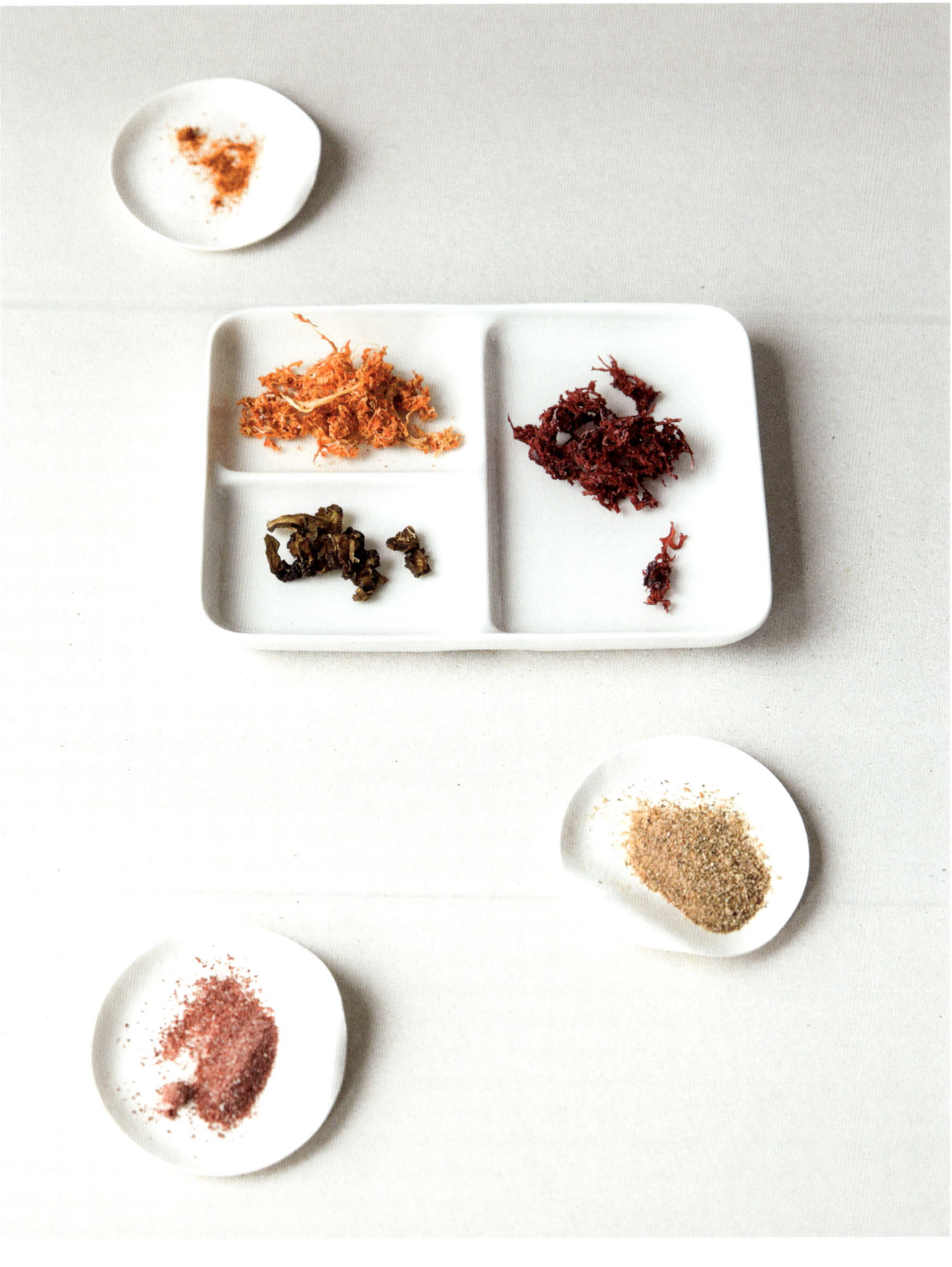

Dried sour gherkin

This is quite unusual in flavour and looks a little like pieces of coloured glass. You can turn it into a tart salt below.

Prep 10 minutes
Dry about 5–6 hours

6 fermented gherkins, thinly sliced P38

— Place the fermented gherkin slices in a thin layer on 2–3 dehydrator trays and dry for about 5 hours P170-1, or until dry.
— Turn off the dehydrator and leave to cool. Once cool check the gherkins for dryness. If they are damp, continue drying.
— Once dry, store in an airtight container for up to 3 months.

Dried sour gherkin salt

Fermented gherkins P38 have a wonderfully sour taste, which can be harnessed in this mouth-puckering salt.

Makes about 70g/2½oz

60g/2¼oz dried sour gherkins above
10g/¼oz/2 tsp pink Himalayan salt

— Place the dried fermented gherkin in a spice or clean coffee grinder and grind until it turns into a fine powder. Work in batches if making larger quantities.
— Mix the fermented gherkin powder with the salt and store in an airtight container for up to a year.

Dried fermented pink turnip

If you have a bit of fermented turnip P50 to use up, dry it to add to salads or turn into a piquant salt below.

Prep 10 minutes
Dry about 7-8 hours
Ready 7-8 hours

½ a jar (about 200g/7oz) fermented pink turnip, drained P50

— Spread the fermented turnip in a thin layer on 2-3 dehydrator trays and dry for about 2 hours P170-1.
— Divide into chunks and dry for a further 5 hours.
— Turn off the dehydrator and leave to cool. Once cool check the fermented turnip for dryness. If it is damp, continue drying.
— Once dry, store in an airtight container for up to 3 months.

Dried fermented turnip salt

Makes about 80g/3oz

60g/2¼oz dried fermented pink turnip above
20g/¾oz/4 tsp pink Himalayan salt

— Place the dried turnip in a spice or clean coffee grinder and grind until it turns into a fine powder. Work in batches if making larger quantities.
— Mix the fermented turnip powder with salt and store in an airtight container for up to a year.

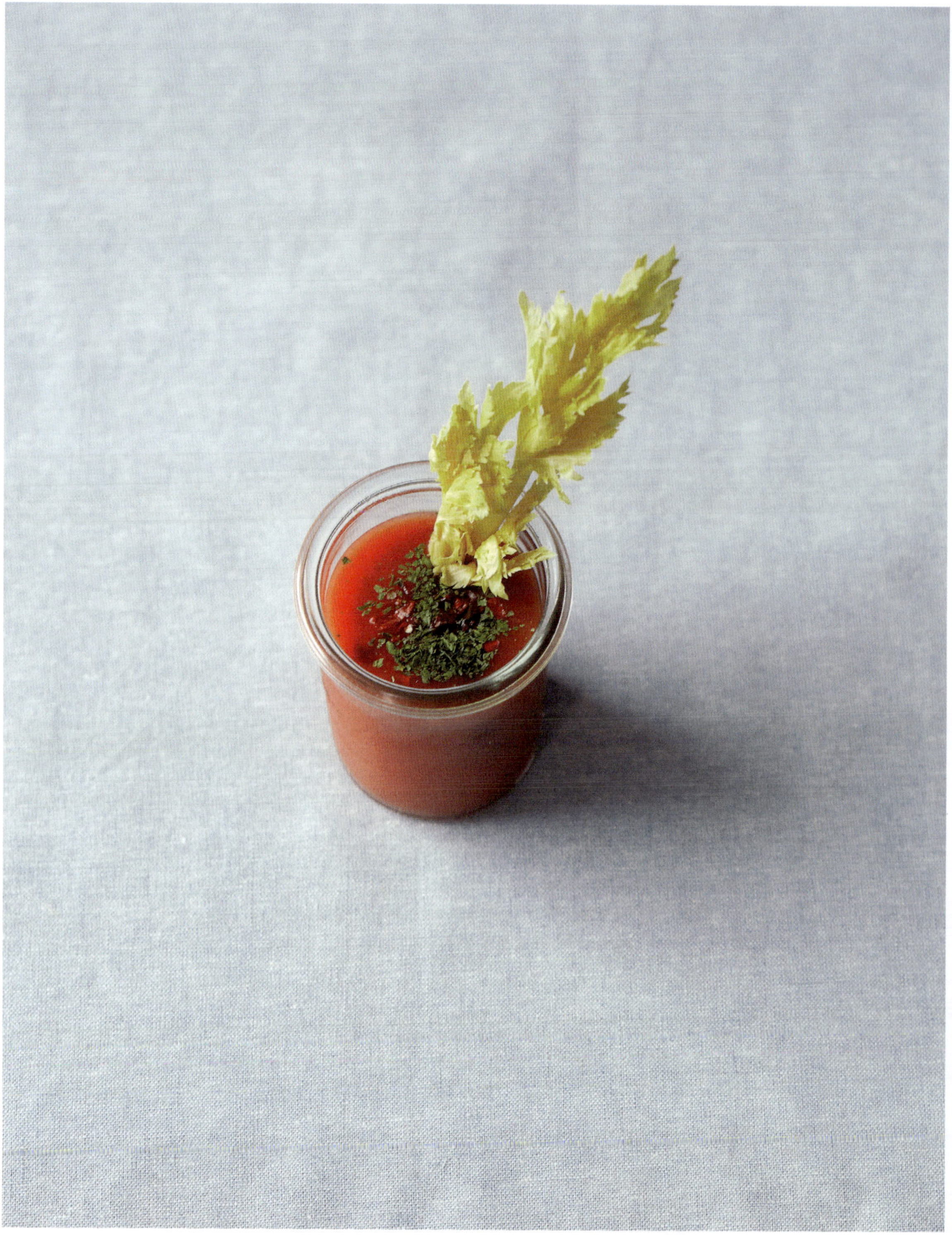

Dried chilli

There are many types of chilli that you can buy fresh, but it can be hard to find a wide selection of dried chilli in the shops. Since it's also possible to grow many interesting varieties at home, it's a good idea to preserve them for the kitchen cupboard – you can keep them whole, crushed, flaked and even ground.

Prep 10 minutes
Dry 4–5 hours

50g/1¾oz chillies, stalks cut off, left whole or sliced into 2cm/¾in pieces

— Place the chillies in a single layer on a dehydrator tray.
— Dry for 4–5 hours P170-1.
— Leave whole, flake or use a spice grinder or clean coffee grinder and grind until it turns into a fine powder.
— Store in an airtight container for up to a year.

Bloody mary II

Another bloody mary (see P132 for the first version with pickled celery): this one has a homemade fiery kick from the dried chilli above, and a sprinkle of dried herbs P218.

Serves 2

Ice cubes
200ml/7fl oz/scant 1 cup tomato juice
Few drops of Worcestershire sauce
½ tsp dried chilli powder above
1 tsp dried mixed herbs, plus extra for sprinkling P218
75ml/2½fl oz/5 tbsp vodka, or to taste
20ml/¾fl oz/4 tsp red wine (optional)
2 lemon wedges
Celery stick

— Add plenty of ice cubes to a large jug. Add the tomato juice, Worcestershire sauce, dried chilli powder and herbs, the vodka and red wine (this gives the bloody mary a richness) and mix well.
— Add the lemon wedges and leave in the fridge for a few minutes to chill.
— Put a celery stick into 2 glasses, pour in the bloody mary and sprinkle with extra dried herbs.

Sweet potato crackling

This was inspired by the American writer Glenn McAllister who used dehydrated foods to create meals for long-distance trekking. He came up with the idea of vegetable 'bark', and this is a homage to that idea. It has flavour added to the mix (to save taking spices on camping trips) and can be used in campfire dishes such as below.

Prep 25 minutes
Dry about 12 hours

440g/14½oz sweet potatoes, peeled
100ml/3½fl oz/scant ½ cup apple juice
Pinch of salt
Pinch of freshly ground black pepper
Pinch of paprika
Pinch of nutmeg
Pinch of ground cumin
Pinch of mixed spice
Pinch of ground coriander
Pinch of ground allspice
Pinch of ground turmeric
Pinch of ground ginger

— Line a dehydrator tray with baking parchment.
— Steam the sweet potatoes until soft, then mash and mix in the apple juice to make a purée.
— Mix in the salt, pepper and spices.
— Spread the purée out in a thin layer on the lined dehydrator tray and dry for about 8–12 hours P170-1.
— Store in an airtight container for several months.

Potato crackling frittata

This was designed for cooking on a camping stove (omit the oven step, and make as an omelette). In the countryside it's often easy to pick up a box of eggs, which combine with crackling above for a filling breakfast.

Serves 2

45g/1½oz sweet potato crackling above
3 tbsp hot water
Knob of butter or 2 tbsp sunflower oil
1 red onion, chopped
8 small closed-cup mushrooms, stalks cut off, quartered
Salt and freshly ground black pepper
Pinch of hot pepper flakes (optional)
70g/2½oz cheddar, cubed
6 eggs, beaten and seasoned
4 tbsp sliced spring onions (scallions), green parts only

— Cut the sweet potato crackling into 1 x 1cm/½ x ½in pieces. Place in a heatproof bowl and cover with the hot water. Soak for 10 minutes, then drain.
— Preheat the oven to 150°C/300°F/gas mark 2.
— Melt a knob of butter in an ovenproof frying pan over a medium heat and fry the onion for 5 minutes, or until translucent.
— Add the mushrooms and fry for a further 5 minutes, or until they start to turn golden brown. Season with salt, pepper and hot pepper flakes (if using) and stir well.
— Add the cheddar and drained sweet potato crackling and spread out evenly over the frying pan. Add the beaten eggs, stir gently, then sprinkle with the sliced spring onion and fry for 3 minutes.
— Bake the frittata for 20 minutes, or until set and turning golden on the top. A knife inserted into the centre should come out clean. Leave to stand for 5 minutes before serving.

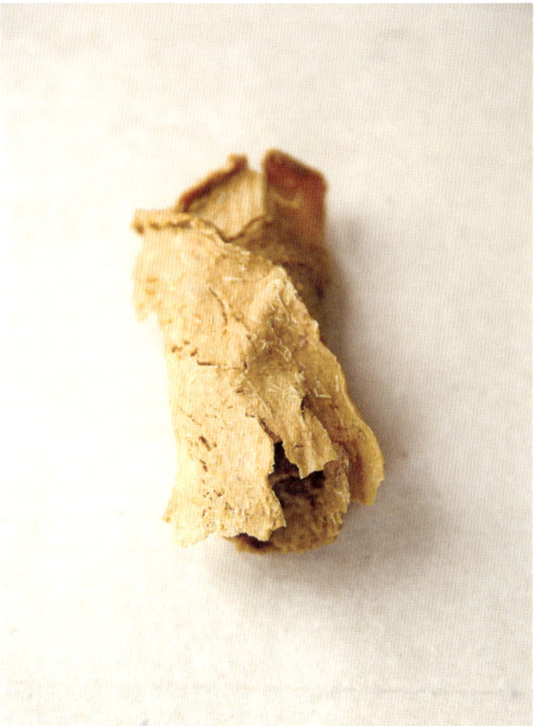

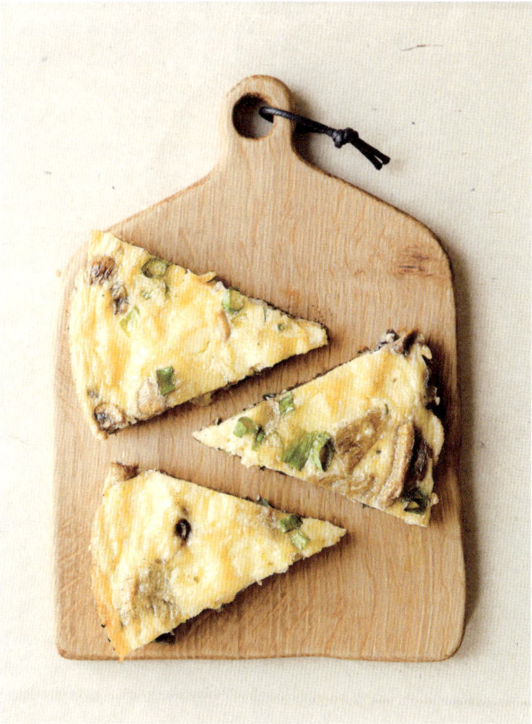

Bean crackling

This dehydrated bean 'bark' was inspired by Mexican refried beans, but also makes use of an adapted version of Georgian spice mix khmeli suneli. We like to do a double batch of the fresh bean mix, eat half fresh as a sandwich filling (with different pickles such as pickled celery P132 or sweet and spicy gherkins P116), and dry the other half. This can be rehydrated for another meal, such as the quick bean tortilla P198.

Prep 1 hour + 12 hours soaking
Dry 2-4 hours
Ready 17 hours

500g/1lb 2oz/3 cups dried pinto beans, soaked overnight in water
3 tbsp sunflower oil
2 medium onions, chopped
1 tsp fennel seeds
4 cardamom pods, crushed and shells removed
1 tbsp coriander seeds, crushed
6 garlic cloves, very finely chopped
1 tbsp dried marjoram
1 tsp ground cumin
1 tsp ground turmeric
1 tsp smoked paprika
1 tsp cayenne pepper
300g/10½oz cherry tomatoes, chopped
2 bay leaves
6 dried plums, chopped P213 (optional)
1 tsp salt
1 tsp ground black pepper
150ml/5fl oz/⅔ cup water

— Line several dehydrator trays with baking parchment.
— Rinse the soaked beans, then bring them to the boil in a medium saucepan. Reduce the heat and simmer for 30 minutes.
— Meanwhile, heat the oil in a large heavy-based saucepan, add the onions and fry for 10 minutes, stirring frequently, until soft and golden.
— Add the fennel, cardamom and coriander seeds and fry for 1 minute, stirring constantly.
— Add the garlic and remaining herbs and spices and fry for a further 1-2 minutes stirring constantly.
— Add the pinto beans, tomatoes, bay leaves, dried plums, salt and pepper and water. Stir, then cover with a lid and bring to the boil.
— Reduce the heat and simmer for 20 minutes, then uncover and simmer for a further 10 minutes, stirring frequently.
— Leave to cool a little, then transfer to a blender in batches and blend into a smooth paste (or use a handheld blender).
— Spread the paste thinly on the lined dehydrator trays and dry for 2-4 hours P170-1.
— Store in airtight containers for several months.
— To rehydrate the bean crackling, put the it in a heatproof bowl, add the boiling water and leave to soak for 20-30 minutes, then mash with a fork. It should be fully rehydrated.

Rehydrated bean crackling
Bean crackling
Sourdough tortilla P85
(Tortilla with bean crackling P198)

Tortilla with bean crackling

Beans and pickled vegetables go really well together. This is a Mexican-style dish with Georgian-spiced beans P196 and Balkan pickles. Unusual but tasty.

Makes 4

120g/4oz bean crackling P196
120ml/4fl oz/½ cup boiling water
4 sourdough tortillas P85
80g/3oz/¾ cup mature cheddar, grated
8 tbsp Balkan pickles P153
5 tbsp chopped coriander (cilantro)
5 tbsp chopped mint
2 long red chillies, sliced
12 tbsp plain yoghurt P20

— Put the bean crackling in a heatproof bowl, add the boiling water and leave to soak for 20–30 minutes, then mash with a fork. It should be fully rehydrated.
— Preheat the oven to 230°C/450°F/gas mark 8.
— Meanwhile, make the tortillas.
— Spread one-quarter of the bean paste across the middle of the tortilla, sprinkle with one-fifth of the cheddar, 2 tablespoons of the Balkan pickles, one-fifth of the herbs and one-quarter of the sliced chillies.
— Fold over the 2 outer edges so they overlap and place on a baking tray.
— Repeat with the remaining 3 tortillas, then sprinkle the remaining cheddar and herbs on top.
— Bake in the oven for 10 minutes.
— Serve hot with fresh salad and plain yoghurt, if you like.

Spiced crackers

These spiced crackers are an alternative to popadoms and can be served with a thali P200, or simply eaten as a snack.

Prep 25 minutes
Dry about 6–7 hours

1 tsp caraway seeds
2 tsp coriander seeds
½ tsp nigella seeds
2 tbsp flaked (slivered) almonds
3 tbsp cashew nuts
4 tbsp sunflower seeds
1 large apple, peeled, grated and juice squeezed out
1 small parsnip, peeled, grated and juice squeezed out
100g/3½oz sprouted green lentils
4 tsp sesame seeds
½ tsp dried chilli flakes
1 tsp salt
1 tsp ground cumin

— Line several dehydrator trays with baking parchment.
— Heat a medium dry frying pan over a medium heat and toast the caraway, coriander and nigella seeds for 30 seconds, or until fragrant, then remove from the heat.
— Repeat with the almonds, cashews and sunflower seeds, removing from the heat when they start to brown.
— Crush the caraway, coriander and nigella seeds together in a mortar with a pestle and set aside.
— Chop the almonds, cashews and sunflower seeds in a blender or food processor into small pieces and place in a bowl.
— Blitz the apple, parsnip and sprouted lentils in a blender or food processor to a smooth paste and add to the bowl.
— Add the seeds to the bowl with all the remaining ingredients and mix together. Spread the mixture on to the lined dehydrator trays.
— When spreading on the trays make sure it is pressed down firmly and between 3 and 4mm/⅛in thick.
— It can be dried as a single sheet with indented cutting lines or cut with a knife or cookie cutter into desired shapes.
— Dry for 6–7 hours P170-1.
— Store in an airtight container for up to 4 weeks.

To sprout green lentils, put them in a jar large enough to accommodate them expanding to three times their size. Cover in water, secure a cloth over the top with an elastic band then leave overnight. The next day, drain off the water and leave the jar somewhere out of direct sunlight. Every 12 hours, add water to the jar, swish it around then drain it. They should begin to sprout after 1–3 days and after 2–4 days their sprouts should be long enough. They can be stored in an airtight container in the fridge for up to a week.

Dried apricot and turmeric rice P202
Spicy pineapple and mango pickle P120
Spiced crackers P199

Spiced aubergine crisps P202
Coriander and yoghurt dip P57
Pickled shallots P141

Dried apricot and turmeric rice

A juicy way to use your dried apricots P231.

Serves 4

8 dried apricots, cut into 5mm/¼in pieces P231
210g/7oz/generous 1 cup brown rice
1 tsp ground turmeric

— Place the apricot pieces in a heatproof bowl and cover with boiling water. Leave to soak for 20 minutes, then drain.
— Cook the rice according the packet instructions.
— Add the turmeric to the boiling rice 5 minutes before the end of the cooking time.
— Drain the rice and combine with the dried apricots.

Spiced aubergine crisps

Something different to serve with the fermented hummus P66, or add to a chunky dhal P203.

Prep 30 minutes + 1 hour marinating
Dry about 5–6 hours

1 large aubergine (eggplant), thinly sliced, use a mandolin for the best results

Marinade
1 tbsp light soy sauce
1 tsp spicy red pepper flakes
Juice of ½ lemon
Juice of ½ orange
½ tsp ground coriander
⅓ tsp ground cumin
2 tbsp honey
1 garlic clove, very finely chopped
5 tbsp sunflower oil
⅓ tsp cayenne pepper

— Mix all the marinade ingredients together in a large bowl.
— Dip each slice of aubergine into the marinade and place in another bowl, then cover the aubergine slices with the remaining marinade.
— Leave the aubergines to marinate for 1 hour, turning over every 15 minutes to make sure all the slices are well covered.
— Place the marinated aubergine slices in a single layer on dehydrator trays and dry for 5–6 hours P170-1.
— Once dry, store in an airtight container for up to a month.

Chunky dhal with aubergine crisps

Serves 2–3

250g/9oz/1¼ cups dried chana dhal lentils, rinsed and soaked overnight in cold water
3 tbsp rapeseed (canola) oil
1 tbsp coriander seeds, ground
1 tsp white mustard seeds, ground
1 tsp ground cumin
1 tsp ground turmeric
1 tsp garam masala
1 large onion, chopped
2cm/¾in piece of fresh ginger, skin scraped off and chopped
4 garlic cloves, very finely chopped
400g/14oz chopped tomatoes
225ml/8fl oz/1 cup water
3–4 whole green chillies, roughly sliced
50g/1¾oz/1 cup spiced aubergine crisps left
Juice of ½ lime
Salt and freshly ground black pepper
10g/¼oz/½ cup chopped coriander (cilantro) leaves
Dried apricot and turmeric rice, to serve left

— Place the chana dhal in a large saucepan of cold water, bring to the boil, then reduce the heat and simmer for 30 minutes. Remove from the heat and drain.

— Meanwhile, heat the oil in a medium saucepan, add all the spices and fry for 30 seconds stirring constantly. Add the onion and fry for a further 5 minutes, stirring constantly. Add the ginger and garlic and fry for 30 seconds.

— Add the chopped tomatoes and the measured water, stir and bring to the boil. Reduce the heat and simmer for 10 minutes.

— Add the chana dhal and simmer for a further 10 minutes, adding more water if it is too thick.

— Add the chillies, dried aubergine and lime juice. Season with salt and pepper and bring to the boil. Reduce the heat and simmer for 10 minutes.

— Stir in the chopped coriander just before serving with the dried apricot and turmeric rice.

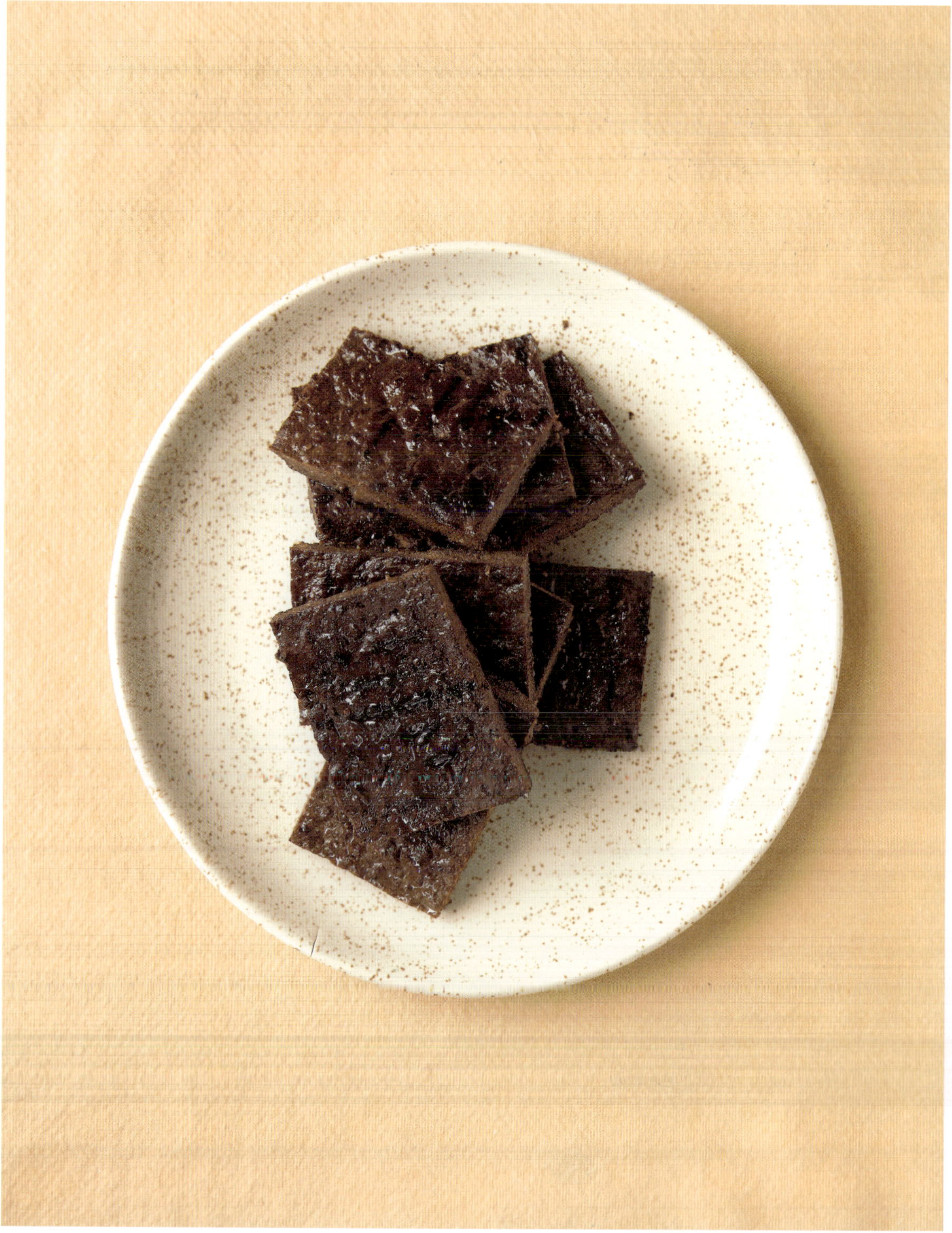

Honey glazed Chinese beef jerky

Drying meat is a useful way to add flavour and to add to its shelf life and is practised the world over. The beef combines wonderfully with the traditional Chinese cooking elements of ginger, honey, soy and five spice.

Prep 90 minutes + 1–8 hours chilling
Dry about 5–7 hours
Makes about 12 pieces

500g/1lb 2oz beef mince (ground) (not too lean, 85% meat and 15% fat would be good)
3 tbsp sweet soy sauce
3 tbsp soy sauce
30g/1oz piece of ginger, skin scraped off and grated
3 garlic cloves, grated
1 tbsp honey
4 tsp fish sauce (optional)
4 tsp oyster sauce (optional)
1 tsp ground black pepper
1 tsp Chinese five-spice
¼ tsp fine sea salt

Basting
2 tbsp honey
1 tbsp rice wine (or other white cooking wine)
¼ tsp sea salt flakes

— Stir all the ingredients, except the basting ingredients, together in a large bowl and until the mixture becomes glue-like. Cover the bowl with clingfilm and leave in the fridge for at least 1 hour, preferably overnight.
— Preheat the oven to 160°C/325°F/gas mark 3. Line the base of a large oven tray with baking parchment.
— Place the meat mixture on the baking parchment and, using a rolling pin, flatten into a 5mm/¼in thick square. When flattening the meat, double the baking parchment, so the meat is rolled between 2 layers to prevent it sticking to the rolling pin.
— Cook the meat in the oven for about 15 minutes, then take it out and gently flip it over. Return to the oven for another 15 minutes, or until cooked. Leave the meat to cool on a chopping board or tray, then cut it into rectangles.
— Place the jerky on dehydrator trays and dry for 5–7 hours.
— Store the cooked meat in airtight containers for several months. It can be gently reheated in a frying pan or the microwave until hot. Or you can baste the meat for sticky finish.
— To do this, mix the rice wine, honey and salt together in a bowl.
— Heat a griddle pan or a barbecue. Baste the meat with the honey glaze, and griddle or grill until they look handsomely caramelised.
— Eat straight away.

Nori seaweed crackers

If Greek god of the sea Poseidon ever made crackers, they probably tasted like this.

Prep 25 minutes + 1-24 hours soaking
Dry about 6-7 hours
Makes about 30 crackers

3 tbsp flaxseeds
6 tbsp pumpkin seeds
1 large apple, peeled, grated and juice squeezed out
1 small parsnip, peeled, grated and juice squeezed out
2 fermented gherkins, grated and juice squeezed out P38
4 tbsp sprouted green lentils
12 sundried black olives, thinly chopped
4 tbsp sesame seeds
2 tbsp chia seeds
½-1 tsp salt
½-1 tsp ground black pepper
3-6 nori seaweed sheets
2-3 tbsp cabbage and apple sauerkraut, chopped P67 or carrot kimchi P47 or grated fermented gherkins P38

— Soak the flaxseeds in a bowl of water for 24 hours.
— Chop the pumpkin seeds into small pieces in a blender or food processor, then place in a large bowl.
— Blitz the apple, parsnip, gherkin and sprouted lentils in a blender or food processor to a smooth paste and place in the bowl.
— Add all the remaining ingredients, except the nori sheets and sauerkraut (carrot kimchi or grated gherkin), to the bowl and mix together.
— To make flat nori crackers (which have no sauerkraut mix), place one nori sheet on a work surface, spread the cracker paste evenly in a 3mm/⅛in layer, cover with a second nori sheet and press down firmly. Place on a dehydrator tray and dry for about 5 hours.
— Once dry, cut the sheets into 2cm/¾in squares with scissors.
— To make 'sushi' crackers, place one nori sheet on a work surface, spread the paste evenly in a 3mm/⅛in layer, press it down firmly and place on a dehydrator tray and dry for about 1½-2 hours.
— Remove from the dehydrator, place 2-3 tablespoons sauerkraut, carrot kimchi or grated fermented gherkin along the edge, which will end up in the middle of the 'sushi', and roll it up tight. Return it to the dehydrator tray with the end edge facing down. Dry for a further 2 hours, then, using a very sharp knife, cut into 5mm/¼in slices. Lay the slices flat on the dehydrator trays and dry for a further 4-5 hours, or until dry.
— Use the remaining paste to make more nori crackers. Or make crackers without seaweed by spreading the mix on a dehydrator tray lined with baking parchment. It can be dried as a single sheet with indented cutting lines or cut with a knife or cookie cutter into desired shapes.
— When spreading on the trays make sure it is pressed down firmly and between 3 and 4mm/⅛in thick.
— Dry for 6-7 hours P170-1.
— All crackers can be stored in an airtight container for up to a month.

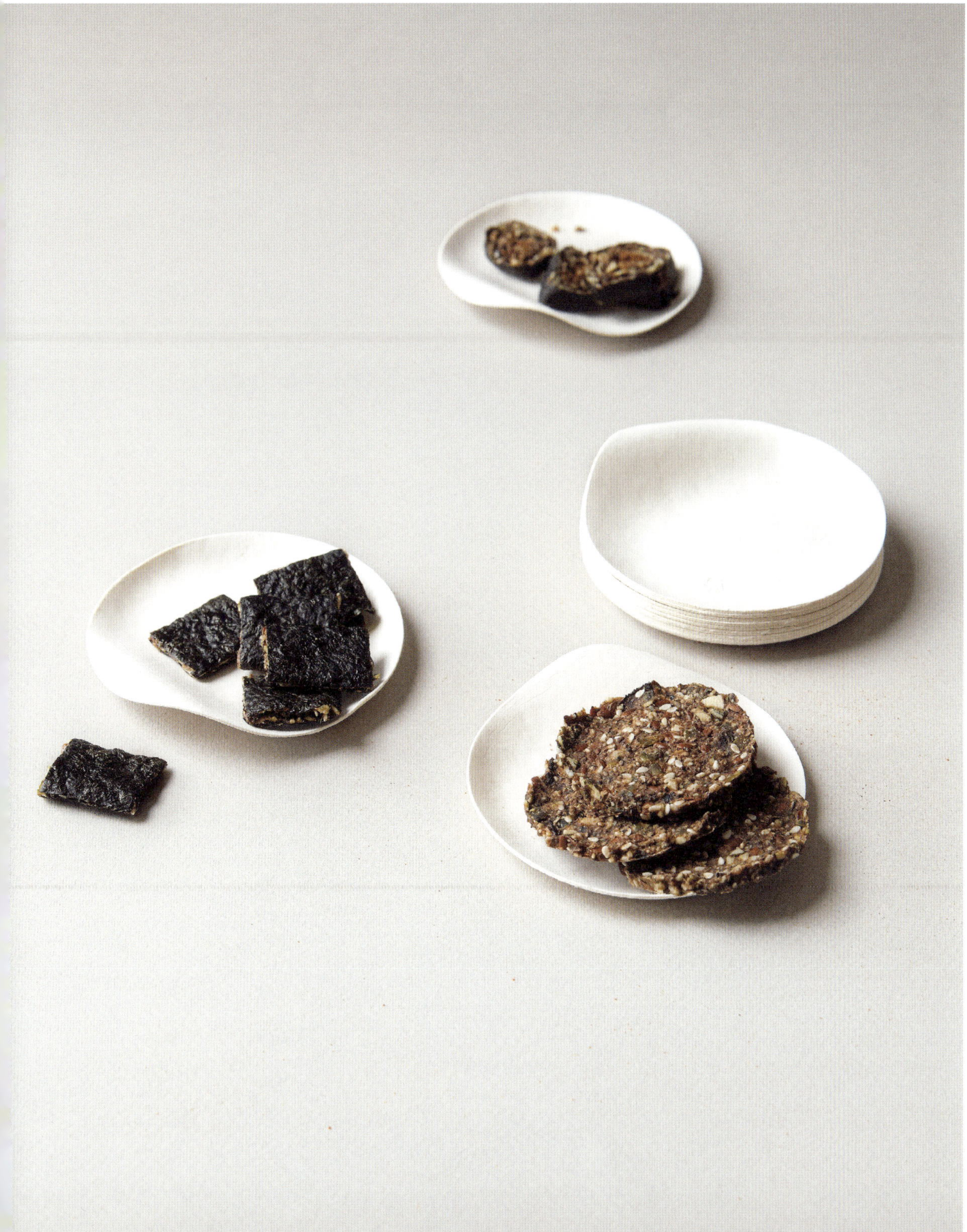

Kimchi crackers P210
Beetroot and apple crackers P212

Beetroot and sauerkraut crackers P210
Fermented turnip and carrot crackers P211
Sauerkraut crackers P210

Kimchi or sauerkraut crackers

We usually use napa kimchi P42 to make these, but other types of kimchi are splendid too.

Prep 30 minutes + 1 hour soaking
Dry 6–7 hours

6 tbsp flaxseeds
2 medium carrots (125g/4½oz each)
2 celery sticks
80–100g/3–3½oz classic napa kimchi P42 or cabbage and apple sauerkraut P67
½ tsp ground black pepper
6 tsp chia seeds
6 tsp sesame seeds
6 tbsp sunflower seeds
6 tsp ground almonds
Pinch of salt

— Soak the flaxseeds for 1 hour. Line dehydrator trays with baking parchment.
— Grate the carrots and squeeze the juice out by hand.
— Finely chop the celery and squeeze out the juice.
— Place the carrot pulp, celery pulp and napa kimchi (or sauerkraut) in a blender and blend until smooth, then combine with the remaining ingredients.
— Place on the lined dehydrator trays. It can be spread as a single sheet with indented cutting lines or cut with a cookie cutter.
— When spreading on the trays make sure it is pressed down firmly and between 3 and 4mm/⅛in thick.
— Dry for 6–7 hours P170-1. Store in an airtight container for a month.

If you prefer spicy crackers add ½ teaspoon cayenne pepper.

Beetroot and sauerkraut crackers

Prep 30 minutes
Dry 6–7 hours

100g/3½oz cabbage and apple sauerkraut P67
1 portion, about 250g/9oz, beetroot and apple cracker mix P212

— Line dehydrator trays with baking parchment.
— To prepare the sauerkraut, drain, squeeze out the juice and chop into very small pieces or blend in a blender.
— Combine with the pre-prepared beetroot and apple cracker mix.
— Place the mixture on the lined dehydrator trays. Spread as a single sheet with indented cutting lines or cut with a cookie cutter.

— When spreading on the trays make sure it is pressed down firmly and between 3 and 4mm/⅛in thick.
— Dry for 6–7 hours P170-1.
— Store in an airtight container for up to a month.

Fermented turnip and carrot crackers

Prep 20 minutes + 30 minutes soaking
Dry about 5–6 hours

3 tbsp flaxseeds
1 small carrot
40g/1½oz fermented pink turnips P50
3 tsp ground almonds
3 tsp chia seeds
3 tsp sesame seeds
1 tbsp sunflower seeds
⅓ tsp cayenne pepper
½ tsp ground black pepper
Salt, a pinch

— Soak the flaxseeds for at least 30 minutes. Line dehydrator trays with baking parchment.
— Grate the carrot into a bowl and squeeze the juice out by hand.
— Place the carrot pulp and fermented turnips into a blender and blend until smooth.
— Combine with the remaining ingredients.
— Place on the lined dehydrator trays. Spread as a single sheet with indented cutting lines or cut with a cookie cutter into 10 pieces.
— When spreading on the trays make sure it is pressed down firmly and between 3 and 4mm/⅛in thick.
— Dry for 5–6 hours P170-1.
— Store in an airtight container for up to a month.

Beetroot and apple crackers

These crunchy, healthy crackers are pretty mellow in flavour despite the punchy ingredients.

Prep 20 minutes + 1-24 hours soaking
Dry about 6-7 hours

70g/2½oz/½ cup sunflower seeds
50g/1¾oz/½ cup walnuts, chopped
45g/1½oz/⅓ cup flaxseeds
1 large beetroot (beet), peeled, grated, juice squeezed out
2 small apples, peeled, grated, juice squeezed out
½-1 tsp salt
1 tsp paprika

— Place the sunflower seeds and walnuts in separate bowls of warm water and the flaxseeds in a bowl of cold water and soak for 1-24 hours. Line dehydrator trays with baking parchment.
— Chop the walnuts and sunflower seeds into small pieces in a blender and place in a bowl.
— Blitz the beetroot and apple in a blender to a smooth paste.
— Combine the walnuts and sunflower seeds with the beetroot paste, then season with salt and paprika.
— Place the mixture on the lined dehydrator trays. It can be spread as a single sheet with indented cutting lines or cut with a cookie cutter.
— When spreading on the trays make sure it is pressed down firmly and between 3 and 4mm/⅛in thick. Dry for 6-7 hours P170-1. Store in an airtight container for up to a month.

Dried plums

Victoria and Polish Wegierka plums are the best for drying, but other varieties will also be successful. We prefer to dry them whole, as they're more fun to eat. But when cut into pieces, the drying time is reduced. Remember, plums that are still a little moist after drying will not keep as long.

Prep 10 minutes
Dry about 12–24 hours

500g/1lb 2oz ripe plums, washed and cut halfway along sideways so the sides stay connected but the plum can be easily stoned

— Place the closed plums in a single layer on a dehydrator tray.
— Dry for 12–24 hours P170-1, or longer if needed. Drying time will depend on the size of the plums and how ripe they are.
— Once dry, store in an airtight container for up to 3 months.

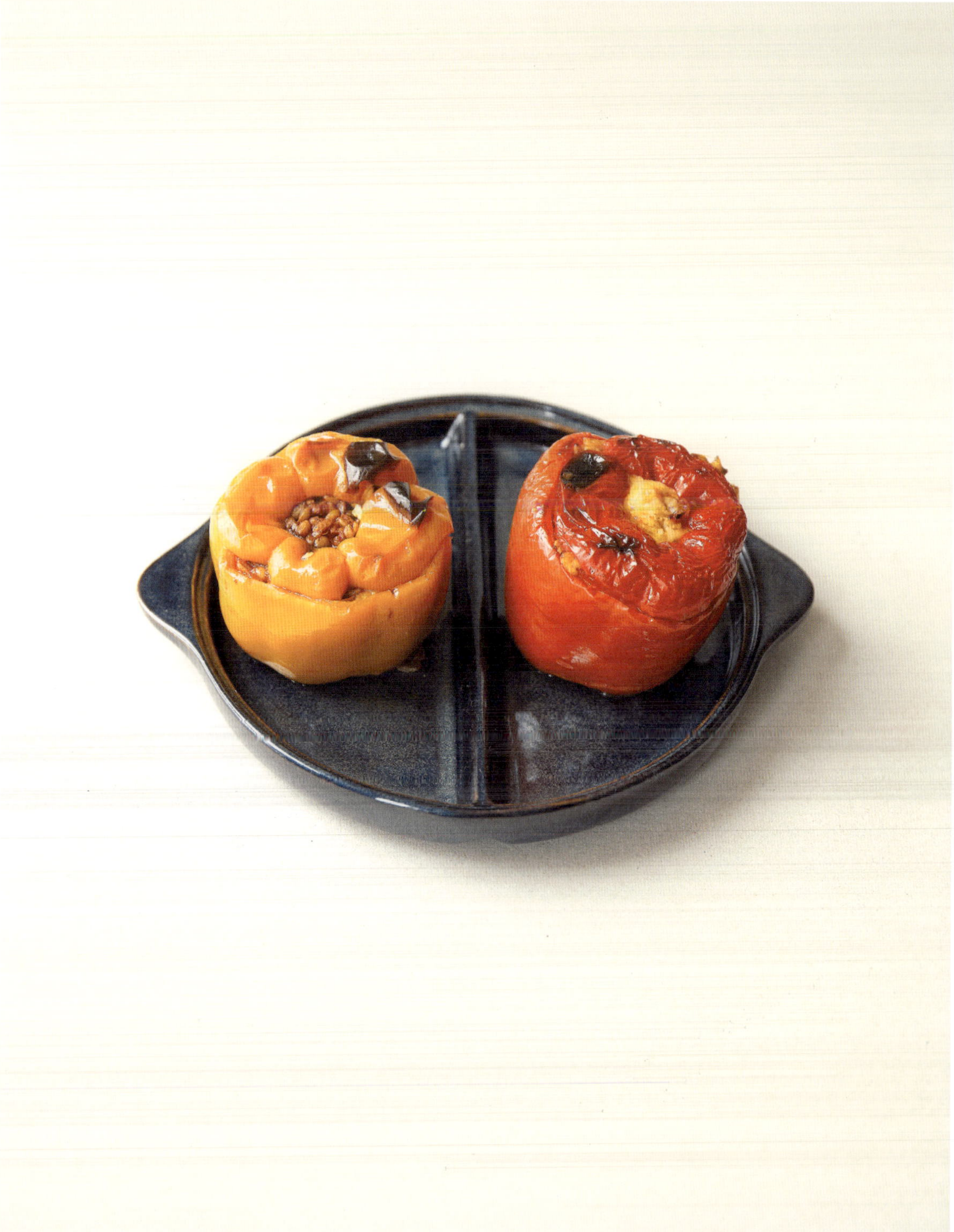

Dried plum-stuffed peppers two ways

Dried plums P213 shouldn't just be for dessert – they are great in savoury dishes as well. This recipe benefits from slow cooking to bring out all the flavours.

Serves 3

180g/6½oz/1 cup cooked orzo pasta (reserve the water it was cooked in)
Salt and freshly ground black pepper
50g/1¾oz/½ cup grated mature (sharp) cheddar or feta
6 large (bell) peppers, red and yellow, tops cut off and stalks removed, deseeded
160g/5¾oz/1 cup cooked wheat grains

Sauce
3 tbsp vegetable or rapeseed oil
1 medium onion, chopped
1 large carrot, chopped
4 celery sticks, sliced
1 tsp paprika
1 tsp smoked paprika
400g/14oz can chopped tomatoes
2 tbsp balsamic vinegar
2 handfuls of dried plums, chopped P213
5 garlic cloves, chopped
2 (halves) pickled ramiro peppers, cut into 1.5cm/⅝in pieces (optional) P106
2 pickled baby courgettes, sliced (optional) P142
50g/1¾oz/¼ cup puy lentils, boiled
150ml/5fl oz/⅔ cup water
8g/¼oz/⅓ cup chopped fresh herbs including thyme, marjoram and flat leaf parsley
125ml/4fl oz/½ cup water in which the pasta was boiled in

— To make the sauce, heat the oil in a pan over a low heat, add the onion and fry for 10 minutes, or until soft and translucent. Add the carrot and celery and fry for a further 10 minutes, stirring frequently. Add the paprika and smoked paprika, stir well and fry for 1 minute. Add the chopped tomatoes, vinegar and chopped plums and stir well. Bring to the boil, then reduce the heat and simmer for 10 minutes.
— Add the garlic, pickled pepper and courgette (if using) and simmer for a further 10 minutes.
— Add the lentils and simmer for a further 10 minutes. If the sauce is very dry, add 150ml/5fl oz/⅔ cup of the water and simmer for another 4–5 minutes.
— Add the fresh herbs and stir well.
— At this point you can serve it with spaghetti or proceed to make stuffed peppers.
— Preheat the oven to 230°C/450°F/gas mark 8.
— Reserve 4–6 tablespoons of the sauce.
— Divide the remaining sauce in half.
— Mix the first half with the cooked orzo pasta and season with salt and pepper.
— Mix it with half of the cheddar or feta and divide into 3 portions.
— Stuff the yellow peppers with the orzo pasta mix, then sprinkle with the remaining cheese and cover each pepper with its top.
— Mix the second half of the sauce with the cooked wheat and season with salt and black pepper.

— Stuff the red peppers with the wheat mix and cover them with their tops.
— Mix the reserved sauce with the reserved orzo pasta cooking water and pour into the base of a large ovenproof dish.
— Carefully place all the peppers in the dish. Cover and bake in the oven for 30 minutes.
— Uncover and bake for another 15–30 minutes until the peppers are soft and slightly browned on top.
— Check the peppers every few minutes, making sure there is some sauce at the bottom of the dish – if not add some of the leftover water. Serve.

Kamut, unripe spelt (known in German as gruenkern), and other grains can be used instead of wheat.

For the best results soak the dry grains overnight before cooking.

Dried mango and apple savoury fruit crisps

In this recipe the quality of spices makes a huge difference to the flavour. The quantities used are very small, so it is worth using really good paprika and chilli.

Prep 10 minutes
Dry about 6–7 hours

1 mango, peeled, stoned and thinly sliced
½ tsp dried chilli flakes
Pinch of pink Himalayan salt
225ml/8fl oz/1 cup water
Juice of ½ lemon
1 large apple, peeled, cored and thinly sliced
½ tsp paprika

— Sprinkle the sliced mango with the chilli flakes and a pinch of salt.
— Mix the water with the lemon juice in a bowl.
— Dip the sliced apple in, drain and sprinkle with the paprika and a pinch of salt.
— Place all the fruit in single layers on the dehydrator trays and dry for about 6–7 hours P170-1, or until the pieces are crisp.
— Store (together, if liked) in an airtight container for up to 1 month.

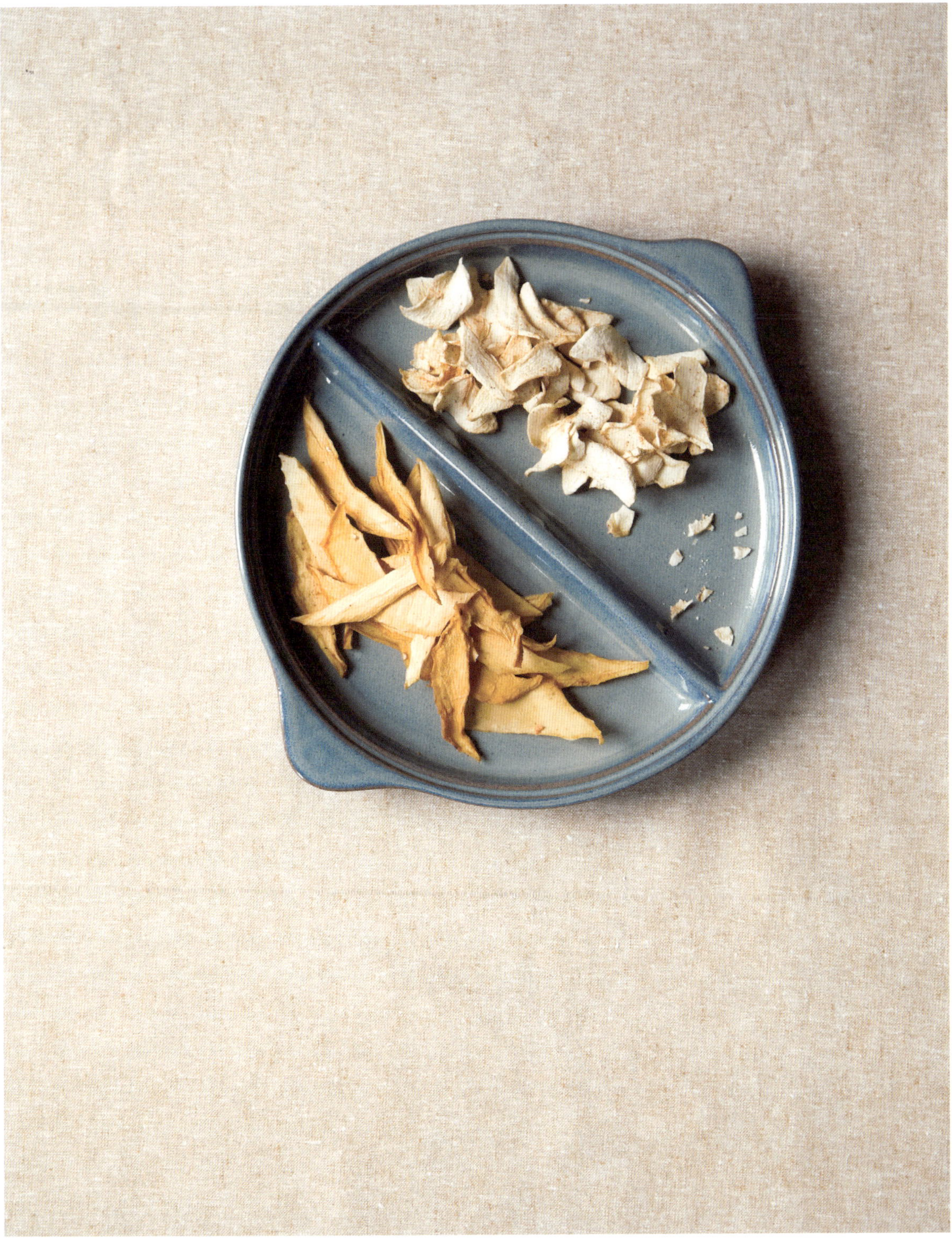

Dried herbs

Herbs can be dried in different ways depending on the plant. Leafy herbs such as parsley, basil and coriander can be dried in a dehydrator. Other herbs can be tied in a bunch and hung up in a warm or airy place. In both cases it's important to avoid direct sunlight.

Prep 10 minutes
Dry about 6-7 hours

A bunch of your favourite herbs, including:
  Basil (stalks removed)
  Parsley (stalks removed)
  Coriander/cilantro (stalks removed)
  Dill
  Marjoram
  Oregano
  Thyme
  Rosemary

— Tie the herbs with stalks together into a bunch with string and hang them from the ceiling, on a staircase, or from a suitable height.
— Make sure that they are hanging in a warm and airy place and not in direct sunlight.
— They should be dry in 6-7 days.
— Alternatively, line dehydrator trays with baking parchment. Place the sprigs or leaves in a single layer on the lined trays and dry on a low heat, uncovered, for about 6-7 hours P170-1.
— Once dry, the herbs should crumble easily, but should not turn into a powder.
— Store in separate airtight containers.

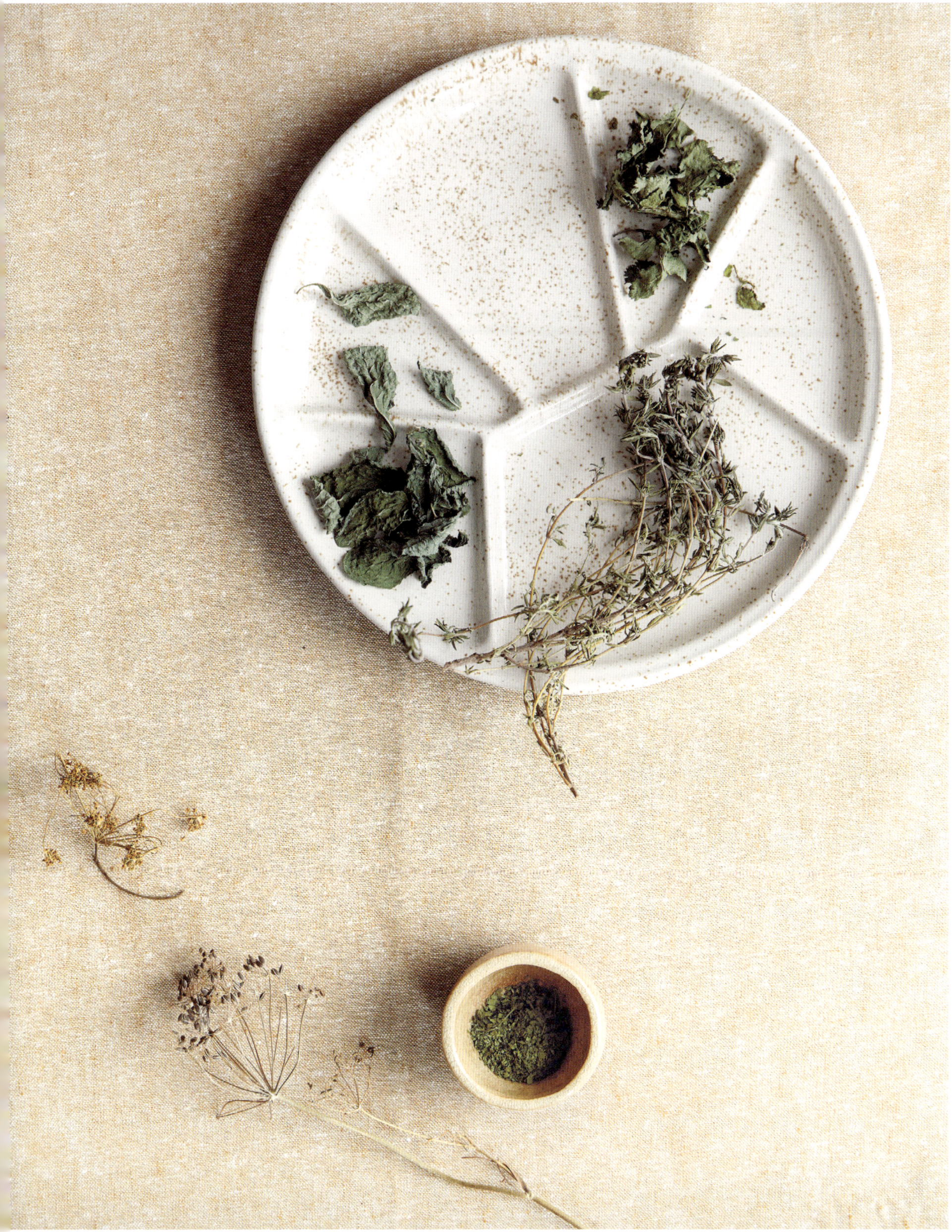

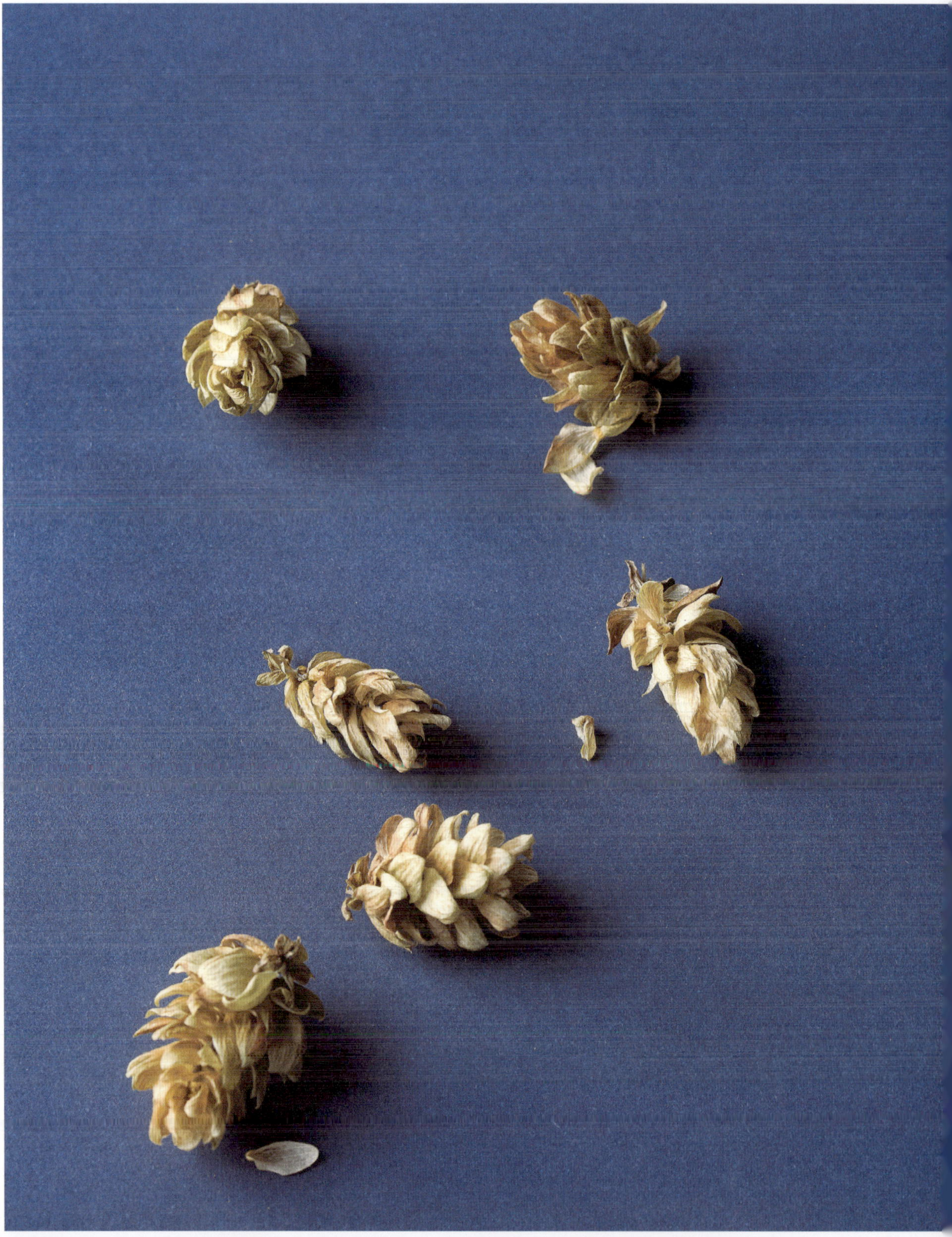

Dried hops

Hops can be found growing wild in hedgerows, marshes or even at the end of gardens. They can be infused in hot water to make herbal tea which helps alleviate sleeping problems: just add 1 tablespoon of dried hop flowers to a teapot, cover with 250ml/9fl oz boiling water, and let it steep for 15 minutes. Of course, the primary use of hops is in the production of beer, or mead below.

Prep 10 minutes
Dry 6–7 days

Bowl of hop flowers (seed cones)

Method 1
— Line a tray or any flat dish with clean paper. Place the hop flowers in a single layer on top.
— Keep in a warm and airy place, away from direct sunlight.
— Turn them over and move them frequently.
— They should be dry after 6–7 days.

Method 2
— Alternatively, line dehydrator trays with baking parchment. Place the hop cones in a single layer on the lined trays and dry over a low heat, uncovered for about 6–7 hours P170-1.
— Store in an airtight container for up to 1 year.

Hoppy mead

Honey was available long before sugar and used in the earliest fermented alcoholic drinks. Although honey has antimicrobial properties, once it is diluted with water it ferments nicely. Many spices have been used to make mead, and dried hops above give a good balance to any sweetness.

Makes about 3 litres/5¼ pints

3 litres/5¼ pints/3 quarts water
1kg/2¼lb/3½ cups honey
30g/1oz hops above
80g/3oz/½ cup raisins, chopped
1 tsp yeast

— Bring the water and honey to the boil in a saucepan and boil for 20 minutes. Add the hops and boil for a further 30 minutes.
— Leave to cool to just above room temperature, about 20–25°C/68–77°F; any higher and the yeast will be damaged.
— Add the raisins and yeast and pour the mixture into a sterilised demijohn P12 and fit an airlock.

— Keep at room temperature until fermentation ceases. This could be up to a month depending on the yeast and temperature.
— Decant into a fresh sterilised demijohn or wine bottles leaving as much of the sediment behind as possible.
— Leave to mature for about 6 months or shorter if patience expires.

Dried linden and elderflowers

The herbal teas you can make with these dried botanicals not only have a great flavour, but also have medicinal properties. If you're worried about any specific condition, however, consult a doctor before drinking these infusions.

Prep 10 minutes
Dry about 1 week

Bowl of linden flowers (also known as lime, but not the same as the citrus) and elderflowers. Linden trees and elder trees can be found in parks, marshes and forests and are easy to forage. They should be picked when they start to blossom (elderflowers on a dry day in April or May; linden flowers in mid-June). The whole heads and blossom, with all the papery leafy bits, should be picked and dried. It is best to avoid plants growing near roads due to pollution.

— Tie the flowers together with string and hang in a shaded, warm and airy place for a few days.
— Alternatively, spread the flowers out on paper-lined trays and keep in a dry, warm and airy place.
— Move and turn the flowers a couple of times a day.
— The drying time depends on the humidity of the air and the temperature, but it should take about 7 days.
— The drying process can be sped up by using a dehydrator. Line dehydrator trays with baking parchment. Place the flowers in a single layer on the lined trays and dry over a low heat for about 6 hours, or until dry.
— Once dry (crunchy, easily breakable) store them in an airtight container in a dark place for up to a year.

Linden and elderflower tea

Both elderflower and linden flower teas are good for colds. Linden also has other properties: it has a calming effect and can be a digestive aid. It is important not to drink more than three cups of linden or elderflower tea a day.

Makes 1 cup

1 tbsp dried linden flowers or elderflowers above
250ml/9fl oz/generous 1 cup hot water
1 tsp raw honey (optional)

— Place the linden flowers or elderflowers in a tea infuser, directly in a cup (strain before drinking) or in a teapot.
— Pour over the boiling water, cover with a lid and leave to infuse for 10 minutes for the elderflowers or 10–20 minutes for the linden flowers.
— Drink the tea by itself or leave it to cool a little and add honey, to taste.

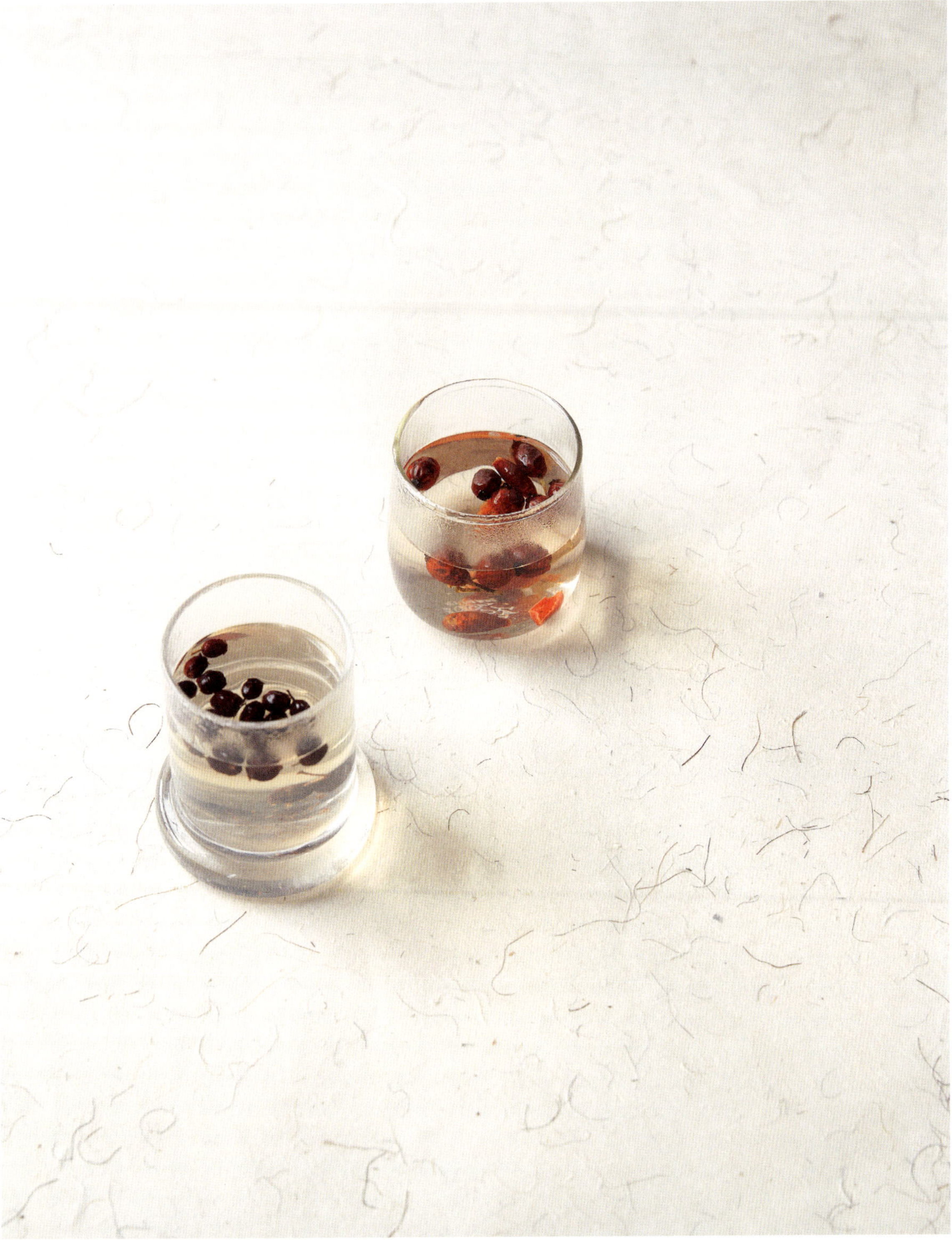

Dried rosehip and hawthorn

Rosehip and hawthorn can be found in hedgerows, but are often overlooked. It's a pity as they make good wine and are great added to apple jelly. They can also be dried to make tea. Both have medicinal properties (consult a doctor if worried, particularly if using heart medication). Hawthorn is used to treat heart conditions, regulate blood pressure, aid the digestive system and relieve anxiety. Rosehip is an excellent source of vitamin C. It contains 50% more vitamin C than lemons or oranges.

Prep 10 minutes
Dry about 1-3 weeks or 4 hours

500g / 1lb 2oz rosehips or hawthorn berries, ripe but firm

When dried they should not change colour, if they look burnt discard them.

Store in an airtight container for up to a year. Avoid metal containers, as metal might react with the fruit acids.

Method 1
— Wash, dry and cut off any stalks. If you prefer, cut each rosehip in half and remove the pips.
— Place in a single layer on trays covered with clean paper or newspaper.
— Dry in a shaded warm, airy place for about 1-3 weeks.
— Check for soft berries, they might start to rot; if they do then discard.
— Remove the dry berries and continue drying until all the berries and rosehips are ready. They should not be elastic or bendy.

Method 2
— The drying process can be speeded up by using a dehydrator or domestic oven P170-1. When drying rosehips in the oven it is important to start off with a higher temperature and slowly lower the temperature to limit the loss of the vitamin C.
— Preheat the oven to 90°C/194°F/ lowest gas mark. Place the rosehips on a baking tray in a single layer and dry in the oven with the door ajar.
— Lower the temperature every 10-20 minutes by 10 degrees until 50°C/122°F is reached and continue drying. Rosehips should be dry after about 4 hours.

Rosehip or hawthorn tea

Makes 1 cup

1 tbsp dried rosehips or hawthorns above
250ml / 9fl oz boiling water
1-2 tsp honey (optional)

Method 1
— Place the rosehips or hawthorns in a cup or teapot and add the boiling water. Cover with a lid and leave to infuse for 10-20 minutes.
— Strain or pour into a cup and add honey, if you like.

Method 2
— Place 2 tablespoons dried rosehips in a medium saucepan, cover with 1 litre / 34fl oz cold water and soak for 12 hours, or overnight.
— Bring to the boil, then reduce the heat and simmer for 10-15 minutes.
— Strain and drink by itself or with honey, if you like.

Dried mint or lemon balm

Prep 10 minutes
Dry about 6-7 days or 6-7 hours

Bunch of mint or lemon balm, stalks removed

Method 1
— Place the mint or lemon balm leaves in a single layer on trays covered with clean paper.
— Keep in a warm, airy place away from direct sunlight.
— Turn them over a couple of times a day. They should have dried after 6-7 days.

Method 2
— Line dehydrator trays with baking parchment. Place the mint or lemon balm leaves in a single layer on the lined dehydrator trays and dry over a low heat, uncovered for about 6-7 hours P170-1.
— The dried herbs should crumble easily but should not turn into a powder. Store in an airtight container for up to 1 year.

Mint or lemon balm teas

Mint tea can aid digestion and lemon balm (also known as melissa) has relaxing properties. Both can be drunk on their own or mixed with other herbs, seeds or flowers. They can be mixed with dried linden flowers or elderflowers P222 in the following proportion: 1 part dried mint or lemon balm with 4 parts dried linden flower or elderflower. They can also be mixed with green tea or fennel seeds. Mint, yarrow and elderflower is a classic cold mix which has been used for centuries: mint for its decongesting action, yarrow for its diaphoretic action (makes you sweat) and elderflower for its anti-catarrhal action.

Makes 1 cup

1-1 ½ tsp mint or lemon balm above
250ml/9fl oz/generous 1 cup boiling water
1 tsp honey (optional)

— Place the dried mint or lemon balm in a cup or teapot.
— Add the with boiling water, cover with a lid and infuse for 10 minutes.
— Strain and drink by itself or with honey, if you like.

Both lemon balm and mint can be used as herbs in cooking.

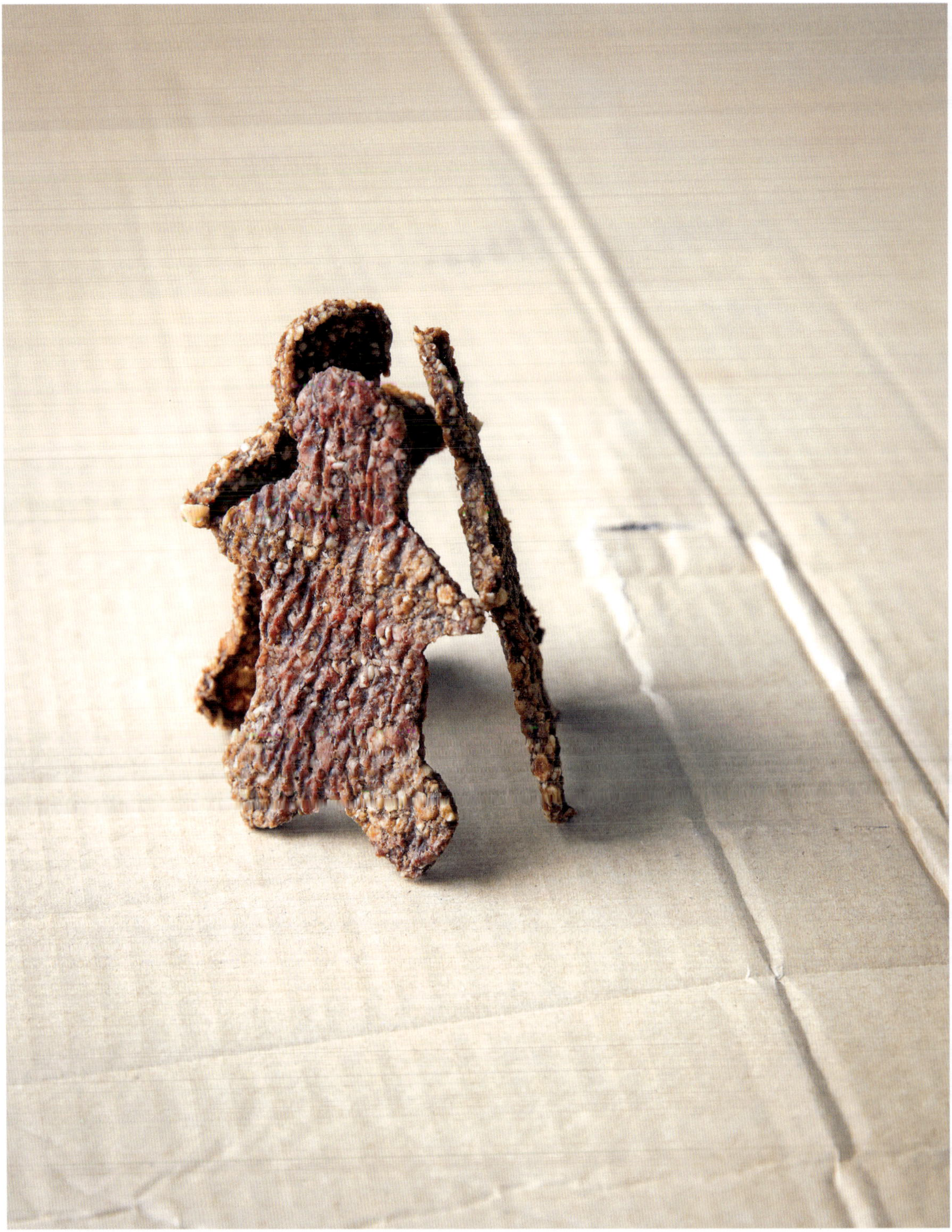

Gingerbread crackers

These are a great alternative to sugary gingerbread biscuits. There's no added sugar: the sweetness comes from the banana, apple and pumpkin.

Prep 25 minutes + 1–24 hours soaking
Dry about 6–7 hours

120g/4oz/1 cup mixed nuts such as walnuts, hazelnuts, cashew nuts, soaked in warm water for 1–24 hours
50g/1¾oz/scant ½ cup sunflower seeds, soaked in warm water for 1–24 hours or sprouted
2 apples peeled, grated, juice squeezed out
50g/1¾oz pumpkin, peeled, deseeded and grated
1 banana, peeled and sliced
3 heaped tbsp ground almonds
1 tsp ground nutmeg
1 tsp ground ginger
½ tsp ground allspice
½ tsp ground coriander
1 tsp mixed spice
1 tsp fresh grated ginger
1 tbsp lemon juice
½ tsp salt
Pinch of ground black pepper

— Line dehydrator trays with baking parchment.
— Chop the mixed nuts and sunflower seeds into small pieces in a blender or food processor, then place in a bowl.
— Blitz the apples, pumpkin, banana, ground almonds, spices and lemon juice in a blender or food processor to a smooth paste. Add to the bowl and mix together. Season with the salt and black pepper.
— Place the mixture on the lined dehydrator trays.
— When spreading on the trays make sure it is pressed down firmly and between 3 and 4mm/⅛in thick.
— It can be spread as a single sheet with indented cutting lines or cut with a cookie cutter.
— Dry for 6–7 hours P170-1.
— Store in an airtight container for up to 4 weeks.

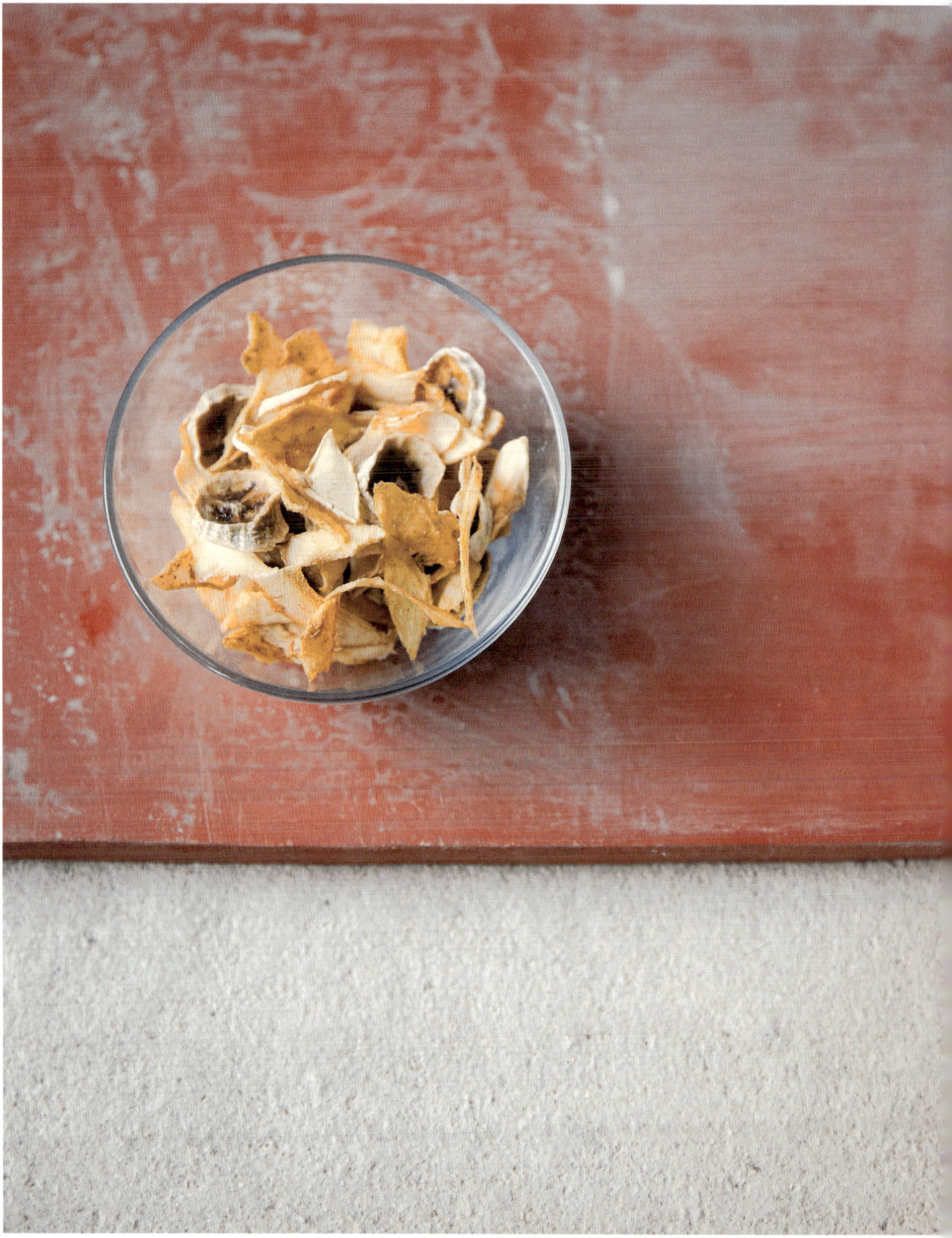

Banana, apple and pear crisps

These tend not to hang around for long, but in theory they can be stored in an airtight container for a month.

Prep 10 minutes
Dry about 6–7 hours

1 large banana, peeled and thinly sliced
1½ tsp ground cinnamon or 1½ tsp ground mixed spice
225ml/8fl oz/1 cup water
Juice of 1 lemon
1 large apple, peeled, cored and thinly sliced
1 large pear, peeled, cored and thinly sliced

— Place the sliced banana in a single layer on a dehydrator tray and sprinkle with ½ teaspoon cinnamon.
— Mix the water and half the lemon together in a bowl. Dip in the sliced apple, then drain and sprinkle with ½ teaspoon cinnamon (or mixed spice).
— Repeat with the pear.
— Dry for about 6–7 hours P170-1, or until the pieces are crisp.
— Store in an airtight container for up to 4 weeks.

Dried soft fruit

Some fruits like cranberries, figs and apricots can become too hard when dehydrated, so we find they benefit from a quick boil in a water and sugar solution before drying.

Dried cranberries

Prep 10 minutes
Dry about 6-8 hours

300ml/10fl oz/1¼ cups water
150g/5½oz/¾ cup sugar
5 cloves
300g/10½oz/3 cups cranberries

— Bring the water to the boil with the sugar and cloves in a saucepan.
— Add the cranberries to the pan, return to the boil and boil for 2 minutes, or until the cranberries start to crack. Drain.
— Spread out in a single layer on dehydrator trays and dry for about 6-8 hours P170-1, or until dry.
— Store in an airtight container for up to 3 months.

Dried figs

Prep 10 minutes
Dry about 36 hours

20 fresh ripe figs
500ml/18fl oz/2 cups water
1 tbsp sugar

— Trim the tails from the figs, then place in a single layer on dehydrator trays and dry for 12 hours P170-1.
— Bring the water and sugar to the boil in a medium saucepan, stirring until the sugar has dissolved.
— Add the figs to the syrup and boil for 1 minute.
— Drain and place the figs back on the dehydrator trays and dry for a further 24 hours, or until dry.
— Store in an airtight container for up to 3 months.

Dried apricots

Prep 10 minutes
Dry about 36 hours

1kg/2¼lb fresh ripe apricots
500ml/18fl oz/2 cups water
1 tbsp sugar

— Using a sharp knife, make a cut on the side of each apricot, being careful not to cut all the way through, and remove the stones.
— Place the apricots in a single layer on dehydrators trays and dry for 12 hours P170-1.
— Bring the water and sugar to the boil in a saucepan, stirring until the sugar has dissolved. Add the apricots to the syrup and boil for 1 minute.
— Drain and place the apricots back on dehydrator trays and dry for a further 24 hours, or until dry.
— Store in an airtight container for up to 3 months.

Dried grapes

Seedless grapes are best here, but you can dry any grapes.

You can eat grapes at different stages of dryness, but if you want to keep them longer than a few days, it's best to dry them completely.

Prep 10 minutes
Dry about 24 hours

500g/1lb 2oz white or red grapes

— Place the grapes in a single layer on dehydrator tray and dry for 24 hours P170-1.
— Store in an airtight container for up to 3 months.

Nutty fruit bar

This is a real energy boost and brings together the dried fruit P230 in a chewy, moreish bar – it makes a fine treat in a lunchbox.

Makes about 8 bars

100g/3½oz/1 cup walnuts, roughly chopped
100g/3½oz/⅔ cup hazelnuts, roughly chopped
100g/3½oz/⅔ cup cashew nuts, roughly chopped
100g/3½oz/½ cup dried apricots, chopped P231
100g/3½oz/⅔ cup dried cranberries P230
100g/3½oz dried grapes, chopped P231
½ tsp ground nutmeg
½ tsp ground cloves
½ tsp ground coriander
½ tsp ground cinnamon
Pinch of freshly ground black pepper
100g/3½oz/¾ cup wholewheat flour
100g/3½oz/⅓ cup honey
100g/3½oz/½ cup brown sugar

— Preheat the oven to 200°C/400°F/gas mark 6. Line a small baking tray with baking parchment.
— Heat a large frying pan, add the nuts and dry-toast until they start to turn brown. Remove the frying pan from the heat immediately to prevent them burning.
— Mix the nuts, dried fruit, spices and flour together in a large bowl.
— Mix the honey and sugar together in a small saucepan and cook over a low heat until the sugar dissolves.
— Pour over the nut and fruit mixture, then spread out evenly over the lined baking tray, pressing down hard.
— Bake for 20–30 minutes, then remove from the oven and cut into desired shapes.
— Store in an airtight container for up to a week.

Dried apricots P231
Dried cranberries P230
Dried grapes P231
Nutty fruit bar

Candied beetroot P236
Spiced candied pumpkin
Candied granola P236

Spiced candied pumpkin

This recipe is a great way to use up pumpkin or butternut squash. These delicious cubes can be dipped in chocolate (a match for praline any day) or they can be used to spice up granola P236, muesli and cakes.

Prep 40 minutes
Dry 10–16 hours + 8-day process

450ml/15fl oz/2 cups water
100ml/3½fl oz/scant ½ cup distilled spirit vinegar 10%
300g/10oz pumpkin, peeled and cut into 2cm/¾in cubes

Syrup
350ml/12fl oz/1½ cups water
350g/12oz/1¾ cups sugar
1 cinnamon stick
6 cloves
½ tsp dried chilli flakes
3 star anise

Day 1
— Bring the water and vinegar to the boil in a saucepan. Add the pumpkin and boil for 4–5 minutes, then drain and place in a sterilised 500ml/18fl oz jar P12.
— To make the syrup, mix the water, 100g/3½oz/½ cup of the sugar, the cinnamon, cloves, chilli flakes and star anise in a saucepan. Bring to the boil and stir constantly for 4 minutes.
— Pour the syrup over the pumpkin and leave for 24 hours.

Day 2
— Strain the syrup from the pumpkin into a small saucepan.
— Add the 50g/1¾oz/¼ cup of the remaining sugar. Bring to the boil and stir constantly for 4 minutes.
— Pour the syrup over the pumpkin and leave for 24 hours.
— Repeat each day for the next 4 days until all of the 350g/12oz/1¾ cups sugar is used up.

Day 7
— Remove the pumpkin from the syrup and place around the edge of a plate or in a single layer in a sieve over a bowl and leave to drain for 2 hours.
— Once drained, place the pumpkin pieces on dehydrator trays and dry for about 10–16 hours P170-1 until touch-dry.
— Turn off the dehydrator after 10 hours and let the pumpkin pieces cool, then check for dryness – warm, candied fruit and vegetables remain sticky. Drying time will vary depending on the size of the pumpkin pieces.
— Store in a jar or other airtight container. Well-dried candied pumpkin will keep for up to 2 months.

This recipe can be made spicy by replacing a proportion of the pumpkin with the same quantity of cubed ginger.

Candied beetroot

These are great for those who like something sweet but unusual flavours. Add to the granola below.

Prep 30 minutes
Dry about 10-16 hours

300g/10½oz beetroot (beet), peeled and cut into 1-1.5cm/½-⅝in cubes
50g/1¾oz/scant ½ cup icing (confectioners') sugar

Syrup
300ml/10fl oz/1¼ cups water
150g/5½oz/¾ cup sugar
½ tsp salt
½ tsp dried chilli flakes
½ tsp celery seeds
6 black peppercorns
6 cloves

— Mix all the syrup ingredients together in a saucepan and bring to the boil.
— Add the beetroot and boil for about 15 minutes.
— Drain the beetroot and toss the pieces into the icing sugar.
— Spread out on dehydrator trays and dry for 10-16 hours P170-1.
— Turn off the dehydrator after 10 hours and let the beetroot pieces cool, then check for dryness – warm, candied fruit and vegetables remain sticky. Drying time will vary depending on the size of the beetroot pieces.
— Store in a jar or other airtight container. Well-dried candied beetroot will keep for up to 3 months.

Candied granola

Dried candied beetroot and pumpkin turn this granola into a bounty of moreish (not-so-healthy) morsels.

Serves 5

200g/7oz/1⅓ cups mixed roasted hazelnuts, walnuts and almonds
100g/3½oz/⅔ cup rolled spelt and/or rye flakes
100g/3½oz/⅔ cup rolled oat flakes
3 tbsp honey
2 tbsp rice bran oil
1 tsp lemon juice
3 tbsp fermented pumpkin syrup P28, or golden syrup, honey or date syrup
50g/1¾oz/⅓ cup raisins
50g/1¾oz/⅓ cup dried cranberries P230
50g/1¾oz spiced candied pumpkin, cut into smaller pieces P235
30g/1oz candied beetroot above

— Preheat the oven to 180°C/350°F/gas mark 4.
— Spread the nuts out in a single layer on a baking tray and roast in the oven for about 4 minutes, checking and shaking or turning frequently. Once they start to turn brown remove them from the oven and immediately transfer them to a plate to prevent burning.
— Increase the oven temperature to 230°C/450°F/gas mark 8.
— Mix the spelt, rye, oat flakes, honey, rice bran oil, lemon juice and syrup together in a bowl.
— Spread the oat, rye and spelt mixture evenly out on a baking tray and bake in the oven for about 10 more minutes.
— Add the nuts, raisins, cranberries, spiced candied pumpkin and candied dried beetroot and mix well.
— Store in a jar or other airtight container. Well-dried granola will keep for up to a month.

Always use unwaxed oranges. It's best to buy oranges with a thick skin, but if you can only get unwaxed oranges with a thin skin they will work too.

Orange peel can be collected over 2-3 days. Simply keep it in a plastic container in the fridge until you have enough to make a portion.

Candied orange peel

The bittersweet flavour of candied orange peel is a classic way to liven up cakes. We like it best when used in sweet breads such as challah. It doesn't take long to make and is far superior to the glucose-heavy commercial varieties. Dip in chocolate to make even better P238.

Prep 3 hour
Dry 4-6 hours

300g/10½oz orange peel
400ml/14fl oz/1¾ cups water
300g/10½oz/1½ cups sugar
1 cinnamon stick
4 cloves

— Place the orange peel in a saucepan and pour in enough water to cover. Bring to the boil and drain, then return to the pan. This step can be omitted if a bitter flavour is desired.
— Add the measured water to the orange peel in the pan and bring to the boil. Reduce the heat and simmer for 15 minutes, or until the peel is soft. Drain and reserve the water to make the syrup.
— Mix the reserved water with the sugar, cinnamon and cloves in a medium saucepan. Bring to the boil and stir until the sugar has dissolved.
— Cut the softened peel into narrow strips or small squares. We like to slice it into long strips about 1cm/½in wide.
— Add the orange peel to the boiling syrup and return to the boil. Take off the heat and leave to cool.
— Once cool, return to the heat and bring to the boil again.
— Repeat the last 2 steps several times until all the water has evaporated.
— Place the peel on dehydrator trays in a single layer and dry for about 4-6 hours P170-1, or until touch dry.
— Store in an airtight container for up to 2 months.

Candied orange peel and spiced pumpkin dipped in chocolate

Dried candied orange and pumpkin that's been dipped in chocolate is a great accompaniment to strong coffee. Placed in an elegant box or a nice tin it can make a lovely alternative present to a box of chocolates. Use good-quality dark chocolate for this recipe – it will make a huge difference.

Makes 1 jar

½ bar of good-quality dark chocolate (at least 70% cocoa solids), broken into pieces
Spiced candied pumpkin P235, or dried kiwi P240, pear, ginger or any other fruit can also be used
Dried candied orange peel P237

— Melt the chocolate in a heatproof bowl set over a pan of simmering water. Make sure the base of the bowl doesn't touch the water.
— Pour the melted chocolate into a small narrow glass or cup, then carefully dip each piece of pumpkin and peel halfway into the chocolate.
— Place each chocolate-coated pieces on to a flat ceramic, metal or plastic tray and leave to set. To speed up this process the trays can be placed for a few minutes in the freezer.
— Once set, carefully remove the fruit from the trays, using a wide knife to prise them off the surface.
— Store in an airtight container for up to a month.

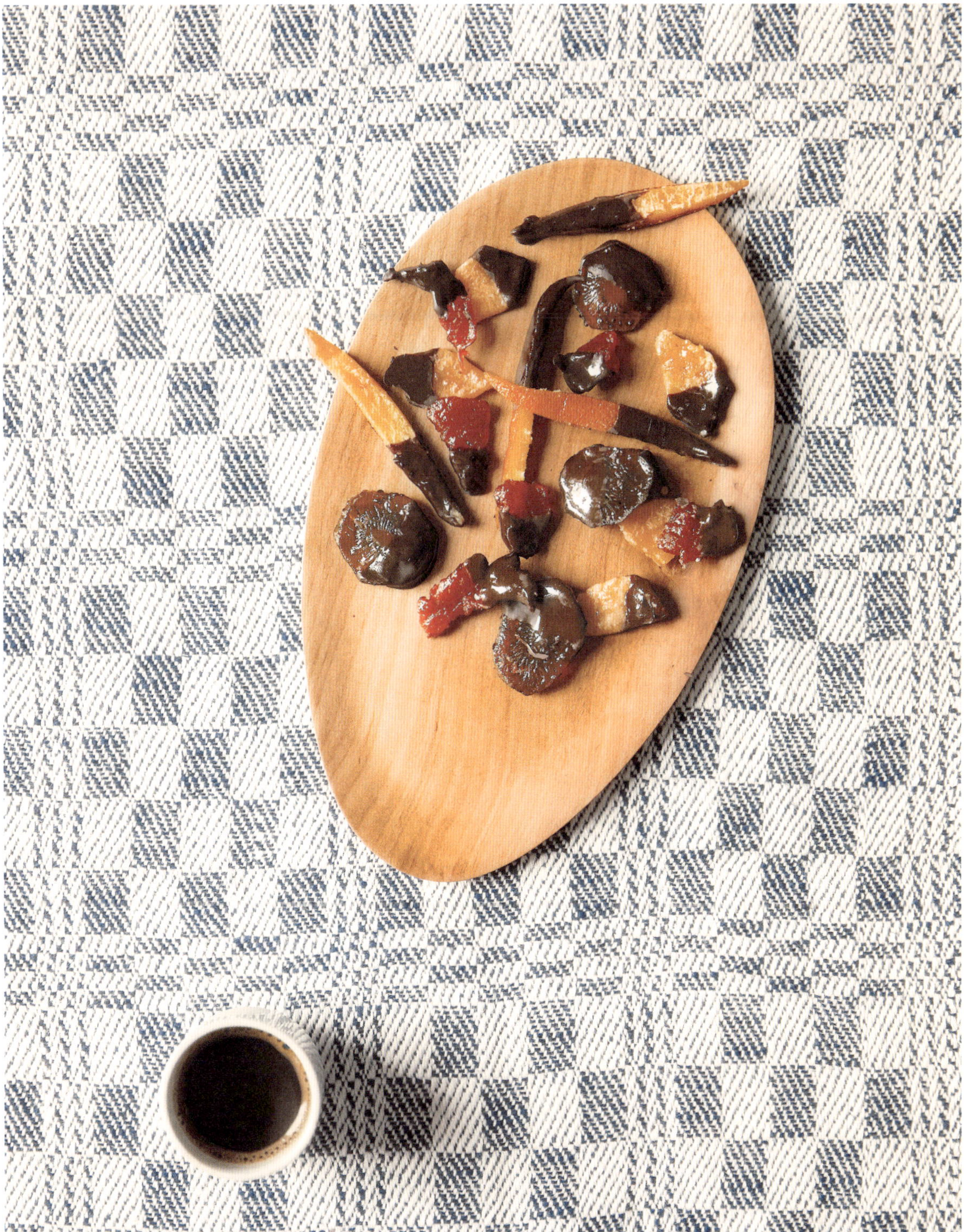

Dried candied kiwi

We love the flavour and chewy texture of dried kiwi. The beauty of this recipe is that you can use the remaining syrup to pour over pancakes. The method used to dry the kiwi in this recipe is also suitable for different fruit and roots, such as watermelon, ginger and pear, as well as cherries and cranberries. Once dry, try dipping in chocolate P238.

Prep 1 hour + 6-day process
Dry 8-16 hours

100ml/3½fl oz/scant ½ cup water
Juice of ½ lemon
300g/10½oz kiwi (or other soft fruit), peeled and sliced

Syrup
300ml/10fl oz/1¼ cups water
300g/10½oz/1½ cups sugar
1 star anise (optional)
1 cinnamon stick (optional)
6 cloves (optional)

The quantities of fruit can be changed, but it's important to keep the proportions of water, sugar and fruit equal: 1:1:1 (eg. 100ml/3½fl oz/scant 1½ cup water, 100g/3½oz fruit, 100g/3½oz/½ cup sugar).

Day 1
— Mix the water and lemon juice together in a bowl.
— Dip the sliced fruit in the lemon water, then drain.
— To prepare the syrup, mix the water with 100g/3½oz/½ cup of the sugar and spices (if using; we prefer to use the spices just for the candied pears) in a medium saucepan and bring to the boil.
— Place the sliced fruit in the boiling syrup, reduce the heat and simmer for 4 minutes, then transfer to a 500ml/18fl oz sterilised jar P12 and leave for 24 hours.

Day 2
— Strain the syrup from the fruit into a small saucepan.
— Return the fruit to the jar.
— Add 50g/1¾oz/¼ cup of the sugar to the syrup, then bring to the boil. Stir constantly for 4 minutes. Pour the syrup over the fruit and leave for 24 hours.
— Repeat for next 3 days until you use up all the 300g/10½oz/1½ cups sugar.

Day 6
— Place the fruit and the syrup in a medium saucepan and bring to the boil.
— Remove the fruit from the syrup and place around the edge of a plate or in a single layer in a sieve over a bowl and leave to drain for 1 hour.
— Once drained place the fruit pieces on dehydrator trays and dry for 8-16 hours P170-1, or until touch-dry. Store in an airtight container for a month.

Dried candied watermelon
Dried candied pear
Dried candied kiwi
Dried candied ginger

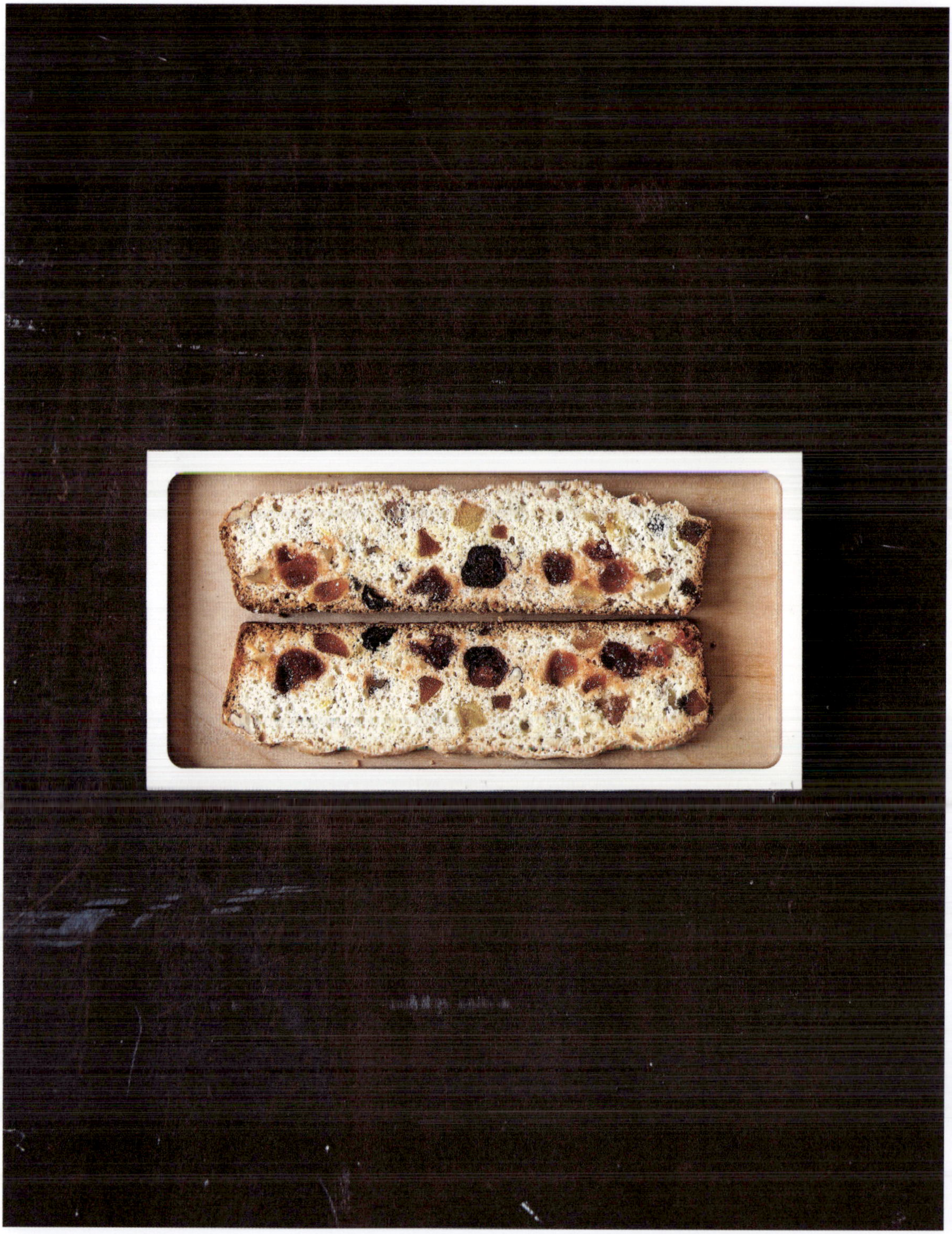

Cwibak

This Polish sweet loaf (pronounced 'chvi-back') is reminiscent of Italian biscotti and is great with coffee or toasted as an indulgent alternative to traditional English teacake.

Makes 450g/1lb cake

7 eggs
About 450g/1lb cups sugar
About 400g/14oz cups plain (all-purpose) flour, plus extra for dusting
About 225g/8oz/1½ cups mixed nuts including walnuts and pecans and/or hazelnuts and almonds, chopped into raisin-sized pieces
40g/1½oz/¼ cup raisins
40g/1½oz/¼ cup dried cranberries P230
50g/1¾oz dried figs/apricots/dates, cut into raisin sized pieces P231
About 220g/7½oz mixed dried candied fruit, raisins, dried soft fruit including a choice of dried candied kiwi, watermelon, pear, pumpkin, ginger, cut into raisin-sized pieces P240 and dried candied orange peel, cut into raisin-sized pieces P237

— Preheat the oven to 180°C/350°F/gas mark 4. Line two 450g/1lb loaf tins with baking parchment.
— Weigh 7 eggs and write down the weight.
— Weigh 6 eggs and write down the weight.
— Weigh the sugar. You will need the same weight as that of 7 eggs.
— Weigh the flour. You will need the same weight as that of 6 eggs.
— Weigh the mixed nuts, raisins, dried fruit and dried candied fruit and peel. You will need the same weight as that of 7 eggs.
— Prepare all the fruit by coating them in a little flour.
— Divide 6 egg whites and yolks.
— Mix 1 egg yolk and egg white with 6 egg yolks and most of the sugar (approx ⅘) in a large bowl until creamy and all the sugar has dissolved. It is best to use a blender, electric mixer with beaters or a balloon whisk.
— Beat the egg whites, gradually adding the remaining sugar.
— Gently add the fruit, nuts, almonds and flour to the egg yolk mixture, mixing carefully.
— Very gently add the egg whites into the egg yolk, flour, fruit and nut mixture. Mix it delicately, being careful not to overmix.
— Place the mixture into the prepared loaf tins and bake for 30–50 minutes until dry on the inside and light brown on the outside.
— To check if the cake is baked insert a cocktail stick, skewer or toothpick into the middle of the cake. If it comes out with some wet batter, crumbs or stickiness on it, the cake needs to bake for a little longer. If it is dry, then the cake is done.
— Leave to cool in the tins, then remove from the tins and serve. Wrap in foil and store in a container for up to a month.

If you do not have all the different candied fruit and dried fruit and nuts simply increase the amount of what you have at hand to reach the required weight.

A tip for beating the egg whites: use a large, deep bowl (a glass or copper bowl is best). Set the bowl of egg whites over a pan of warm water. It is best to begin at a slow speed and gradually speed up. Once the egg whites are white and opaque gradually add the sugar.

It is ready when the egg whites become fluffy and form stiff peaks. Stop at this stage – if you overbeat them, they will liquefy again. Use the beaten egg whites straight away. Do not let them sit.

Cranberry leather

Prep 15 minutes
Dry about 6–8 hours

300ml/10fl oz/1¼ cups water
150g/5½oz/¾ cup sugar
5 cloves
300g/10½oz/3 cups cranberries

— Line a dehydrator tray with baking parchment.
— Put the water into a saucepan, add the sugar and cloves and bring to the boil. Add the cranberries and return to the boil. Boil for 5 minutes until all the cranberries have cracked and the mixture is starting to go mushy. Drain, then mash with a fork.
— Spread the paste in a thin layer on the lined dehydrator tray and dry for about 6–8 hours P170-1, or until dry.
— Once the mixture is dry enough to peel from the baking paper, remove the paper. At this stage you can roll up the leather and continue drying for another hour if you like the leather harder.
— Store in an airtight container for up to a month.

Mango and chilli leather

Prep 10 minutes
Dry about 6–8 hours

1 large ripe mango, peeled and stoned
½–1 tsp dried chilli flakes

— Line a dehydrator tray with baking parchment.
— Place the mango in a bowl and mash with a fork or mix with a handheld blender to a paste.
— Mix the paste with the chilli flakes.
— Spread the paste in a thin layer on the lined dehydrator tray and dry for about 6–8 hours P170-1, or until dry.
— Once the mixture is dry enough to peel from the baking paper, remove the paper. At this stage you can roll up the leather and continue drying for another hour if you like the leather harder.
— Store in an airtight container for up to a month.

Fruit leather is a great additive-free sweet snack and is a good method of using up excess fruit. It can be served cut into strips, while thin curls are very good for decorating cakes.

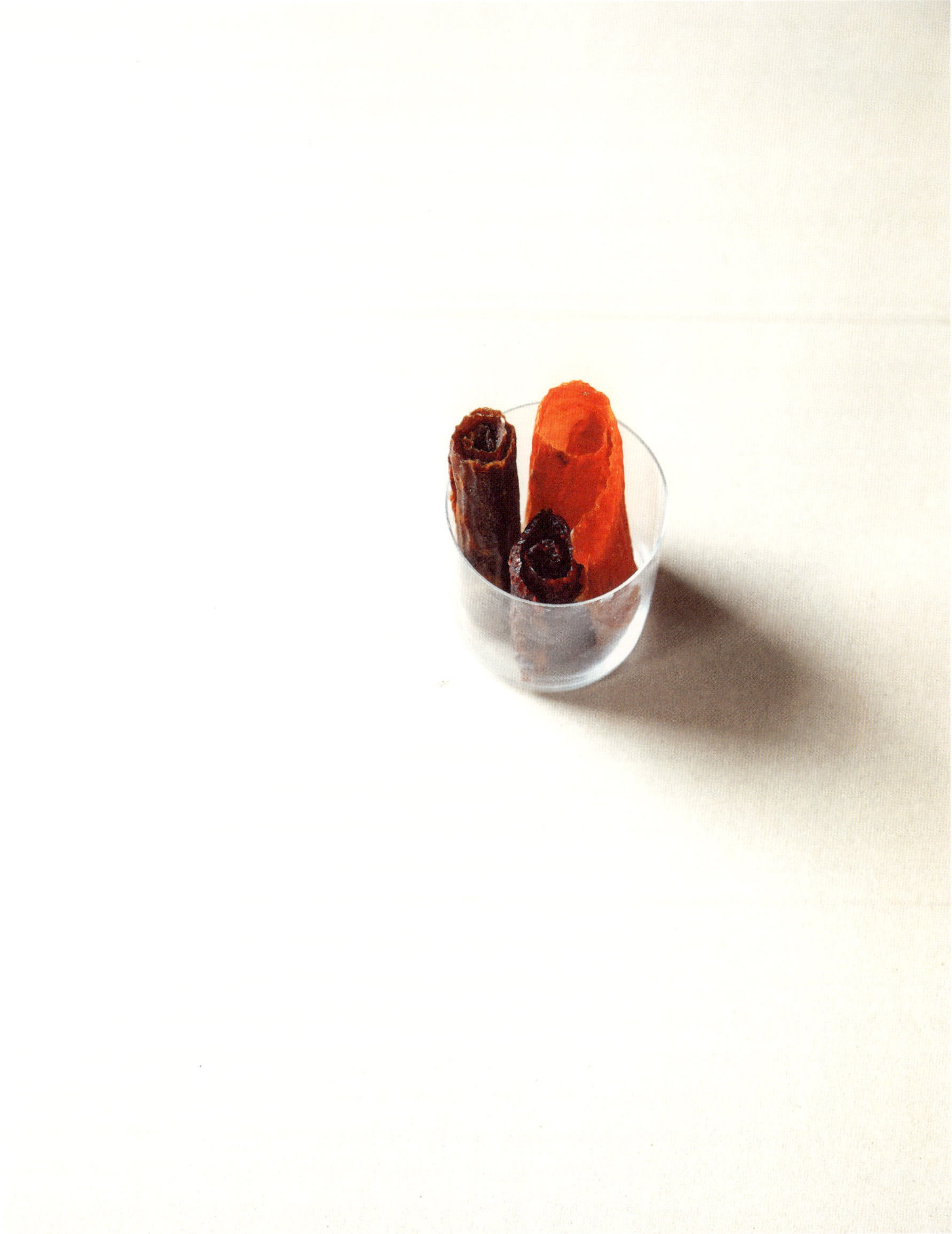

Spiced apple and banana leather

Prep 20 minutes
Dry about 6-8 hours

4 large cooking or dessert apples, peeled, cored and cut into slices
Juice of ½ lemon
1 banana
1 tsp ground cinnamon
1 tsp ground ginger

— Preheat the oven to 230°C/450°F/gas mark 8. Line a dehydrator tray with baking parchment.
— Place the apple slices in a bowl and pour over the lemon juice. Mix together well, then transfer to a small baking dish and bake, covered, for about 10 minutes.
— Blitz the apples, banana and spices in a blender or food processor until to a paste.
— Spread the paste in a thin layer on the lined dehydrator tray and dry for about 6-8 hours P170-1, or until dry.
— Once the mixture is dry enough to peel from the baking paper, remove the paper. At this stage you can roll up the leather and continue drying for another hour if you like the leather harder.
— Store in an airtight container for up to a month.

Dried candied plums

One of the best varieties for this is the Polish plum Wegierka which appear in Eastern European shops at the end of summer. The Victoria plum is a capable alternative, but any variety could be given a try.

Prep 1 hour + 6-day process
Dry about 8–16 hours

300g/10½oz plums
100ml/3½fl oz/scant ½ cup water
Juice of ½ lemon

Syrup
300ml/10fl oz/1¼ cups water
300g/10½oz/1½ cups sugar
1 star anise (optional)
1 cinnamon stick (optional)
6 cloves (optional)

Day 1
— To prepare the plums, using a sharp knife, make a cut on one side of the plum, being careful not to cut in half and remove the stones.
— Mix the water and lemon juice together in a bowl.
— Dip the plums in the lemon water, then drain.
— To make the syrup, add the water to a medium saucepan. Add 100g/3½oz/½ cup of the sugar and the spices (if using; we prefer to use the spices just for the candied pears) and bring to the boil.
— Place the plums in the boiling syrup, then reduce the heat and simmer for 4 minutes.
— Pour the plums and syrup in a sterilised 500ml/18fl oz jar P12 and leave for 24 hours.

Day 2
— Strain the syrup from the fruit into a small saucepan.
— Return the plums to the jar.
— Add 50g/1¾oz/¼ cup of the sugar to the syrup and bring to the boil. Stir constantly for 4 minutes.
— Pour the syrup over the fruit and leave for 24 hours.
— Repeat each day for the next 3 days until you use up all the 300g/10½oz/1½ cups sugar.

Day 6
— Remove the fruit from the syrup and place around the edge of a plate or in a single layer in a sieve over a bowl and leave for 1 hour to drain.
— Once drained, place the fruit pieces on dehydrator trays and dry for 8–16 hours P170-1, until touch dry.
— Store in an airtight container for up to 3 months.

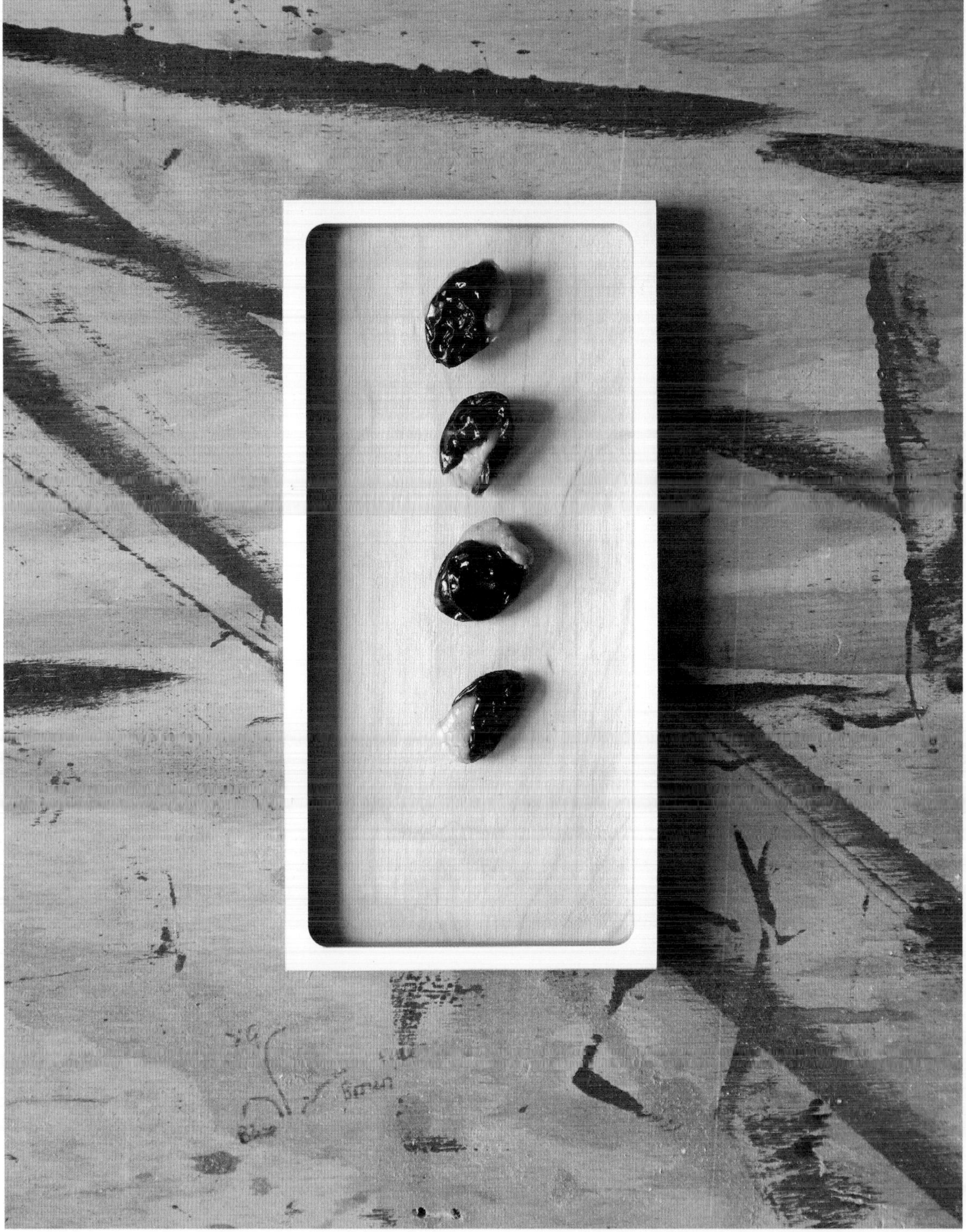

Dried plum and walnut bites

This recipe is inspired by a delicious sweet bite made by Gaba's great aunt Babcia Koko. Unfortunately she did not leave the recipe, so it had to be recreated with the help of family.

Makes about 20 bites

40g/1½oz/scant ½ cup walnuts, finely chopped or roughly ground
55g/2oz/¼ cup sugar
1–2 tbsp water
Portion of dried candied plums (about 20) P247

— Mix the walnuts, sugar and water together in a small saucepan, then heat gently, stirring constantly until the sugar has dissolved and the mixture has thickened.
— Fill each plum with 1 teaspoon of the walnut paste.
— They can be stored in an airtight container for up to 2 weeks.

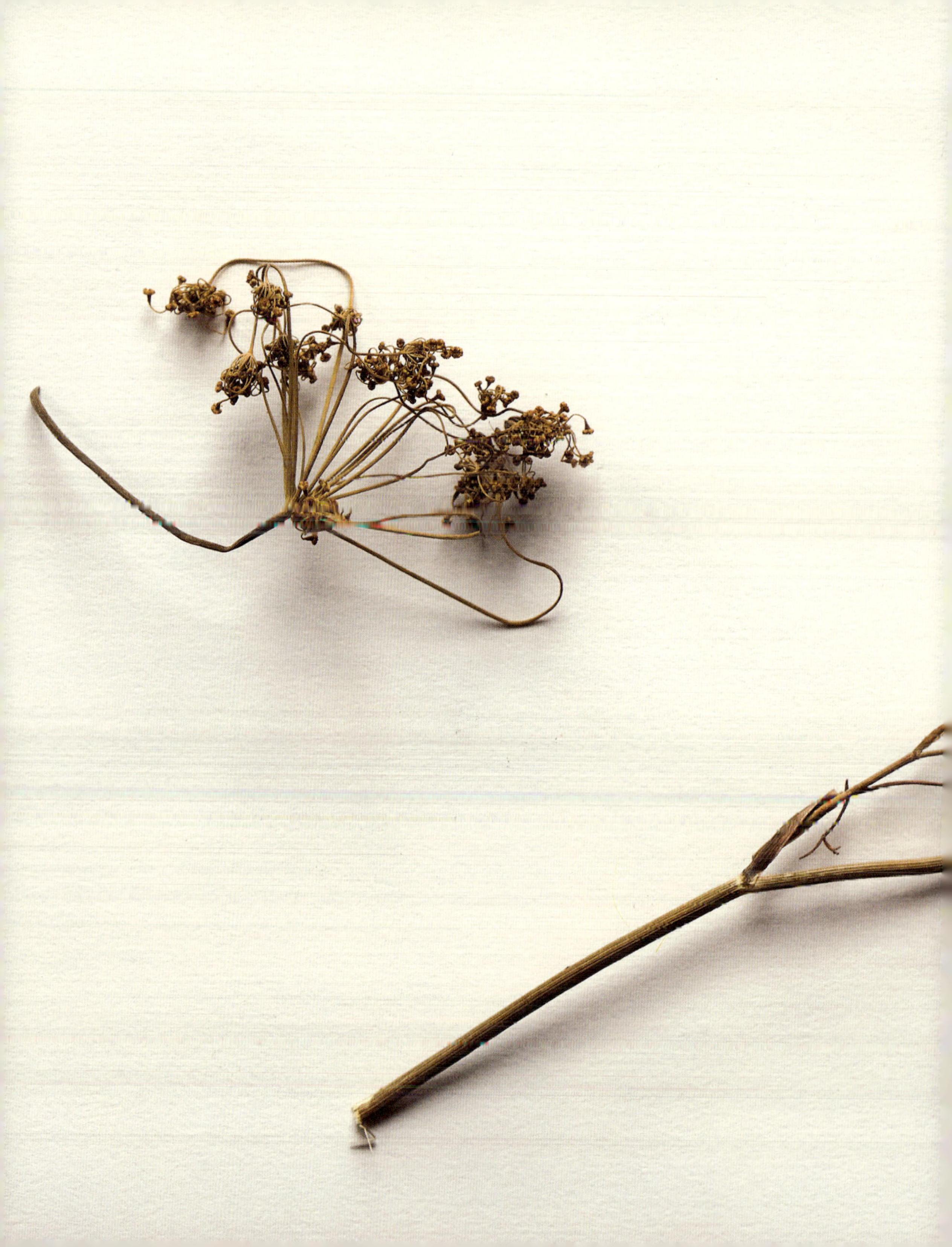

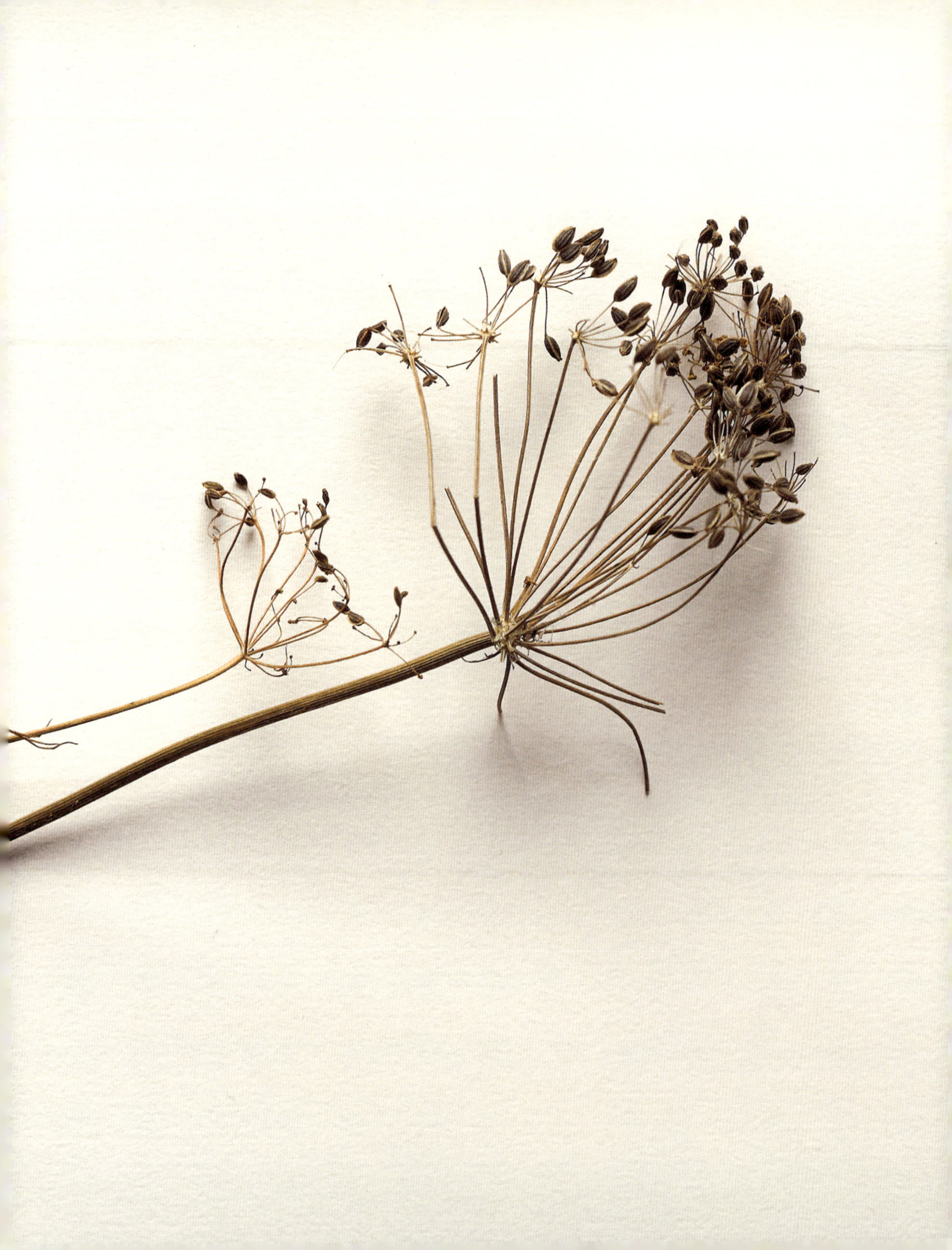

Index

Page numbers in **bold** refer to main entries.

ajvar **138**
   grilled sirloin steak with ajvar and leaves **138**
amazake **94**, 95
apples
   apple and yoghurt herring salad **152**
   baked apple with sweet and spiced viili cream **31**
   banana, apple and pear crisps **229**
   beetroot and apple crackers 210, **212**
   cabbage and apple sauerkraut **67**, 69, 206, 210
   dried mango and apple savoury fruit crisps **216**
   fermented apples **99**, 100
   fermented fruit muffins **100**
   gingerbread crackers **227**
   nori seaweed crackers **206**
   spiced apple and banana leather **246**
   spiced crackers **199**
apricots
   dried 165, 202, **231**, 232, 243
   dried apricot and turmeric rice **202**, 203
aubergines
   ajvar **138**
   aubergine hummus **66**
   fermented gherkin and nasturtium caponata **41**
   roasted vegetable and buckwheat salad **145**
   spiced aubergine crisps **202**, 203
avocado and smoked prawns with chilli and tomato paste **114**

bacon, zurek **77**
Balkan in a pickle **153**, 198
bananas
   banana, apple and pear crisps **229**
   blackcurrant smoothie or yoghurt ice cream **24**
   spiced apple and banana leather **246**
beans *see* French (green) beans;
pinto beans; soya beans
beef
   grilled sirloin steak with ajvar and leaves **138**
   honey glazed Chinese beef jerky **205**
beetroot
   beetroot and apple crackers 210, **212**
   beetroot kvass **75**, 76
   beetroot and red pepper pickle **117**
   beetroot and sauerkraut crackers **210**
   borscht **76**
   candied **236**
   carrot kimchi, beetroot and coriander salad **47**
   dried chilli **182**
   fermented pink turnips **50**
bell peppers
   ajvar **138**
   beetroot and red pepper pickle **117**
   chilli and tomato paste **114**
   dried plum-stuffed peppers two ways **215**
   napa kimchi solyanka **48**
   peppe rosso 10-inch pizza **61**
   pumpkin kimchi curry **46**
   spicy tempeh in Vietnamese wraps **74**
biscuits, kimchi or pink turnip **53**
blackcurrant smoothie or yoghurt ice cream **24**
blinis **37**
Bloody mary **132**, 193
borscht **76**
bread *see* pitta bread; pizza; sourdough
bubble and squeak sauerkraut rosti **69**
buckwheat
   blinis **37**
   kimchi or pink turnip biscuits **53**
   roasted vegetable and buckwheat salad **145**

cabbage
   Balkan in a pickle **153**
   cabbage and apple sauerkraut **67**, 69, 206, 210

classic napa cabbage kimchi **42**
napa kimchi solyanka **48**
nukadoko **62**
nukazuke with udon noodles **63**
carrots
   Balkan in a pickle **153**
   carrot kimchi **47**, 53, 188, 206
   carrot kimchi, beetroot and coriander salad **47**
   carrot and onion pickled herrings **149**
   dried carrot kimchi **188**
   dried carrot kimchi salt **188**
   dried carrots three ways **183**
   fermented turnip and carrot crackers **211**
   misozuke carrots and cauliflower **158**
   kimchi or pink turnip biscuits **53**
   nukadoko **62**
   nukazuke with udon noodles **63**
   pumpkin kimchi curry **46**
   roasted vegetable and buckwheat salad **145**
cauliflower
   fermented veggie sticks **64**
   misozuke carrots and cauliflower **158**
   nukadoko **62**
   nukazuke with udon noodles **63**
celeriac
   Balkan in a pickle **153**
   borscht **76**
celery
   Balkan in a pickle **153**
   crispy kale stir-fry **187**
   fermented gherkin and nasturtium caponata **41**
   pickled **132**, 187
cheese
   Greek salad **113**
   labneh cream **34**
   peppe rosso 10-inch pizza **61**
   pickled plum flammekueche **123**
   sourdough toasties with fermented toppings **58**
   walnut and goat's cheese parcels **162**
chickpeas
   fermented hummus **66**
   pickled bean falafel **155**
   pumpkin kimchi curry **46**

chillies
    Bloody mary II **193**
    chilli and tomato paste **114**
    chilli-pickled radish and cottage cheese salad **147**
    dried 62, **193**
    dried chilli beetroot **182**
    green chilli and red onion pickle **121**
    mango and chilli leather **244**
chocolate, candied orange peel and spiced pumpkin dipped in **238**
chorizo
    peppe rosso 10-inch pizza **61**
    sourdough toasties with fermented toppings **58**
chutney, marrow and fennel **162**
cocoffins **96**
coffee meringue cake **165**
coriander
    carrot kimchi, beetroot and coriander salad **47**
    coriander and yoghurt dip **57**
cottage cheese salad, chilli-pickled radish and **147**
courgettes
    baby courgette kimchi **43**
    Balkan in a pickle **153**
    pickled baby **142**, 145, 215
    spiced courgette crisps **183**
couscous, preserved lemon **79**
crackers
    beetroot and apple 210, **212**
    fermented turnip and carrot **211**
    gingerbread **227**
    kimchi or sauerkraut **210**
    nori seaweed **206**
    spiced **199**
cranberries
    cranberry leather **244**
    dried 46, 165, **230**, 232, 236, 243
crisps
    banana, apple and pear **229**
    dried mango and apple savoury fruit **216**
cucumbers
    lightly pickled **124**
    sweet and spicy gherkins **116**, 61
curry, pumpkin kimchi **46**
cuttlefish, pickled oranges, spiced cuttlefish and squid ink linguini **128**
Cwibak **243**

dill and mustard sauce, herrings in **152**
duck with pickled pears **131**

eggs
    hot pink pickled **141**
    miso pickled **156**, 161

potato crackling frittata **194**
tartar sauce **27**
zurek **77**
elderflowers
    dried botanicals **222**
    linden and elderflower tea **222**

falafel, pickled bean **155**
fennel chutney, marrow and **162**
figs, dried 165, **230**
flammekueche, pickled plum **123**
French (green) beans
    napa kimchi solyanka **48**
    pickled bean falafel **155**
    pickled French beans **155**
fruit
    candied **237-40**, 247
    Cwibak **243**
    dried fruit pickled in brandy **165**
    dried soft **230-1**
    fermented fruit muffins **100**
    leathers 165, **244-6**
    nutty fruit bar **232**

garlic, honey-pickled **133**
gherkins
    dried sour **190**
    dried sour gherkin salt 132, **190**
    fermented gherkin and nasturtium caponata **41**
    fermented gherkins and grapes **38**, 190
    gherkin and mushroom labneh dip **37**
    kimchi or pink turnip biscuits **53**
    napa kimchi solyanka **48**
    sweet and spicy gherkins **116**, 61
    tartar sauce **27**
gin
    gintopf 95, **166**
    sour grape pickle-tini **38**
ginger
    dried **177**
    ginger beer **89**
    ginger bug 28, **88**, 89
    gingerbread crackers **227**
gochugaru, kimchi 42-3, 47
granola, candied **236**
grapes
    dried **231**, 232
    fermented gherkins and **38**
    sour grape pickle-tini **38**
Greek salad **113**

hawthorn
    dried **224**
    tea **224**
herbs, dried 218, **194**
herrings

apple and yoghurt herring salad **152**
in black tea 148, **149**
carrot and onion pickled **149**
in dill and mustard sauce **152**
orange and lemon pickled **149**, 152
sweet and spicy **148**
honey
    fermented honey mustard **54**
    honey glazed Chinese beef jerky **205**
    honey-pickled garlic **133**, 134
    hoppy mead **221**
    raw 15, 24, 57, 99
hops
    dried **221**
    hoppy mead **221**
horseradish
    dried **177**
    mushroom risotto topped with **177**
hummus
    aubergine **66**
    fermented **66**

ice cream
    blackcurrant yoghurt **24**
    gintopf fruit and **166**

kale
    crispy curly **187**
    crispy kale and black rice stir-fry **187**
kefir
    milk **32**
    water **33**
ketchup, fermented **57**, 58
kimchi
    baby courgette **43**
    carrot **47**, 53, 188, 206
    carrot kimchi, beetroot and coriander salad **47**
    classic napa cabbage **42**, 48, 53, 210
    crackers **210**
    dried carrot kimchi **188**
    dried carrot kimchi salt **188**
    kimchi or pink turnip biscuits **53**
    napa kimchi solyanka **48**
    pumpkin **43**
    pumpkin kimchi curry **46**
kiwi, dried candied **240**, 243
kombu seaweed, nukadoko **62**
kombucha 6, 9, 54, **90**
    kombucha punch **93**
kvass
    beetroot **75**, 76
    zur kvass **75**
    zurek **77**

labneh **34**
   blinis with labneh dips **37**
   labneh cream cheese **34**
lemon balm **225**
   tea **225**
lemons
   orange and lemon pickled herrings **149**, 152
   preserved **79**
   preserved lemon couscous **79**
lentils
   chunky dhal with aubergine crisps **203**
   dried plum-stuffed peppers two ways **215**
   nori seaweed crackers **206**
   spiced crackers **199**
lime (linden) flowers
   dried botanicals **222**
   linden and elderflower tea **222**

mackerel, Chinese cabbage and nasturtium caper salad **110**
mangoes
   dried mango and apple savoury fruit crisps **216**
   mango and chilli leather **244**
   pickled watermelon rind salad **137**
   spicy pineapple and mango pickle **120**
marrow and fennel chutney **162**
mead, hoppy **221**
meringue cake, coffee **165**
milk kefir **32**, 37, 96
mint
   mint balm **225**
   mint balm tea **225**
miso paste
   miso pickled eggs **156**, 161
   miso pickled mushrooms **156**, 161
   misozuke carrots and cauliflower **158**, 161
   misozuke and soba noodle salad **161**
   nukazuke with udon noodles **63**
mooli
   classic napa cabbage kimchi **42**
   nukazuke with udon noodles **63**
muesli, whey-fermented **23**
   with plain yoghurt and fruit **23**
muffins
   cocoffins **96**
   fermented fruit **100**
mushrooms
   borscht **76**
   bubble and squeak sauerkraut rosti **69**

dried mushroom sauce 69, **175**
dried wild **172**, 174, 175
gherkin and mushroom labneh dip **37**
miso pickled mushrooms **156**, 161
mushroom risotto topped with horseradish **177**
napa kimchi solyanka **48**
pickled porcini **110**
potato crackling frittata **194**
tartar sauce **27**
wild porcini soup **174**
zurek **77**
mustard seeds
   fermented **54**
   fermented honey mustard **54**

napa cabbage
   kimchi **42**, 43, 48
   mackerel, Chinese cabbage and nasturtium caper salad **110**
   napa kimchi solyanka **48**
nasturtium capers
   fermented gherkin and nasturtium caponata **41**
   mackerel, Chinese cabbage and nasturtium caper salad **110**
   napa kimchi solyanka **48**
   pickled **109**
nectarines, grilled, pulled pork with swede mash, honey-pickled garlic and **134**
noodles
   misozuke and soba noodle salad **161**
   nukazuke with udon **63**
nori seaweed crackers **206**
nukadoko **62**
nukazuke with udon noodles **63**
nuts
   baked apple with sweet and spiced viili cream **31**
   candied granola **236**
   Cwibak **243**
   easy pickled 123, **142**, 145
   gingerbread crackers **227**
   nutty fruit bar **232**
   whey-fermented muesli **23**

oats
   candied granola **236**
   whey-fermented muesli **23**
olives
   fermented gherkin and nasturtium caponata **41**
   Greek salad **113**
   peppe rosso 10-inch pizza **61**
oranges
   candied orange peel **237**, 238,

243
   candied orange peel and spiced pumpkin dipped in chocolate **238**
   orange and lemon pickled herrings **149**, 152
   pickled **127**
   pickled oranges, spiced cuttlefish and squid ink linguini **128**

Parma ham, pickled watermelon rind salad **137**
parsnips
   dried curried **182**
   nori seaweed crackers **206**
   roasted vegetable and buckwheat salad **145**
   spiced crackers **199**
pears
   banana, apple and pear crisps **229**
   duck with pickled **131**
   gintopf **166**
   pickled **127**, 101
peppers *see* bell peppers; chillies; ramiro peppers
pesto, dried tomato **178**
pineapple and mango pickle, spicy **120**
pinto beans
   bean crackling **196**, 198
   tortilla with bean crackling **198**
pitta bread, sourdough **87**
pizza
   fermented pizza sauce **58**, 61
   long-fermented pizza dough **61**
   peppe rosso 10-inch pizza **61**
plums
   dried 196, **213**, 215
   dried candied **247**, 249
   dried plum-stuffed peppers two ways **215**
   dried plum and walnut bites **249**
   fermented **99**, 100
   fermented fruit muffins **100**
   pickled **117**, 123
   pickled plum flammekueche **123**
pork, pulled, with swede mash, grilled nectarines and honey-pickled garlic **134**
potatoes
   bubble and squeak sauerkraut rosti **69**
   zurek **77**
prawns, avocado and smoked, with chilli and tomato paste **114**
production leaven **81**, 85, 87, 96
pumpkins
   candied orange peel and spiced

pumpkin dipped in chocolate **238**
fermented fruit muffins **100**
fermented pumpkin syrup **28**, 31
gingerbread crackers **227**
pickled plum flammekueche **123**
pumpkin kimchi **43**
pumpkin kimchi curry **46**
roasted vegetable and buckwheat salad **145**
spiced candied **235**, 236, 243

radishes
  chilli-pickled radish **147**
  chilli-pickled radish and cottage cheese salad **147**
ramiro peppers, pickled 37, 58, **106**, 215
raspberries
  drunken rice pudding **95**
  gintopf **166**
red onion pickle, green chilli and **121**
rice
  amazake **94**
  crispy dried kale and black rice stir-fry **187**
  dried apricot and turmeric rice **202**, 203
  drunken rice pudding **95**
  mushroom risotto topped with horseradish **177**
rosehip
  dried **224**
  tea **224**
rye
  sourdough starter **80**, 81, 84
  sunflower rye sourdough **84**

salads
  apple and yoghurt herring **152**
  carrot kimchi, beetroot and coriander **47**
  chilli-pickled radish and cottage cheese **147**
  Greek salad **113**
  misozuke and soba noodle **161**
  pickled watermelon rind salad **137**
  roasted vegetable and buckwheat **145**
salt
  dried carrot kimchi **188**
  dried fermented turnip **191**
  dried sour gherkin **190**
sauerkraut
  beetroot and sauerkraut crackers **210**
  bubble and squeak sauerkraut rosti **69**
  cabbage and apple **67**, 69, 206,

crackers **210**
shallots, pickled **141**, 145
smoothie, blackcurrant 24
soups
  borscht **76**
  wild porcini **174**
  zurek **77**
sourdough
  sourdough pitta bread **87**
  sourdough toasties with fermented toppings **58**
  sourdough tortilla **85**, 198
  spelt **82**
  starters **80**
  sunflower rye **84**
soya beans
  spicy tempeh in Vietnamese wraps **74**
  tempeh **70**
spelt
  candied granola **236**
  cocoffins **96**
  sourdough **82**
  sourdough starter **80**, 81
  whey-fermented muesli **23**
spinach, lightly pickled baby **159**, 161
spring onions, kimchi **42–3**, 47
squid ink linguini, pickled oranges, spiced cuttlefish and **128**
stock, instant vegetable 177, **179**
sunflower rye sourdough **84**
swede mash, pulled pork with grilled nectarines, honey-pickled garlic and **134**
sweet potatoes
  pickled plum flammekueche **123**
  potato crackling frittata **194**
  pumpkin kimchi curry **46**
  roasted vegetable and buckwheat salad **145**
  sweet potato crackling **194**

tartar sauce **27**, 110
tea
  herring in black tea **148**, 149
  kombucha **90**
  kombucha punch **93**
  linden and elderflower **222**
  mint or lemon balm **225**
  rosehip or hawthorn **224**
tempeh **70**
  spicy tempeh in Vietnamese wraps **74**
tomatoes
  chilli and tomato paste **114**
  dried **178**
  dried tomato pesto **178**
  fermented gherkin and nasturtium caponata **41**

fermented ketchup **57**
fermented pizza sauce **58**
napa kimchi solyanka **48**
pickled cherry **113**
pickled green tomatoes **116**
pumpkin kimchi curry **46**
tortillas
  sourdough tortilla **85**, 198
  tortilla with bean crackling **198**
turnips
  dried fermented pink **191**
  dried fermented turnip salt **191**
  fermented pink **50**, 110, 191, 211
  fermented turnip and carrot crackers **211**
  kimchi or pink turnip biscuits **53**

vegetables
  dried **179**
  fermented veggie sticks **64**
  instant vegetable stock 177, **179**
vermouth
  kombucha punch **93**
  sour grape pickle-tini **38**
viili cream **27**, 34
  baked apple with sweet and spiced **31**
  sweet and spiced **28**, 31
vodka
  Bloody mary **132**, **193**
  kombucha punch **93**

walnuts
  dried plum and walnut bites **249**
  walnut and goat's cheese parcels **162**
water kefir **33**, 57, 66
watermelon
  pickled watermelon rind **137**
  pickled watermelon rind salad **137**
whey **34**
  fermented hummus **66**
  fermented ketchup **57**
  whey-fermented museli **23**
wraps, spicy tempeh in Vietnamese **74**

yoghurt
  apple and yoghurt herring salad **152**
  blackcurrant smoothie or yoghurt ice cream **24**
  coriander and yoghurt dip **57**
  labneh **34**
  plain live **20**, 23, 24, 34, 57, 96, 114, 152, 198
  viili yoghurt **27**

zur kvass **75**
zurek **77**

255

We would like to thank everybody who helped to create this book especially Zena Alkayat for her enthusiasm, ongoing support and patience and for not following through on her barbaric threats when deadlines were missed. Further thanks to Kim Lightbody for the photography, Marente van der Valk for the food styling (and for writing most of the meat recipes), Glenn Howard for book design, Kathy Steer for recipe editing, Euan Ferguson for proof reading, and Eliefs for the Onggi fermenting crock pictured on P14.

More thanks to…

Our friends and colleagues David Lopez and Anna Drozdova at The Fermentarium for sharing their knowledge and advice.

Our family and friends, Gaba's mum Ewa Smolinska, dad Jerzy Smolinski, aunt Anna Latkiewicz, and uncle Edek Smolinski, Nel Topor-Madry, Dada Felja and Dada's mother Julka Felja, Heike Gaulitz, Ona Risoviene, Edyta Gach, Steph and Sandy Miller and Sarah Gray MNIMH for their knowledge, experience, ideas and some of the recipes in this book as well as feedback on the new recipes they tried.

Also thanks to Ala Kozlowska, Clare Paul, Malgosia Latkiewicz-Pawlak and Krzysiek Pawlak, Uli Siegg, Marta Sosnowska-Conradi and Jon Conradi for trying different recipes and for their constructive feedback.

Thanks also to our little Marek for putting up with the writing and for tasting much of the food.